MEDIA DIPLOMACY

MEDIA
DIPLOMACY

The Foreign Office in the
Mass Communications Age

Yoel Cohen

FRANK CASS

First published 1986 in Great Britain by
FRANK CASS AND COMPANY LIMITED
Gainsborough House, 11 Gainsborough Road,
London, E11 1RS, England

and in the United States of America by
FRANK CASS AND COMPANY LIMITED
c/o Biblio Distribution Centre
81 Adams Drive, P.O. Box 327, Totowa, N.J. 07511

British Library Cataloguing in Publication Data

Cohen, Yoel
    Media diplomacy: the Foreign Office in
    the mass communications age.
    1. Mass media—Great Britain
    2. News agencies—Great Britain
    3. Great Britain—Foreign relations
    — 1945—
    I. Title
    327.41   DA589.8
    ISBN 0-7146-3269-4

Library of Congress Cataloging-in-Publication Data

Cohen, Yoel, 1953—
    Media diplomacy.

    Bibliography: p.
    Includes index.
    1. Great Britain—Foreign relations—1945—
    2. Great Britain. Foreign and Commonwealth Office.
    3. Diplomacy.   4. Mass media—Political aspects—
    Great Britain.   I. Title.
    JX1543.C64   1986   327.41   86-1296
    ISBN 0-7146-3269-4

Typeset by Williams Graphics, Abergele, North Wales
Printed and bound in Great Britain by
A. Wheaton & Co. Ltd., Exeter

CONTENTS

TO MY PARENTS

FOREWORD

Yoel Cohen has done a valuable job in amassing a whole wealth of evidence to illustrate the evolving relationship between diplomats and the media. It is a diligently researched dossier of the way events in recent British diplomatic history have been presented to the media and covered by the press and television. I am sad that he was not able to be more forthright in his conclusions about what he calls 'Media Diplomacy'. I believe that it is partly because of the secretive and suspicious nature of the British bureaucracy in its relations with the media, an attitude that politicians in power do little to disperse, that Britain is seen somehow to be a nation without élan.

Yoel Cohen details the British government's nervous news management of the Falklands War: how much more respect would the country have won from the outside world if it had opened its doors to the media with the open confidence of a mature democracy fighting a jaded dictatorship?

But this book is an important contribution to a little covered corner of British history, and it will provoke lively discussion.

Peter Snow

PREFACE

This book is a study of the relationship of news media and modern diplomacy. The growth of mass communications and the interest of the citizens of democratic societies in international affairs have certain implications for diplomacy. By examining British diplomacy, this study attempts to pinpoint those areas where the media impinge on the foreign policy process either in terms of having an influence on public opinion, by providing new information to policy makers, or in terms of being used by officials as channels to other governments and to the public at home and abroad.

In addition to published sources, the study is based on 250 interviews in Britain and abroad with government ministers, parliamentarians, civil servants, editors, journalists, and interest group leaders. For reasons of confidentiality the identity of many interviewees quoted cannot be given. Elite interviews have to be used in qualitative rather than quantitative terms, and extracts from interviews have been used to illustrate analytical points being made rather than as conclusive proof of their validity. A combination of interviews and published sources allows a picture of the relationship of the media and diplomacy to emerge. Interviews alone do not always show all the factors leading up to a particular decision, and published sources alone do not provide answers to some questions including perceptions of officials and journalists about one another. Access to key individuals and institutions remains a problem for the social scientist investigating the British Civil Service, and the time has still to come when he or she is able to observe the workings of a government agency such as the Foreign and Commonwealth Office from the inside for a fixed period of time. In contrast, in examining the connections between Washington reporters and US government officials, one academic was granted the opportunity to be an inside observer at five federal agencies, including the White House, the Department of State, and the Department of Defence, and had access to staff meetings and internal documents. Moving between reporters and officials, he was able to observe the same event from the two perspectives.[1]

The author is grateful to the many people who agreed to be interviewed, and who gave of their time to share their thoughts and opinions. I wish to thank Professor Jeremy Tunstall for his advice and helpful comments. The patience of my wife, Sara Rivka, and my daughter and son, Haviva and Hezki, eased the task of completing the manuscript. Without the encouragement and support of my parents, Aaron S. and Florida M. Cohen of London, the study would not have been undertaken.

Jerusalem   Yoel Cohen
November 1985

NOTE

1. Stephen Hess, *The Government/Press Connection*, Washington DC, The Brookings Institution, 1985; Stephen Hess, 'The Golden Triangle: The Press at the White House, State and Defence', in *The Brookings Review*, The Brookings Institution, Summer 1983.

CHAPTER ONE

INTRODUCTION

At weekends the machinery of British foreign policy comes to a halt. But on Sunday, 23 February 1969, a hum of activity filled the Foreign and Commonwealth Office (FCO). There was no crisis in the sense of war. But a diplomatic crisis was brewing, one that graphically illustrates the effect which mass media can have on modern diplomacy. Normally on a Sunday afternoon a single duty officer in News Department is available to answer journalists' inquiries. But on this Sunday the chief spokesman, the head of News Department, was telling the assembled journalists that President de Gaulle of France had traduced his European partners, and was seeking British support to liquidate NATO in return for British admission to the European Economic Community. To back him up, the under-secretaries who constitute the office's senior echelon were in attendance. Nearly every known foreign affairs journalist was there, as well as some who were unheard of.

What became known as the Soames affair began in 1968 with the political appointment by the foreign secretary, George Brown, of Christopher Soames to the post of ambassador in Paris. He had the task of persuading de Gaulle to favour British membership of the EEC. De Gaulle was critical of NATO and the EEC in general, and had proposed the creation of an enlarged European economic association with a small inner council composed of France, Britain, West Germany and Italy. An atmosphere of mutual suspicion existed between London and Paris. It was, therefore, not surprising that de Gaulle in making the proposal – which he said should have come from Britain rather than France – was less trying to fulfil British aspirations and more exploiting the opportunity to drive a wedge between Britain and her allies in Europe, with Britain being perceived as trying to destroy the rights and liberties of smaller states like the Netherlands and Belgium.

Although the de Gaulle–Soames conversation was confidential, Harold Wilson, the prime minister, saw the need to inform European governments about the conversation lest once it became known, as it inevitably would, Britain would become suspect in European eyes.

Europe's governments were informed in confidence in mid-February. Indications of a British–French crisis began to appear in the media. Who leaked first – London or Paris – is unclear. *Le Figaro* and *France Soir* published a version of the conversation on Thursday, 20 February. On the same day diplomatic correspondents in London were told by the FCO about the conversation, although they would have to 'wear' the story at their own risk and could not indicate its source.

An interesting aspect of the affair was that No 10 Downing Street was kept in the dark about this briefing. Instead, on the next day, Friday, 24 February, the FCO suggested to Wilson's chief press spokesman, Joe Haines, that since the French media had broken the story the previous day the British had to get their position across. 'On this occasion, the FCO were after a bigger prize than a "purely procedural" victory', Haines noted.[1] It would be an opportunity to expose the perfidy of the French and display the innate decency and desire to be good Europeans of the British. The FCO's News Department proposed that the British version should be leaked to the Rome newspaper, *Il Messagero*.

The Italian government rather than the British government would be thought of as being the source of the leak. Wilson vetoed this proposal: if the French decided to leak the story Britain could not stop them, but he did not want London accused of being responsible.

The FCO decided to brief correspondents that same day notwithstanding No 10's veto, telling them that there was a grave difference of opinion between France and Britain over the EEC, NATO, and Europe in general. Correspondents could even hint that the information came from 'sources close to Whitehall'. This was followed on Sunday by what amounted to a full-scale press conference. 'We've seen the blighter off', a journalist was told by an FCO official.[2] A rupture in Anglo-French relations as bad as occurred in 1963, when de Gaulle first vetoed Britain's application to join the EEC, resulted from the affair. But the rupture did not last long because within 18 months de Gaulle and Wilson both relinquished office enabling their successors, President Pompidou and Edward Heath, to start afresh. As a diplomatic manoeuvre the leaks and counterleaks were in the best style: a classic illustration of how the media have become the tools of trade of the professional diplomat.

Another example of media diplomacy was the expulsion from the Soviet Union of six British foreign correspondents – from BBC Television, the *Daily Telegraph*, the *Daily Mail*, *The Observer* and two from Reuters news agency – in September 1985. It served as a reminder of the difficulties facing a foreign correspondent there. The first hurdle is to obtain a visa from the authorities. Most correspondents live in the foreigners' ghetto enabling the authorities to keep watch over their activities as well as, according to some journalists, to stop correspondents from seeing the realities of Soviet life. The Novosti Press Agency and the Soviet Foreign Ministry's Press Department are the official points of contact, with the latter deciding on all requests for press interviews and for trips outside of Moscow. News reporting is monitored by the Soviet embassy in London and reporters displeasing the authorities may be summoned to the foreign ministry or denounced by name in the Soviet press. More severe measures range from unexplained interruptions on telephones and telex machines, to not granting requests for interviews, to physical assault, and finally to non-renewal of visas or expulsion.

It would, however, be wrong to suggest that reporting is impossible because while formal interviews require approval it is possible to speak to ordinary citizens as long as they are not quoted by name. In addition to limited off the record official contacts for purposes of calculated leaks or disinformation, some correspondents have been used for competitive leaking by middle or higher ranking officials who have failed to achieve a particular objective by working within the system. Dissidents seek contact with, and in varying degrees are sought after by, correspondents, although their views are not necessarily typical of the population as a whole. However, when compared to the pluralist society, from which the British correspondent comes, with its open debate and investigative journalism, reporting from Moscow is very restrictive. The expulsion of the six journalists emasculated the British press corps in Moscow from 14 to 8 journalists, and in effect reduced further an already limited flow of information which British audiences receive about the superpower.

The relationship between the media and international affairs has been examined using a number of approaches. One is to analyse the nature of news content. This is particularly relevant to a study of international affairs given that distorted images and perceptions compound conflicts of interest between states. Accordingly, within the study of international relations there is a trend away from examining disputes in terms of objective issues and events towards a subjective dimension of asking why and how the image of world affairs held by other nations may differ from our own.[3] The analysis of news content is valid in considering the formation of attitudes of the wider public, most of whose information about international affairs is drawn from the media, but it is less relevant in the case of ministers and officials most of whose information is in the form of the flow of messages from the diplomatic missions and internal reports.

Another approach is to focus on the institutional and occupational characteristics of journalism. Tunstall has examined the characteristics of correspondents, news sources, and news organisations for factors

explaining differences in news-gathering behaviour and outputs.[4] Sigal
has observed the internal operations and news flow of the *New York
Times* and the *Washington Post*,[5] and Argyris has examined inter-
personal communication between reporters and editors.[6]

A third approach, which will be emphasised in this study, is to
examine the relationship between the media and foreign policy. Early
studies of democracy and foreign policy dealt in terms of an undifferen-
tiated public. Almond identified four key participants in the opinion-
policy process each of which play different roles: the general public,
which participate in an indirect and passive way; the attentive public,
before whom informed discussion takes place; policy and opinion elites,
which compete for public support and influence; and the official leadership, which makes policy.[7] Few studies examine the opinion-policy
process as a two-way one, in terms of both the effects of the media on
policy, and the effects of policymakers on the media. In their review
of works on the relationship of media and government, Rivers, Miller
and Gandy postulate four categories: governmental impact on the media,
governmental information systems, the media's impact on government,
and the nature of the media.[8] Several studies have examined governmental impact on the media in terms of the channels, techniques, and
processes by which officials disseminate information to journalists.
Nimmo studied relations between government information officials and
specialist correspondents.[9] Chittick examined relations between US
State Department information and policy officials, reporters, and
interest groups in terms of cooperation and antagonism.[10]

Although these studies generated new hypotheses about the interaction of reporters and officials, the question remains what is the final
impact of these interactions on the media. It is, similarly, not enough
to know which media are seen by policymakers, but also necessary to
ask what impact the media have on policy. Rosenau has argued against
tracing the flow of influence in a political system because the researcher
has to examine both the behaviour which precipitated the influence and
the behaviour to which that influence may have contributed, and must
then examine what the latter behaviour might have been if it had not been
modified by the influence. The measurement of 'might-have-beens'
is only possible through the manipulation of variables in controlled
experiments.[11] The effect of the media may, however, be observed
when behaviour is a necessary and sufficient cause of something – that
is, nothing else could cause it and the media need no assistance. In a
lesser sense the media's effect is also observable when the media are
a catalyst or occasion an event which might have happened anyway but
not otherwise in that form or at that time.[12]

MEDIA–DIPLOMACY RELATIONSHIPS

The different types of relationships between the media and diplomacy may be categorised as follows.

1. The media, overseas and British, are a source of information to members of diplomatic missions abroad and to officials and ministers in London. The British media influence foreign policy as a result of their effect on policymakers, MPs, interest groups, and the wider public. The media are in addition sources of information and agenda setters for these and are used by interest groups and MPs as channels to reach the official policymakers and the public.
2. The media are also channels of communication among policymakers, British and foreign. They are used by British government departments, individual officials and ministers at the policy formulation stage to disclose information in order to advance or hinder policy options. At the stage of policy implementation, as illustrated by the Soames affair, the media are used in international negotiations by Britain and other governments as a device through which to manoeuvre another government.
3. The media are also used to gain public support for policy. The channels include, abroad, the building by diplomatic missions abroad of relations with the local media, and the distribution of printed and visual material to them; and in London, with the foreign press corps and the BBC External Services. The British media are means for the FCO to explain policy to the British public.

Are there any common elements among the aforementioned interactions between media and foreign policy from which a theory of media diplomacy may be generated? These interactions appear initially to vary in type and to differ in the roles they play in the policy process. As a source of information to policymakers and the public, the media behave as channels connecting them to the world outside. In terms of the relationship of the media to public opinion, and of public opinion to policy, the media do not act as a channel but influence the substance of policy. As a channel of communication the media supplement the official diplomatic network through which governments communicate with one another. In being used by a policymaker to disclose information, whether in the formulation or implementation of policy, the media do not serve as diplomatic channels but create certain political effects that hinder or advance policy. And the explanation of policy to overseas and domestic publics should be distinguished from the implementation of policy, since the former takes place outside the policy process after policy has been implemented between two countries.

To busy professional diplomats an all-encompassing theory of media diplomacy would seem improbable. The role of the media in reporting international affairs makes the media one additional source of information to policymakers, in a way that has nothing to do with the use of the media by officials to reflect public thinking. Officials and ministers deny that they use the media to disclose information at the stages of policy formulation and policy implementation, or that they channel messages and signals to other governments through the media. And if this technique is admitted to, it is only one among a number of diplomatic channels between policymakers. None of these media roles has anything in common with overseas information programmes – in which the role of the media is recognised by diplomats – nor with the foreign ministry's relations with journalists from their own country. If diplomats do have a concrete media policy, it involves questions of the type of overseas information policy to adopt, such as the distribution of information attachés in diplomatic posts. Any policy of media diplomacy would, therefore, be simply the sum of overseas information policies around the world.

Yet, notwithstanding seemingly non-integrated connections of the media and diplomacy, media diplomacy does exist as one type of diplomacy. Other types of diplomacy – also with differentiated, and seemingly unintegrated, elements – include, for example, economic diplomacy with such diverse diplomatic tools as loans and grants, embargoes, the terms of trade, the manipulation of financial currencies, and technical assistance. Each involves an overlap of economics and of diplomacy, and each is designed to change directly or indirectly the behaviour or policies of a government. Media and diplomacy are two different types of communication which run along different paths, in many instances never crossing. This book deals with those points where overlap occurs. The rise of a mass circulation press and expansion of foreign news coverage have brought the public closer to international affairs. The British Empire with its far-flung commitments, national conscription, the two world wars and developments in mass communications including the telegraph, radio, cable, telephone and television have each added to the media–diplomacy relationship. Television, for example, has revolutionised foreign news gathering. Actuality brings the drama of an event into the living room of the viewer in a way that print cannot. Portable cameras and satellites enable the viewer to watch an event as it is happening and become a participant in it, giving the event an added dimension in the form of public pressure. The 'new diplomacy' has replaced the 'old diplomacy' in which diplomats made foreign policy without due regard for any public reaction, few governmental structures existed for explaining policy, and governments communicated to one another through the conventional diplomatic channels.

Still, the overlap between media and diplomacy is partial. Many aspects of the media, such as domestic news, coverage of the arts, sport, and entertainment, to name a few, are not the concern of diplomacy. And many aspects of diplomacy, including international economic relations, bilateral political relations, and cultural ties are not defined as 'news' by the media. Yet crises, war and peace are the stuff of both journalists and diplomats. Policymakers and the public use the media as a source of information. The media influence the public, thereby bringing pressure on policymakers. The media are often used to cause tactical manoeuvres during international negotiations. The media are primary means by which policymakers gain public support for their policies. Media diplomacy is thus to be distinguished from 'public diplomacy' in that the latter encompasses not only information work and cultural activities, where the media are involved, but all public aspects of foreign policy – speeches, trips, public appearances by the prime minister, the foreign secretary, and other senior officials, and the support and cultivation of political groups and forces abroad that may serve the long-term interests of Britain and the West generally. Media diplomacy includes all those aspects of public diplomacy where the media are involved as well as others not associated with public diplomacy including the sending of signals by governments through the media, and the use of the media as a source of information.

Furthermore, the elements of media diplomacy are interrelated. A chain of linkage between these elements begins with the image of the world as portrayed by the media. The image will determine those policies and issues where the media exert influence. Information which does not make the threshold of news includes that from culturally distant regions like Latin America, or which concerns economic and scientific developments, or which cannot be reported because journalists are barred access by a government. The influence of that information which passes through the news threshold is dependent on the reactions of Parliament, interest groups, and the wider public. These rely on the media for their primary sources of information about international affairs. Further, in the absence of Parliament discussing international affairs in depth, the media set the agenda for 'issues' of debate and act as forums of discussion. The extent to which this process results in a change of policy somewhat depends on the attitudes about such domestic pressures as the media held by ministers and officials. To officials, domestic opinion does not necessarily coincide with the longer-term national interest. Few elections have been fought on foreign issues. Ministers, who have an interest in avoiding criticism of government policy, try to take this

MD-B

into account if not in altering the substance of policy at least in changing the way policy is presented. An additional linkage between the media and Parliament and interest groups is that the former are used by MPs and interest groups to reach the wider public. If the influence of the media is limited by the national interest and international pressures, public reaction will influence the nature of governmental explanation of policy to the public through the media.

Moreover, in a wider sociological sense, many of the elements of media diplomacy share common patterns.

1. The media are a source of information and ideas at several stages in the foreign policy process: to diplomats abroad; to ministers and officials in London; and to the wider public, MPs, and interest groups.
2. The media link the public to policymakers in terms of acting as a forum of debate on foreign policy and in terms of reflecting this debate in public opinion to policymakers.
3. Media diplomacy is associated with the concept of influence: the media determine what areas and subjects are covered by the media; and the media change policy.
4. Media diplomacy concerns the way the media link policymakers to foreign governments and to the public by including British government attitudes in editorial matter and by disclosing information which has the political effect of changing policy.

The occupations of the diplomat and the journalist also highlight similarities and differences between media and diplomacy. Both diplomats and journalists deal with relations between states – gathering information and influencing public opinion about international affairs. There is an interdependence between the diplomat and the journalist in each of these functions. Diplomats and journalists each have sources of information in a foreign country which the other may not have; for example, in some countries while a journalist can keep in touch with opposition groups, for a foreign diplomat to do so might be considered an interference in local politics. And diplomats are privy to confidential information about international diplomacy from which the media are excluded. As a moulder of opinion, a journalist has a wider public audience than the diplomat can hope for. He can also freely criticise his own, or other, governments. Both diplomat and journalist believe they are contributing to society's well-being: the diplomat by defending the national interest and negotiating on his country's behalf, and the journalist by playing the critical role of watchdog on government and the rest of the society.

Other similarities and differences involve training and work organisation. Both are engaged in nonroutine work. First, the journalist is producing a new product each day and the diplomat is responding to the changing world situation. Second, there is an increasing tendency towards specialisation and delegation of work: in the FCO decisions are taken at the desk officer level without rising further up the structure towards the ministerial level than necessary, and in news organisations work is divided between, and within, the categories of news processors (sub-editors and editorial executives) and news gatherers (reporters and correspondents). In terms of background, diplomats are university graduates while journalists in many cases are not. However, journalists are professionally trained while in diplomacy the generalist is still preferred.

THE MEDIA AND FOREIGN POLICY

A useful way to examine the media–diplomacy relationship is to evaluate at each stage in the making and implementing of foreign policy any media effect or media role. Taking British foreign policymaking as our case study, it is first necessary to describe the policymaking process. The main foreign-policymaking organisation is the Foreign and Commonwealth Office. Although home departments are increasingly involved in those foreign policy decisions with domestic implications, the FCO is linked to the world through about one hundred and forty diplomatic missions. It is clear, therefore, that in contrast to some small countries, where most decisions are made by a handful of people, this is not the case with Britain. Even at times of crisis when an important decision can be attributed to the prime minister or the foreign secretary, it will be based on a culmination of smaller decisions made by officials. It would be wrong to assume that only the executive branch of government is involved in foreign policy formulation, although in contrast to the United States, the executive is dominant. Parliament and other sections of the 'domestic environment', including interest groups, commercial interests, public opinion, and the media, exert influence on a small range of key issues. Nevertheless, on most issues of external policy there has generally been bipartisan agreement between the political parties.

The making of foreign policy begins with the gathering and interpreting of information about international affairs – with the media having an obvious function. This information will be the basis of policy proposals made by officials to ministers. In preparing the proposals, international interests and any domestic pressures, such as from the media and public opinion, need to be weighed. Decisionmaking in the FCO begins at the desk officer level, rising to the levels of undersecretaries and ministers only when a particular issue falls outside the existing policy guidelines or is likely to have domestic ramifications.

Consultation with other government departments is routine; this will be done generally behind closed doors although occasionally interdepartmental fighting is played out in public, notably in the media. Once a policy decision is reached, instructions are drawn up for its implementation. Occasionally, the media will be chosen as the most suitable channel through which to signal to or manoeuvre another government. Public support for a particular policy may be important at home or abroad. In an interview with the author, Lord Home, former prime minister (1963–64) and foreign secretary (1961–63 and 1970–73) remarked, 'It is in the minister's interest that the public be kept informed and understand the foreign situation as he sees it'. Although the media play an important role in explaining foreign policy, most transactions between governments are 'technical' and of little public concern.

In the literature on British foreign policymaking – itself small – only a few aspects of media diplomacy are covered. These include the British media's image of world affairs, the influence of public opinion on policy, the FCO's relations with the media, and overseas information policy. Other aspects which have not been dealt with include the use of the media as a source of information, the media's influence on policymakers, and the use of the media by governments during international negotiation. Furthermore, those aspects which have been examined have not been considered specifically in relation to the media.[13] This study attempts to fill these gaps. Adopting as its reference point the process by which foreign policy is made and implemented, the framework of the study will be to examine at each stage of the policymaking process any effects or roles of the media. This will guard against the tendency in some media research to exaggerate the role of the media in politics.

Chapter 2 traces briefly the origins of media diplomacy. Chapters 3 and 4 examine the role of the media as a source of information. Chapter 5 looks at the influence of the media in the formulation of policy. Chapter 6 deals with the role of the media in interdepartmental infighting which sometimes accompanies the stage of the formulation of policy. It also analyses the use of the media in international negotiation when, following its formulation, policy is implemented. The building of support abroad and at home is examined in Chapters 7 and 8 respectively. Three case studies, on the TWA hijacking to Beirut in 1985, and the 1982 Falklands and Lebanon wars, examine different aspects of media diplomacy discussed in earlier chapters. In conclusion, Chapter 12 considers the implications of the revolutions in communications and diplomacy for future trends in media diplomacy.

CHAPTER TWO

ORIGINS

'Well, sir, this is a change from what it used to be. Before the
war these Press gentlemen used to line up in the courtyard outside the Office at about 4 o'clock and one of us would come and
say "Nothing doing today, gentlemen", and they went away'.
– Foreign Office doorman, on being told by an official to admit
journalists to witness the signing of the Treaty of Locarno,
1925.[1]

The evolution of media diplomacy in Britain is to be explained partly
by changes in the international system over the last hundred years. First,
European diplomacy, in which discussions between governments took
place in an atmosphere of confidentiality within the formal channels
of ambassadorial contacts with statesmen, evolved into democratic
diplomacy, with a greater use of propaganda in diplomacy and a need
for democratic governments to consult their electorates. Second, many
new actors, both state as well as non-state ones including revolutionary
groups, foreign interest groups, international organisations, and multinational companies, also use propaganda. These changes have been
reflected in the structure of the Foreign Office, which has departments
responsible for information and cultural work.

In part, the evolution of media diplomacy may be explained by
Britain's political and educational system. Popular enfranchisement,
beginning with the 1832 Reform Act, created a greater public interest
in foreign affairs. By 1851 over two-thirds of men and over half of
women were able to read, and the 1870 Education Act made education
available to all. The First World War, with its heavy loss of life, added
to this interest. And politicians saw a need to gain public support for
foreign policy, and to present complex ideas about international
relations in terms meaningful to the public.

And, in part, the evolution of media diplomacy came about through
the growth of mass communications. Although William Caxton set up
the first printing press in England in 1476, it was nearly a century and
a half before the country had a genuine newspaper, known as the
corantos, which appeared in 1621. While it appeared infrequently it

nevertheless satisfied other criteria for being a newspaper including being produced by mechanical means, available to anyone prepared to pay the price, and possessing timely contents. The first regular newspaper was the *Daily Courant* in 1702, which appeared six days a week. Restrictions on the publication of certain types of news, including local news and the proceedings of Parliament, and stamp taxes placed on the newspaper itself and on its advertising which were not removed until the 1850s, impeded the growth of the press. So did the level of printing technology. In 1800 the Stanhope Press printed 250 copies of a newspaper in an hour. But by 1850 with the introduction of a rotary cylinder printer, 8,000–12,000 copies could be printed per hour; this together with the rapid multiplication of printing plates, and the introduction of typesetting machines had revolutionised the production of print media. Another factor was that whereas at first newspapers had been distributed by stagecoach, the growth of the railways increased circulation in the first half of the nineteenth century from nine million to 18 million.

FOREIGN NEWS

Foreign news became an important area of news in the second half of the nineteenth century. Until then, only *The Times* took it seriously. Elsewhere, foreign news consisted of international financial and economic news. This changed with the advent of news agencies like Reuters' foreign news service and with the rise of the telegraph. In 1858 seven London daily newspapers subscribed to Reuters, and in 1868 the Press Association began distributing foreign news to the provincial press. Due to the expense of maintaining correspondents throughout the world, Reuters and the French and German agencies, Havas and Wolff, respectively, agreed to post correspondents in the territories associated with their country and to exchange news with one another. A couple of newspapers began to send their own correspondents abroad or hire local correspondents. By 1914 the *Daily Telegraph* had correspondents in Paris, Berlin, St Petersburg, and New York. Only *The Times* kept a network of correspondents in far-flung capitals, doing so at the expense of lowering its price to compete with the penny dailies. Reuters emphasised speed, and their reports often preceded those of *The Times'* own correspondents. The value of *The Times* to the reader lay, first, in its commentaries and background articles, and second, in its role as a balance to the agencies' reports which were sometimes written by journalists who were identified with the local government. The penny dailies' need for more popular angles to foreign news than were supplied by Reuters was satisfied by another news agency, Dalziel's.[2]

War reporting also came into its own as a form of journalism in the second half of the nineteenth century with the accounts of the Crimean War in *The Times* from its own correspondent, William Howard Russell. Until then, war coverage tended to be based on reports which had appeared in foreign newspapers or which were sent by junior officers from the battlefront. The latter were not very satisfactory because they were highly selective, written by people who were soldiers first and correspondents second, and because the writers understood little about what constituted 'news' or the importance of speed. Rival papers followed *The Times*'s example in sending their own reporters to the battlefield. The Civil War in America was covered by British journalists in the North and South. War coverage helped to increase newspaper circulation – the *Daily News* trebled its circulation during the Franco-Prussian War – and this enabled papers to report even more distant events. Military establishments, slow to realise the media's interest, placed few restrictions on what reporters could report.[3]

The press was also an important source of intelligence for ministers and officials. Sir Edward Grey, as Foreign Secretary, for example, received a daily clippings file containing key foreign news reports which had appeared in the press. Occasionally, the accounts in the press were more informative than the reports received from diplomats. As Paris correspondent of *The Times* from 1873 to 1903, M. de Blowitz achieved an enviable network of contacts with many European statesmen. For example, at the 1878 Congress of Berlin he obtained an advance copy of the final treaty for his paper to publish on the day that the treaty was signed. The reports from Emile Joseph Dillon, the St Petersburg correspondent of the *Daily Telegraph* during the 1904–5 Russo-Japanese War, carried considerable weight because of Dillon's friendship with the Russian minister of finance, Sergius Iu Witte. Reports by foreign correspondents often arrived before those by diplomats, including those by G. E. Morrison, the Far East correspondent of *The Times*, regarding Russian activities in China.

The British Broadcasting Corporation, established in 1922, became a source of foreign news only in the Second World War, because press interests feared the competition this might pose. When war broke out in 1939, a six o'clock broadcasting rule was lifted allowing for 24-hour broadcasting. The BBC started the war with one 'observer', Richard Dimbleby, stationed with the British Expeditionary Forces in France, but by 1944 it had a substantial number of correspondents in the various theatres of war. By 1940 the nine o'clock evening news was attracting an audience of 43–50 per cent of radio listeners. In the immediate postwar years the number of correspondents went down to three – in Paris, Berlin, and Washington.[4] Foreign news on television began in the

1950s in the current affairs programmes, 'Panorama' and 'Tonight'. With technical and creative innovations, including new styles of interviewing, investigative journalism, more sophisticated cameras and editing processes, electronic news gathering, video, and satellites, television had by the mid-1970s become the most important source of news.

PUBLIC OPINION

In the period from the 1850s to the outbreak of the First World War, a number of cases occurred in which the media had an influence on foreign policy. In 1909 Sir Arthur Nicolson, the British ambassador in St Petersburg, advocated the strengthening of the 1907 Anglo-Russian Agreement into an alliance but the foreign secretary, Grey, overruled him arguing that public opinion would not accept it. Similarly, Grey overruled a proposal by Foreign Office officials in the pre-war years to strengthen relations with France on the grounds that public opinion would oppose it. These were cases when the media influenced the policymaker regarding future policy options. There were also cases when the media contributed to changing an existing decision. A proposal in 1903 by the British government to participate with Germany in the financing of the Baghdad Railway, which had the backing of the City, had to be abandoned because cooperation with Germany was unpopular among backbenchers at Westminster and with public opinion. In 1855, the foreign secretary, Lord John Russell, returned from negotiations in Vienna terminating the Crimean War, but the terms leaked out and, in the face of considerable parliamentary disapproval, he resigned and the prime minister abandoned the proposed treaty.

In the inter-war years, public reaction to the First World War created pressure on politicians, including Conservatives, to follow a policy of appeasement, and only in the late 1930s did it become publicly acceptable to take a stand for rearmament. Politicians were led by the public and the media, rather than vice versa. Improvements in rail communications enabled Conservative papers in London like the *Daily Mail* and *Daily Express*, which supported Britain's imperial ambitions, to reach the provinces and thus compete with regional dailies, among them many with a liberal outlook. On the eve of the Second World War the British media had achieved a greater degree of social penetration than the media in any other country, with the exception of the US, with 14.5 million daily sales of newspapers, 9 million radios, and cinema audiences for newsreels of 20 million each week. Yet there were few instances when the media or public opinion changed an existing decision. One notable exception was the Hoare–Laval affair, in which Sir Samuel Hoare, the foreign secretary, resigned because of public criticism after the terms of the Hoare–Laval agreement with France, concerning stopping an Italian invasion of Abyssinia, were leaked to the press in Paris. The plan itself had to be jettisoned.

Staffed by officials of whom many had an aristocratic background, the Foreign Office viewed these public pressures and the interventions of politicians like Lloyd George as an interference in the diplomatic process which was best conducted in secret. It was argued that the public did not understand the complexities of external relations, nor was there a common ground between the public's values and the national interest of strengthening the state's power and influence. The counter-argument presented by the advocates of open diplomacy was that the public had a right to be informed about government policy, including foreign policy.[5] The concept of open covenants, put forward by Woodrow Wilson, did not envisage ministers responding to the public in the middle of international negotiations or coming under domestic pressure, but that the final form of an agreement once signed would be submitted to the citizenry.[6]

INTERNATIONAL NEGOTIATIONS

One of the practical results of the greater interest by the media and the public in diplomacy was to encourage those involved in negotiation to use the media to leak sensitive information to the public in order to hinder or advance a particular policy goal. It would be wrong to assume that a smaller Civil Service, or fewer relationships between the diplomatic community and the media, or the ability to confine sensitive information to a handful of officials resulted in no bureaucratic use of the media for competitive leaking. The media were frequently used in the first years of this century as a tool in conflicts between the Ministry of Defence and the Foreign Office and the Colonial Office. The media were also used in inter-governmental communication. During the British negotiations with France over Newfoundland in the winter of 1900–1, the Foreign Office intentionally leaked to the media. When during negotiations with China in 1902 reports in the British press indicated that the Chinese had yielded too much, *The Times* was approached to help create the impression that the chances of the British government accepting the particular Chinese proposals had gone down.[7] Notwithstanding the occasional use of the media during negotiations with foreign governments, the possibility that it might encourage the other side to play the same game generally discouraged its use until the Second World War, when contacts between the Foreign Office's News Department and journalists became more frequent.

MOULDING OPINION ABROAD

As early as the Greek city-states governments had made appeals to people, particularly in wartime. Yet it was only at the end of the nineteenth century that governments began to organise information programmes on a regular basis. The British did so after other governments, including the French, began applying the new techniques of advertising to foreign trade. The First World War made clear the need to explain policy not only to foreign governments but also to foreign publics. At the beginning of the war two organisations, outside of the Foreign Office, one dealing with press material and the other with literary and pictorial material, produced a large quantity of pamphlets and pictures which were designed to influence neutral opinion abroad and stiffen determination at home. In 1916 these became linked to the Foreign Office through the newly established News Department which coordinated their work. By 1918 the work had increased so much that a separate Ministry of Information was established under Lord Beaverbrook. When the war ended the ministry was disbanded on the grounds that propaganda had been a wartime expedient. A lasting peace, safeguarded by the League of Nations, would remain as testimony to the achievements of British ideals. The Treasury was alarmed at the expenditure that a propaganda apparatus would involve. However, Beaverbrook and Lord Northcliffe, who had headed a Department of Enemy Propaganda, were in favour of a skeleton structure remaining. In the end, the ministry was absorbed into the Foreign Office's News Department.

By the early 1920s there was considerable economic competition in British markets from France, Russia and Italy with each engaged in information and cultural work. In 1927 press attachés were appointed to the British embassies in Paris and Berlin with the functions of advising the ambassador about local public opinion, and maintaining contact with local and visiting journalists. In New York the British Library of Information was established, becoming the forerunner of the present-day British Information Services. But it was only in the 1930s that a serious response to the cultural propaganda of other countries was made, with the establishment in 1932 of the Empire Service of the British Broadcasting Corporation, around which the External Services were created, and with the creation of the British Council to encourage foreign visits to Britain and to foster friendship societies between British and other countries. Underlying British thinking on propaganda were the beliefs that propaganda was an adjunct to normal diplomacy and not, as the Soviet government saw it, a substitute for it, and that British propaganda should be intertwined with the truth and that the recipient could check the message for validity. In the First World War atrocity stories and conflicting promises had been the tools of the trade.

As soon as the Second World War broke out, the Ministry of Information was re-established with the functions of centralising government information policy and providing government departments with their information requirements relating to home publicity and allied and neutral countries. Given the ministry's need for credibility, responsibility for covert propaganda among the enemy rested with a political warfare organisation within the Foreign Office. Discussions about arrangements for peacetime publicity began as early as 1943. The Ministry of Information argued that since an efficient information structure had been set up it was neither necessary nor desirable that the Foreign Office, Commonwealth Office and Colonial Office should maintain their own separate information services. Britain's publicity overseas reflected not merely its foreign policy but embraced every aspect of the British way of life. It required the services of professional journalists and advertising men to gather all this material, process it and present it abroad in the most effective manner. The Foreign Office argued that information work was an integral element of overseas representation. A compromise was reached under which the Foreign Office, Commonwealth Office and Colonial Office determined information policy and a Central Office of Information (COI), in a truncated form without a minister, was to supply such technical services as producing press material, photographs, films, magazines and books.[8]

With the post-war amalgamation of the Commonwealth and Colonial offices into the Foreign and Commonwealth Office, the information functions of the first two were absorbed by the latter. Information priorities have changed with less importance given to British Commonwealth countries and more to the communist countries among others, and with commercial targeted information work replacing general image building. There have also been separations and amalgamations among the FCO departments responsible for overseas information policy, for preparing guidance on governmental positions, and for information services. But the various tasks carried out by the FCO, and the nature of its relationships with the BBC External Services, the British Council and the COI are similar, if not identical, today to what they were in 1945.

MOULDING OPINION AT HOME

Despite Britain's powerful international position in the nineteenth century, no apparent need was felt by the Foreign Office to mould the attitudes of the press. One of the first reported instances was during the Fashoda crisis in September 1898 when a *Daily Mail* journalist was briefed by the permanent under-secretary, Sir Thomas Sanderson, on the policy that the government was adopting.[9] Nor was there any formal access for journalists with inquiries until the same year when a system was begun by which at four o'clock each day journalists could submit inquiries on paper which would be sent up to the private secretary to the foreign secretary, and any items of intelligence which were thought suitable for publication were sent down. In 1911 Earl Grey defined the Foreign Office's relations with journalists thus: 'Certain representative newspapers receive any communications in regard to foreign affairs which are suitable for publication. These are confined for the most part to appointments and changes in the Diplomatic Service. If inquiries are made at the Foreign Office with regard to specific facts, they are answered when it is possible without prejudice to public or private interests'.[10] There were ad hoc meetings with senior journalists like Sir Valentine Chirol, foreign editor of *The Times*, Lucian Wolf of the *Daily Graphic*, and Charles Watney, foreign editor of the *Daily Mail*. The first regular briefing consisted of a twice-weekly meeting which Flora Shaw, the colonial editor of *The Times*, had with two under-secretaries.[11] These contacts also provided officials with an additional source of intelligence.

The access became institutionalised with the setting up of the News Department in 1916, making the Foreign Office the second government department, after the General Post Office, to establish a section to deal with the press. It reflected an acceptance by some, though not all, officials that public opinion was playing a less passive role in external matters. A Foreign Office official planning the 1929 London Naval Conference surprised Sir Maurice Hankey, secretary to the cabinet, by suggesting that the press would require as much space as the delegates themselves. The 1955 Geneva summit conference was attended by some 2,000 journalists and technicians; keeping the press informed was, according to one journalist, 'a sort of mass production job with press officers working in relays'.[12] The News Department's ability to brief the press was dependent on the extent to which they themselves were kept informed of diplomatic developments by the geographical departments in the Foreign Office. It was only after the Second World War that this need became more widely recognised.

In the First World War journalists were faced with considerable restrictions owing to the military's suspicions of the media. In 1911 the Official Secrets Act had made it an offence for an official to disclose official information without authorisation. In 1912, when during the Agadir crisis the press revealed sensitive information, the government decided that publication of secret military or naval information would be liable to prosecution. A voluntary system between the press and the government, known as the 'D' Notice system, was agreed under which certain types of news, including accounts of air raids, food shortages, and shipping losses would not be published. When the war broke out war correspondents were not allowed near the battlefront. Censorship became a controversial issue in Parliament and the press, partly due to the government's failure to supply the press with information which could be printed, such as gallant stories of British successes. In 1915 greater access was given.[13]

In the Second World War officials showed a greater awareness of the need to maintain public support, with the need for access soon recognised by most sections of the armed forces. Censorship was based again on the 'D' Notice system. The rationale for having a voluntary system was that under a compulsory system a large number of people would be required, and that it would in any case be opposed by the press. The voluntary system worked well: out of 400,000 different issues of newspapers in the Second World War, only four prosecutions for infringement of the regulations were brought. Censorship for reporters from the foreign media was, however, mandatory.

The Times, from its editor downwards, had a close relationship with the foreign secretary and other officials from before the turn of the century. In the months before the First World War Wickham Steed, its foreign editor, was in daily contact with the permanent under-secretary. However, during the winter of 1914–15 relations between the Foreign Office and *The Times* broke down over the latter's coverage of Turkish affairs. What had been considered a 'special relationship' became more formal in 1937 when the Foreign Office suggested that the paper should appoint a regular diplomatic correspondent to collect news and views. The head of the News Department, Rex Leeper, hoped that feeding *The Times* – the editorial views of which were construed in European capitals as those of the British government – would enable foreigners to distinguish clearly between the paper's policies as expressed in the editorials and those of the government.[14] *The Times* correspondent continued to receive his own briefing after the Second World War when the diplomatic correspondents of other news organisations were given regular briefings in self-formed groups. While *The Times'* man may have been more privy to classified information, the flow of questions to a spokesman from a group of journalists makes it less easy for the spokesman to 'sow' a particular line. By the mid-1970s *The Times'* man had joined the group briefing, and there was no indication that *The Times* received preferential treatment than other respected news organisations such as the BBC, Reuters, or the *Financial Times*.

While the Foreign Office has no veto over what the media say, it has made attempts to press its views on them. When an editorial in *The Times* in 1949 criticised Turkey's claim to be a member of any European federation, the Foreign Office, which received a protest about the editorial from the Turkish government, sent for the paper's foreign editor to reprimand him.[15] The BBC, anxious after the war to return to its former editorial independence, issued a directive to its newsroom to ignore all approaches by the Foreign Office unless they came from the News Department via the BBC diplomatic correspondent.[16] William Clark, a diplomat turned journalist who was *The Observer*'s diplomatic correspondent in the 1950s, said:

> By its control of the sources of information, with the implied threat that criticism of policies would lead to a less full flow to that correspondent, by co-opting all of us diplomatic correspondents into a cosy club of those in the know, I fear that the government (under both parties) did manage the news of our foreign policy.[17]

CONCLUSION

By the middle of this century, media diplomacy had come into its own. During the previous hundred years, foreign news coverage had evolved into a major form of journalism, taken seriously by editors in a competitive market. Together with other factors, the increase in foreign coverage has led to an increase in public interest in foreign policy. The increased public interest has, in turn, led to a felt need by ministers and officials to explain policy to the public in order to build support. Various channels have emerged for this purpose, notably such media channels as the diplomatic correspondents.

While it is true that changes have occurred in media diplomacy since the Second World War, these changes have been mostly in terms of degree rather than type: more foreign news, more or less public interest, more or less governmental explanation of policy. An exception has been the growth of visual media, which has been far more dramatic. These historical trends form the basis of media diplomacy in Britain today.

CHAPTER THREE

INFORMATION

'Governments don't decide policy based on information from
the media. Even if they hear of something first in the media they
will check with that country's embassy or with your embassy
abroad. You have your own superior sources.'
                                                    – prime minister

The making of a country's foreign policy begins with the gathering of
information about developments abroad. A key element in the success
of a foreign policy is whether the policymaker's image of the world is
accurate, because if there is a disparity between his image and the reality
there is a strong possibility that the policy will end in failure. The
policymaker has to examine the situation with which he is dealing and
its implications for the country's policy objectives, consider the different
courses of action to deal with the situation, and then, depending on
whether he is a minister or an official, recommend or decide upon the
course of action which best fits the national interest.

News media are basic sources of information about world affairs.
Diplomatic missions prepare their reports to the FCO in London by
gathering information from the local media, as well as from other
sources. In London the British media are secondary sources of information for officials to the reports and cables which they receive from
overseas posts. It is true that while news media provide the information
for policy decisions, it is officials and ministers who interpret the
information within their concept of the national interest. For example,
when the Shah of Iran was overthrown, which the FCO had failed to
envisage, the then British Ambassador in Tehran, Sir Anthony Parsons,
said, 'our lack of perception derived not from a failure of information
but from a failure to interpret correctly the information available to
us'.[1] The role played by news media is, however, important because
the efficiency of policymaking is already hampered if the information
supplied to the policymaker by news media is quantitatively or
qualitatively inadequate.

Topics to be discussed in this chapter include the use of news media
by diplomatic missions to gather information; the use of the British

media by ministers and officials; whether the media can be substitutes for the diplomatic reporting done by diplomatic missions; and the use of news media by MPs, interest groups, and the wider public.

DIPLOMATIC MISSIONS

In structural terms information gathering is done by diplomatic missions rather than by officials in London, who are responsible for drawing up policy recommendations. A diplomat must gain an understanding of the country to which he is posted. Political analysis forms a large part of the diplomatic mission's work and is designed to discover where power lies in a country, how it is exercised, and who is likely to possess it in the future. Increasingly, such analysis focuses upon defence and economics. In addition to sending London political reports, diplomatic missions need to gather information for their own purposes including the diplomatic exchange of views with the local government and the promotion of British policies at the public level.

Much of this information can be obtained from the media. In some cases, such as during a crisis, the media may be the only source of information available. During the refugee disaster in East Bengal, Pakistan, in 1971, the British High Commission in Calcutta relied upon the local press, journalists, refugees, and Oxfam workers for their information rather than sending any diplomats to the stricken area because 'one felt the whole thing was going to be played up rather much if the British representative was going round the border areas', as the British deputy high commissioner said. 'We were trying at the time to talk with the Pakistan government, and we have tried to maintain a capacity to speak to them.'[1a] The type of media available to a diplomat for information gathering clearly varies, from developing countries where there may be only a few poorly produced newspapers to developed ones like the United States where foreign diplomats can draw upon a wide range of specialised magazines. In countries where the media are small, foreign diplomats have to find alternative sources of information such as government departments, trade unions, and research institutes. But generally the media are primary sources. A British diplomat in a West European capital estimated that 75 per cent of the information gathered by his embassy came from published sources while the remaining 25 per cent was gathered by more active diplomacy, cultivating relations with local politicians, and exchanging classified information with government officials.[2] Cord Meyer, former director of the Central Intelligence Agency, estimates that 90 per cent of the information required by the policymaker is in the public domain.[2a]

Information gathering in the large missions is a fairly sophisticated matter. The Information Department of the British Embassy in Washington organises a press cuttings service in the embassy. It covers the *Washington Post*, the *New York Times, Baltimore Sun, Christian Science Monitor, Wall Street Journal*, and the *Journal of Commerce*. Magazines used include *Time, Newsweek, Business Week, Foreign Policy*, and the *New Yorker*.

Journalists are an additional source of information since often they have spoken to sources in and outside the government which are less accessible to the foreign diplomat. 'My relationship with journalists is a continual trade-off. It's very informal. It would be much more difficult for me to exist without them and more difficult for them without me,' said a diplomat. In some countries with a state-controlled media, including the Soviet Union, local journalists are more inhibited in speaking to foreign diplomats while in others they remain a useful source of information not published in their own media. In capitals with a corps of British foreign correspondents these will often provide diplomats with their most reliable media source. 'In the sense that the British correspondents meet everybody of note in Washington and they often inform us on how key people are thinking, they contribute to our reporting,' a counsellor in Washington noted.

The contribution of the media to information gathering is weakened by several factors. The tangibility of printed media and the relative intangibility of broadcast media have resulted in the latter's exclusion from being a source of information to foreign diplomats. Linguistic obstacles limit the use made of media in foreign languages. State-controlled media are by definition another branch of government, and while they need to be monitored in order to follow what the government is saying they cannot provide diplomats with an independent source of information.

The dominance of printed media over broadcast media may be seen from the fact that until the 1980s few missions possessed a television set let alone equipment to record radio and television programmes, whereas many missions now do. In the past, special current affairs programmes were followed by a designated member of the mission and transcripts of selected programmes were sometimes obtained from the news organisation. Most broadcasts needed to be followed by diplomats at home. But since much of their time was taken up with the diplomatic social life, such diplomats could not hope to compensate for the lack of monitoring of broadcasting done within the mission. Despite the introduction of video equipment only key current affairs programmes are generally recorded. There is no attempt to cover the entire output of radio or television. The argument that foreign broadcasting seen through the summaries of the BBC Monitoring Service, which are read inside the FCO, can make up for this absence is incorrect given that

MD–C

these only summarise important political statements. Nor is it correct to say that printed media, which can be read at a time of the diplomat's choosing, can replace broadcast media because their respective contents are not identical, and because in many countries the latter is more influential than the former.

In those countries where French, German, Spanish, or Italian are the main languages, foreign diplomats are in many cases able to use the media with little difficulty. Diplomats in the Arab world, the Far East, and Latin America, not infrequently spend a considerable part of their career at postings in the same region and thus build up a vocabulary. But in other countries only a handful of the mission's staff are likely to have more than a smattering of the language. To cope with these problems diplomatic missions prepare daily summaries of the local press, and in some cases the foreign ministry produces summaries of articles. These are poor substitutes for reading the newspapers in original since it is difficult to obtain local feeling from them. In certain countries where English-language newspapers are published, a basic knowledge of local events may be gleaned but since these are not usually the media which local politicians read their use is limited.

A 1979 survey found that the media were controlled by the government in 67 countries, partly controlled in 75 countries, and free in 68 countries.[3] In reflecting what the government is telling the people, state-controlled media become an important element of an overseas mission's political reporting. They are one additional channel in a government's network of communications with other countries. In addition, state-controlled media reflect the changing balance of political power in the government. 'Speeches, articles, the place where they occur in the newspaper, the presence or absence of a party leader at an official function, the people chosen to meet or see off visiting dignitaries, the designation by which officials are described, the order of people displayed at national celebrations, the selection, handling and suppression of news, and a multitude of clues, taken together, may throw some light on the darkness which normally covers the struggle for power or shifts of policy in a communist party', an ambassador to Moscow noted.[4] The difficulties in developing contacts with the local population make for an even greater use of the media in these countries. In 1978 the Soviet government placed restrictions on the movement of British and other western diplomats to outside of Moscow, and British defence attachés, whose task is to gather Soviet military information, were followed, photographed, and attacked by the KGB.

THE FOREIGN AND COMMONWEALTH OFFICE

The function of officials in London is less to gather information and more to formulate policy submissions and plan their implementation. Nevertheless, the media contribute to the information flow in London in a number of ways. Each official in the FCO receives a daily cuttings file containing press clippings on matters relevant to him. The desk officer for Poland and Czechoslovakia in the FCO's Research Department said: 'I see the cables from the British posts in Warsaw and Prague, letters from these missions, and the ambassadors' assessments of public opinion and press trends. In addition I see the British newspapers and BBC Monitoring which are a major source to me. Often reports in the British press are better than the cables from missions.'

More often the media supply information before the cables from the missions arrive rather than being suppliers of exclusive information. 'From my experience I haven't seen anything striking in the papers which we were not aware of through other channels. The media more foreshadow embassy reporting,' a departmental head said. The press also helps the official to understand the diplomatic cables, as well as being a gauge of the domestic pressures in Britain which ministers come under from interest groups and the political parties. The proximity of Britain's national press to the political parties gives added significance to this function. A permanent under-secretary said: 'If there is a Conservative government I read *The Guardian* in order to assess the opposition which my foreign secretary may face in Parliament. If there is a Labour government I read the *Daily Telegraph* – I wouldn't need to read *The Guardian* because I know the government's policies.' An additional reason for following the press is to see whether due regard is being given to the government's views. Thus, similar and even identical reports on the same subject in different newspapers are included in the cuttings file.

Specialised journals such as *Africa, West Africa, Latin American Newsletter*, and *Soviet Analyst* are circulated to the relevant departments. The FCO is connected to the BBC Monitoring Service, which together with the US and West Germany monitors radio broadcasts from 120 countries. It sometimes provides officials with the first news of important developments. It was the first source to monitor the German radio announcement of Hitler's suicide, of Tokyo radio's announcement that Hiroshima had been bombed, and of the Russian invasion of Czechoslovakia. The main source from the media of up-to-the-minute news about international developments is the Reuters news agency. The FCO's reliance upon a single international news agency contrasts with the US State Department which subscribes to AP, UPI, *Agence France Presse* and Reuters. The agencies are said to beat the cables received from the US overseas missions by four to five hours and sometimes by up to 24 hours, which can be crucial during diplomatic crises. While the United States' requirement for information may be stronger than Britain's, there is a strong case for subscribing to more than one agency – for instance, AFP often carries news from Africa and Asia not carried by the other agencies.

In the FCO the News Department advises the foreign secretary, the permanent under-secretary, and the relevant departments regarding news developments. In the State Department the news agency tickers are monitored constantly; eight copies of the news come off each ticker, and additional copies are often duplicated in order to distribute the copy to all relevant bureaux in the department. The secretary and deputy under-secretary of state have their separate tickers.[5]

The absence of monitoring broadcasting found abroad with overseas missions is also found with British broadcasting. Until the mid-1970s the FCO did not possess a television set. Today, the foreign secretary junior ministers, the permanent under-secretary, and the News Department each have one. The last also has video equipment to record programmes. While it is questionable whether each government department should monitor broadcasting and prepare transcriptions, there is a case for, say, the Central Office of Information supplying on a centralised basis the relevant government departments with transcriptions of the appropriate programmes and interviews on such programmes as the 'World at One' and 'News at Ten'. One source of broadcast news which FCO officials receive is the broadcasts of the BBC External Services.

With the exceptions of the *International Herald Tribune* and *Le Monde*, few foreign papers are read in London. It is left to the overseas mission – which is in a better position to assess the reliability of a journal and its reporters – to follow the local media. The potential for officials to absorb even more paper is limited.* Foreign ministries in other countries make a greater use of the foreign press. A study of Norwegian foreign policymaking found that out of 230 newspapers and magazines

---

* The head of the North American Department described his department's reading of the foreign media regarding the US thus: 'I am fortunate in reading the *International Herald Tribune* (a digest of the *New York Times* and *Washington Post*). In addition I see the *Washington Post* three days after publication. The assistant head of department and the US desk officer also read it because of its good coverage of Congress. None of us read the *New York Times*: that is left to the official in Research Department covering the United States who acts as our memory bank and ensures that as staff change in our department we are kept aware of established lines of policy. We also get *Time, Newsweek*, and *US News and World Report*. The embassy sends occasional items by telex and, infrequently, articles and news reports by diplomatic bag. The editorials by telex indicate certain lines of thought. We also get a summary of US press opinion prepared by the ambassador based on reports from consulates across the United States.'

read in those government departments engaged in external relations, 157 were from overseas.[6] A study of foreign policymaking in Senegal found that both the Office of the President and the Ministry of Foreign Affairs subscribed to a considerable number of European quality newspapers and magazines.[7]

The usefulness for officials of seeing the foreign press lies in being able to gain much more information about affairs in a country from the local media than from reports in the British press, and in offering officials an alternative source of information to the cables received from the overseas post. The importance of an alternative source of information was illustrated during the Biafran war. The aggrievement and determination of the rebellion in Nigeria's eastern province led by Colonel Ojukwu were underestimated by the High Commissioner in Lagos, Sir David Hunt, who recommended London to back Gowon. The deputy high commissioner responsible for the eastern province, James Parker, however, recognised the determination of the Biafrans. One writer alleges that Parker's comments either were cut out from Hunt's reports to London or had derisive remarks put on them.[8] With little coverage in the British press of the Biafran situation from 1966 when the uprising began until the spring of 1968, officials and ministers in London were dependent on one source of information, the official cables. If Nigerian media had been read in London a more accurate assessment of the rebellion might have been made.

According to a senior FCO official, this was not the only occasion when a head of mission may have failed to report to London the views of subordinates whom subsequent events proved correct. Now that foreign newspapers from many key capitals are available in London 24 hours after publication, the argument for the FCO to widen their use of the foreign press is strong. The importance for officials of receiving alternative sources of information was noted by the Franks Inquiry into British government actions in the period before the Argentine invasion of the Falkland Islands.

As with diplomatic missions, journalists are also a source of information and interpretation in London. 'A journalist who goes shooting off to Afghanistan — his impressions may well be useful to us. We work quite hard to maintain our contacts with the journalistic world but it hasn't been easy because there have been constraints about how much we can say to them and show them,' said a head of the Research Department. After the Russian invasion of Czechoslovakia in 1968 the diplomatic correspondents of Reuters and *The Guardian* suggested to the News Department that Britain should sponsor a UN resolution that a UN delegation be despatched to the centre of Prague with the aim of discouraging the Red Army's repression of the Czech population.

The geographical departments took up their idea, but instead of sponsoring the resolution itself Britain suggested that a non-aligned state should do so. Yugoslavia was asked, but the resolution failed to materialise.[9]

How officials use these media is illustrated by the case of the desk officer for the Arab–Israeli conflict in the Near East Department. His main sources of information are the reports and assessments from British posts in Egypt, Israel, Jordan, Lebanon, and Syria. Unlike the media these are tailor-made for his use and are written within the framework of British policies towards the region. He sees a cuttings file in order to follow local developments. He also sees, uncut, *The Times, The Guardian, Daily Telegraph*, and *Financial Times* because he needs to follow the activities of pro-Arab and pro-Israeli interest groups in Britain, which frequently spill over into the correspondence columns of the quality press, in order to gauge the pressure his ministers may come under. He saw no foreign newspapers from the region with the exception of selected articles sent from the overseas posts. He also saw specialised journals including *Arab Report and Record*, the *Middle East Economic Digest*, the *Jewish Chronicle*, and *Middle East International*. These may be divided between those which gather information and those which are published by or reflect an interest bloc.

Successive government inquiries on Britain's overseas representation have examined the question whether the flow of political reporting done by overseas missions to London is not too much or of the wrong type. While acknowledging that in fulfilling their representative functions these missions need to gather a store of information about the respective countries, the Duncan Report said they should be 'extremely selective in deciding how much of it to report' to London.[10] The first question which has been asked is whether the FCO is simply an information gatherer or whether its work should be geared to managing the country's external relations. In fact, one answer which needs to be given is that as the barrier between domestic and external policies blurs, the FCO's role is becoming increasingly one of a coordinating department. In that sense the FCO's function of being an information gatherer will increase. Another question which has been asked is whether alternative, and cheaper, sources of information such as the media can replace the reporting done by diplomats.

In recommending a reduction in political reporting, the Berrill Report divided reporting into the immediate ad hoc requirement for information relevant to a specific policy decision, and the standing need for a store of background information. It recommended a continuation in the former because as missions have more direct access than the media to required information (for example, about other participants' views), they will anyway be sending London an assessment and advice about the matter and it is not always possible to separate an assessment from a factual report of the issue being discussed, and they can tailor their reports more exactly to policymakers' requirements. Regarding the latter it recommended that greater reliance be placed on the British press and BBC Monitoring:

Missions should assume unless otherwise instructed that policymakers in London can get the news from the media or the BBC Monitoring Service .... (In one large post we visited a factual account of an event which was amply reported in the British press was drafted by a first secretary and submitted through two counsellors and a minister before being despatched by the ambassador.)[11]

The Duncan Report rejected the use of the media to supplement a reduction in the volume of political reporting because

the number of press and broadcasting representatives in the world is nowadays much smaller than is sometimes supposed. In any case the news media have their own ends to serve and cannot be expected to act as the British Government's only source of international political information. Comment is the largest element in good political reporting by diplomatic posts; and if a post is doing its job properly its comments will tend to be more useful to the British Government than any available from other sources.[12]*

In fact, the Berrill Report did not suggest that the media could provide information required for specific policy decisions; rather it recommended that the media provide the background information. The opposition of diplomats to cuts in the volume of political reporting is understandable given that it takes up an important slice of the work of overseas representation; but is it justified? An assessment by the Civil Service or the FCO Inspectorate might suggest, for example, that a more efficient use of the media, as outlined here, could allow for a reduction in the reporting by overseas missions. A study by the author of whether the media could substitute for the background reporting found that this was indeed so regarding military and diplomatic crises. But the media are not an adequate substitute for diplomatic reporting on Britain's bilateral relations; with the exception of media coverage of certain aspects of EEC affairs such as the community budget, bilateral relations

---

* The Diplomatic Service Whitley Council, a staff association of diplomats, rejected the Berrill Report's recommendation because 'the Press is not, unfortunately, an adequate guide to what is happening in far too many countries of the world'.[13]

Sir Humphrey Trevelyan, a former ambassador, has written that a journalist is 'concerned more with the blaze in the foreground than with the permanent realities behind it. He must try and draw conclusions, however speculative, secure in the knowledge that what he writes will be used the next day to wrap up the fish, and that he will have plenty of opportunities to correct his errors.... The ambassador is not required to try and beat the agencies or to compete with all the instant news and comment on the press and radio. His despatches should be the basis of his government's considered judgement of the international scene.'[14]

are deemed unnewsworthy by editors. (These findings are in accordance with the Berrill Report's recommendations.) Some background economic reporting could be supplemented and substituted for by specialised economic and financial media. There is no case for using the national press in diplomatic reporting on defence except in providing general background to international developments.[15]

MINISTERS

The styles of following the media vary with the individual minister.* But in general most prime ministers saw all the national press, some cabinet ministers saw most national newspapers, while junior ministers tended to read the quality newspapers and assumed that the secretary of state read the popular papers. 'I see all the newspapers – including the popular papers because they are popular,' a chancellor of the exchequer said. 'The trained eye can get through the daily press in half an hour,' said a minister of state at the FCO. They also receive a cuttings file, prepared by their private office, of various clippings including key reports and articles, editorials, and letters to the editor.

In reading the national press, most prime ministers are more interested in doing so to follow domestic affairs. For foreign affairs they tend to rely on the private secretary responsible for foreign affairs to brief them and select the important cables for the FCO. The private secretary will have read the main foreign affairs coverage in the quality papers and he might reflect it in his briefing with the prime minister. Edward Heath and James Callaghan read all the national papers. Winston Churchill and Harold Wilson, in addition, read some of the next day's first editions before retiring to bed. Clement Attlee read, as a matter of duty, *The Times* and the *Daily Herald*. Mr Heath also read a summary of editorial opinion and Mr Callaghan a summary of the provincial press prepared by the Press Office at No 10 Downing Street. Lord Home described his newspaper reading as:

I see all the papers. I go to the sports pages first. You get to know the correspondents who pick up the good information. You can't clutter yourself up with too much paper and you rely on your private secretaries to weed it out and to give you the stuff which they think is relevant to something which is happening or which might happen.

*The individuality of reading habits was expressed by a minister of state at the Ministry of Defence who said: 'I have all the newspapers laid out in my office. I glance at all of them and read two or three – *The Guardian, The Times*, and the *Daily Telegraph*. I'm not a great *Financial Times* man – it's the pink that puts me off. The populars are for glancing at – the *Daily Express, Daily Mail*, and *Daily Mirror* may be read in thirty seconds, just headlines and leading articles unless Chapman Pincher has a centre spread. On Sundays we have at home the *Sunday Times, Sunday Express*, and *Sunday Telegraph*. I haven't taken the *Observer* for years – the papers are so expensive that you have to cut something out, but I see it at the mother-in-law's.'

Very little broadcasting is seen or heard by ministers due to its relative intangibility as compared with the printed media. 'The only broadcasting I can listen to is in my car', a deputy foreign secretary said. The programmes ministers listen to regularly are early morning radio and TV news programmes. If their schedule allows, ministers try to listen to editions of current affairs programmes dealing with subjects in their area of responsibility. Until recently few ministers had a television set in their office. Some videotaping of key programmes and interviews is done by the press department in the ministry and by the party headquarters. 'As prime minister you have very little time in your day really to look at TV. Occasionally I listened to the one o'clock news at lunchtime but not regularly. But you got a report every day, if you wanted one, on what was being said on BBC and ITN', Lord Home said.

Very little of the foreign press is seen even among ministers at the FCO. They rely on their staff to bring particular pieces to their attention, and on ambassadors to include summaries of the local media in their reports to London.

The effects of reading the press are as a secondary, and sometimes faster, source of information to the official reports, as a gauge to public opinion, and as a source of ideas about policy. The latter two effects will be examined in the next chapter. As a source of information the media play an important role during international crises when reports from a confused and changing situation may not be sent to London by the overseas mission quickly. Richard Wood, as minister of overseas development, said:

The main use of the media to me is during disasters when some of the best reports come from the media. I rely as much on a good reporter during a disaster as upon an embassy cable. During the 1971 Pakistan refugee disaster there was a lot of press coverage and it was due to those reports that I decided to go to see the situation for myself.

In cabinet, although ministers receive a selection of the telegrams sent to the FCO during a foreign crisis, only the prime minister, foreign secretary, and minister of defence are likely to have seen the latest cables. For example, the Soviet invasion of Czechoslovakia and the imminence of war in the Middle East in 1967 were discussed in cabinet without the prepared papers having been circulated.[16]

The vast amount of information which arrives at a foreign policy bureaucracy rarely reaches the ministerial level. The information is refined so that the minister receives a single departmental view. As an alternative source of information the media serve as a corrective to this single view. 'You get a bland recommendation and if there are other courses of action these are presented with a slant in the hope that they won't be taken up. You feel a need for a counter-balance and there are

only two ways of getting this – by having a political adviser, which
I do not have, and by keeping up one's own careful study of the media,'
a minister of state at the Ministry of Defence said. 'I am often quite
surprised that I often learn of information from the press which hasn't
come through the diplomatic channels,' a junior minister at the FCO
said.

The same is true at the cabinet level. Since the selection of telegrams
for cabinet ministers is controlled by the FCO and the Cabinet Office,
there remains the possibility that those which strengthen the FCO view
are distributed while those which do not are left out. It has been claimed
that when the Labour cabinet discussed membership in the EEC in 1967
the supply of telegrams about West European reaction was controlled
because only a minority of ministers favoured entry.[17] Ministers had
to turn to other sources for information, including the media.

THE WIDER PUBLIC, MPs, AND INTEREST GROUPS

In contrast to ministers and officials, those outside the official bureaucracy – Members of Parliament, interest groups, and the wider public –
do not see the telegrams from overseas but are dependent almost wholly
on the media for their information about international developments.
The dependence of the public on the media may be seen from a survey
of the uses of broadcasting made during the 1975 referendum for entry to the EEC. Forty-four per cent said that the BBC and IBA broadcasting had helped a lot in presenting the cases of the anti- and pro-
Marketeers; 26 per cent a little; 23 per cent said it didn't help; and
7 per cent were undecided.[18] Television is the most useful source of
information about foreign affairs. A survey found that 58 per cent
thought television the most useful source of foreign affairs information,
in contrast to 24 per cent who thought the morning press was and 8 per
cent who thought radio was.[19] The wider public receive little foreign
media, presumably finding their needs satisfied by the British media.
Even senior businessmen, a sector of the public presumably more likely
than others to see the foreign media, do not. A survey found that less
than 1 per cent among them read *Le Monde, La Stampa*, or *Die Welt*.
Time and *Newsweek* were read by 5 per cent, *Business Week* by 10 per
cent and the *International Herald Tribune* by 2 per cent.[20]

A survey among ten MPs who take an active interest in foreign affairs
found that they read one or two of the four quality newspapers – *The
Times*, the *Financial Times*, *The Guardian*, and the *Daily Telegraph*.
Not one of them read a popular paper. Although the political weeklies
are read widely among MPs – one study said *The Economist* was read
by 66 per cent of MPs, the *New Statesman* by 60 per cent, *The Spectator*

by 36 per cent, and the *Tribune* by 23 per cent – only *The Economist* was listed as a source of information specifically regarding foreign affairs.[21] The *International Herald Tribune* is increasingly recognised as an important source of information. The only other foreign media seen by MPs are *Le Monde* and the *Christian Science Monitor*, the latter being sent free to them. The parliamentary timetable meant that few MPs saw much television.

In the House of Commons there are television rooms, one for each channel. Videotaping facilities are available. But MPs said that during the parliamentary session they saw at most occasional editions of such current affairs programmes as 'Panorama' and 'This Week'. The only broadcasting seen or heard in any frequency is early morning radio and television programmes.

The newspapers are an MP's prime source of information. 'MPs don't expect to get information from government departments', said one MP. Another said that 'the FCO sends background papers which are not much more useful than the press. They don't send them to all MPs'. An inquiry from an MP to the FCO is usually directed to the minister. The lack of information from government departments, despite the existence of a Select Committee on Foreign Affairs, contributes to the lack of parliamentary scrutiny of foreign policy. The US Congressman appears to have greater access to official sources than his British counterpart, although he also complains of 'the trickle of information from the Department of State'.[22] Nor is the Conservative Party's Research Department or the Labour Party's International Department of great use to the backbencher for information because these poorly staffed organisations concentrate on supplying the needs of the party's front bench. 'If you are a backbencher you have to run your own foreign office. I cut the papers out, they are my intelligence system. I have a cuttings library going back 25 years', said an MP. Nor is the opposition front bench in a much better position in obtaining official information. For the most part the Civil Service goes to great pains to avoid political contacts with the opposition.[23] As the Labour Party's foreign affairs spokesman, Denis Healey kept his own file of press cuttings.[24] As an opposition foreign affairs spokesman, Douglas Hurd found that while generally he obtained a particular piece of information he requested from the FCO, his main sources of information were '*The Times, Daily Telegraph, Financial Times*, and *The Guardian* and a mass of paper from the EEC'.

A major source of information is the House of Commons Library which itself depends heavily on the media for building its information store. It subscribes to a wide selection of overseas newspapers including *Le Monde, Die Welt, La Stampa, Frankfurter Allgemeine, L'Humanité,*

Der Spiegel, the *New York Times*, the *International Herald Tribune*, the *Toronto Globe and Mail*, various Indian and Pakistani and other Commonwealth papers. In addition, a wide selection of specialist journals are taken. The library's International Affairs Section maintains a comprehensive press cuttings service based on *The Times* and with additional material from *The Guardian* and the *Financial Times*. The library also receives transcripts of certain BBC and ITV programmes and has arrangements by which it can receive transcripts of other programmes.

The media are the main sources of information not only for MPs and the wider public, but also for research institutes, such as the Royal Institute of International Affairs (Chatham House) and the International Institute for Strategic Studies, and for interest groups. For both of these the printed media predominate and may be divided between the national press and specialised journals. The two institutes maintain their own press cuttings service. The IISS, for example, receives about 200 regular publications.

Many interest groups find the national press inadequate for their needs. They read the national press more in order to follow daily developments and to monitor whether their group's point of view is being correctly presented, and less for information which for an interest group is usually superficial and not comprehensive. Finance is a factor influencing the range of publications which an interest group can subscribe to. The heavy cost of subscribing to newspapers and journals from the country or region towards which the group is promoting friendly relations meant in some cases that a group took the relevant journals published in Britain instead.[25]

CONCLUSION: PATTERNS OF MEDIA CONSUMPTION

A number of patterns emerge in the type of news media used by different people. The wider public, MPs, interest groups, and research institutes are to be contrasted with the FCO and the overseas missions in not being privy to official sources of information. As an information gatherer, the overseas mission, like the wider public, MPs, interest groups, and research institutes, is dependent on the media for its primary source of information on foreign affairs. This contrasts with the FCO which draws its primary information from the cables received from over 140 overseas missions.

The sources of information may be divided between primary and secondary sources. The daily press is the primary source of information on foreign affairs to MPs, interest groups, and research institutes, and to about one-quarter of the wider public. Television is the primary source

TABLE 3.1

PRIMARY AND SECONDARY SOURCES OF FOREIGN AFFAIRS INFORMATION

	Overseas Missions	FCO	Wider public	MPs	Interest groups	Institutes
Non-media: overseas cables	Secondary	Primary	–	–	–	–
UK press	–	Secondary	Primary	Primary	Primary	Primary
UK specialist journals	–	Secondary	–	Secondary	Primary	Primary
Overseas press	Primary	Secondary	–	–[3]	Secondary	Primary
UK radio	–	–	Primary	–	–	–
Overseas radio	Primary	Secondary[2]	–	–	–	–
UK TV	–	–	Primary	–	–	–
Overseas TV	–	–	–	–	–	–
News agencies	–[1]	Primary	–	–	–	–

[1] Up to a dozen major missions receive the national or an international agency.
[2] Via the BBC Monitoring Service.
[3] A small number of MPs read foreign newspapers and periodicals.

to the majority of the public. But it is neither a primary nor secondary source to ministers and MPs, whose timetables clash with broadcasts, to diplomats and officials, who find it easier to use the printed media, or to interest groups and research institutes. Radio is a primary source of information to only a small section of the public. Of the political weeklies only *The Economist* is a source of information to MPs, interest groups, research institutes, and a small section of the public. That these various groups of people are not exposed to the same media has obvious implications for foreign policy. 'It is an interesting paradox that while your constituents draw most of their material from television we see hardly any. You are very conscious during election campaigns that you have not been exposed to the same material that they have', an FCO minister said.

Foreign printed media are primary sources to overseas missions and, on a smaller scale, to research institutes. They are a secondary source to the FCO and to some interest groups. Foreign broadcasting is a primary source of information to overseas missions and a secondary source to the FCO. Specialised journals are a primary source to research institutes and to interest groups and a secondary source to the FCO and MPs. News agencies, apart from being a source to other news media, are a primary source only to the FCO.

CHAPTER FOUR

IMAGE OF THE WORLD

'In assessing news priorities you look at the rest of the news around you. You look at the details of the new dam being built and at the details of the assassinated man. It's an instinctive thing.'

– BBC editor

News media are the prime sources to the British public of information about international affairs. Even those people who have other means of widening their knowledge of world affairs, such as through education or travel, cannot encompass the entire spectrum of international developments or gain an up-to-date picture without the media. A difference, however, has to be drawn between the wider public, which, as was argued in the previous chapter, uses the media as its primary source of information, and officials and ministers, who use them as a secondary source to supplement the official reports they receive.

Compared with many other populations, Britons are well served in the quantity of media reporting about international affairs. There are ten national daily newspapers, a large number of provincial newspapers, Sunday newspapers, political and economic periodicals, and BBC and commercial television and radio. The national newspapers, television and radio maintain their own foreign correspondents. London is the head office of one of the four western-based international news agencies, Reuters, which is part-owned by Britain's national daily press. That the British press is somewhat concentrated in the country's capital – national newspapers collectively sell more than provincial newspapers – reduces the degree of parochialness, a feature of provincial journalism. A considerable number of specialised magazines dealing with different world regions and countries are also published in London.

Some significant changes since the Second World War in the number and type of media have affected the flow of information about international affairs. There are four television channels, a cable television is making its debut. Also imminent is direct broadcasting by satellite, which will enable the British viewer to receive transmissions from European countries. Two additional developments have been the rise in the numbers of ethnic papers (about 50) and that of the fringe or alternative press (about 170 papers). Both groups handle foreign news about a country or foreign issue of interest to their readers. Television gives greater relative space on foreign affairs than do radio and newspapers but the latter give greater absolute space.[1] Yet polls have shown that television is regarded as the 'most useful source' of foreign affairs information;[2] this, however, has to be weighed against the fact that twice, or nearly twice, the number of people who see a television news bulletin read a daily newspaper.

The popularity of television is partly due to its being a faster source of news than the printed media. Thus, a poll during the Falklands War found that – despite the absence of television pictures received by satellite – television was the most popular source of information. Television is, in fact, ill-suited as a source of foreign news given the need for background to explain complex international problems. While pictures and graphs are a plus in favour of the visual media, the printed media have more space to communicate. Nor do visual media easily explain, for example, a shift in the balance of power, the significance of the visit of a foreign statesman, or, say, the fact that crucial pressures in a foreign conflict may be coming from outside factors.

GATHERING THE NEWS

British news organisations have two main sources of information about international affairs: their own correspondents and the news agencies. A difference must be drawn between the London-based newspapers and broadcasting organisations which have their own correspondents, and those organisations outside which generally do not. The London-based news organisations should be divided between the popular newspapers and commercial broadcasting, with correspondents in only a handful of key cities such as Washington, New York and Paris, and the quality newspapers and the BBC with correspondents in many major cities. The *Financial Times*, which has the most foreign correspondents, in 1985 had staff correspondents in New York (3 correspondents), Washington (2), Paris (3), Brussels (3), Bonn (2), Frankfurt (2), Rome (1), Milan (1), Madrid (1), Stockholm (1), Tokyo (2), Hong Kong (1), Singapore (1), New Delhi (1), Rio de Janeiro (1), Tel Aviv (1), Johannesburg (1) and Moscow. The BBC, *The Times*, and the *Daily Telegraph* have slightly fewer staff correspondents in many of these cities. Other newspapers, including *The Guardian*, the *Sunday Times*, and *The Observer* have fewer staff correspondents. Most news organisations also have part-time correspondents either 'stringing' for them (i.e. being paid by the item of news) or part-time correspondents receiving a minimum fee.

The *Financial Times* has part-time correspondents, who work almost exclusively for the paper or earn the largest proportion of their income from it, in Amsterdam, Buenos Aires, Cairo, Dublin, Geneva, Mexico City, New York, Peking, San Francisco, Sydney and Toronto. In addition the paper has 75 to 80 stringers. The *Financial Times, The Times, The Guardian* and *The Economist* also have foreign specialists based in London. The use of specialists has contributed to an increase in analysis and background articles. But with fewer newspaper columnists such as the *New York Times'* James Reston, general questions of foreign policy and international issues are debated, beyond newspaper editorial columns, less than in the US press.

These news organisations also subscribe to at least three news agencies: Reuters, United Press International (UPI), and the Associated Press (AP). Some subscribe to additional agencies or news services: a number receive *Agence France Presse* (AFP), and the BBC and *The Times* receive *Tass*. News agencies are of greater importance to organisations without their own correspondents such as the provincial media. Under a long-standing agreement Reuters news is distributed outside London via the Press Association, which edits a selection of Reuters copy and a smaller one from AP. In 1984 Reuters had 566 staff correspondents in 84 bureaux. These were supplemented by 1000 stringers in nearly every country and territory of the globe. The cost of subscription among the agencies varies for each customer, but in general Reuters is more expensive than the American agencies. In return for the greater outlay, news organisations in Britain are getting a news service more geared to the British market. Newspapers which have their own correspondents rely on the agencies more for providing the initial information, and use their own correspondents to report the 'hard news'. This is less true with the BBC which uses its correspondents not only for the 'hard news' but also for background comments and analytical reports.[3] 'We do not ask our correspondents to try to beat the news agencies. Their main job is to present the news in the form in which we can most effectively use it, using their judgement and specialised knowledge to put it into perspective,' a BBC foreign news editor said.[4]

Communication technology has profoundly affected the speed of foreign news gathering. Whereas in the Second World War the only means by which correspondents could send their despatches to their offices were the manually operated telephone system and a primitive form of telex, today there is an array of automatic communications including telephone, telex, and a fast telegraphic system capable of speeds of several thousand words per minute. In Vietnam, television's first war, the medium was film. Film reports had to be flown out by aircraft to the nearest satellite facilities − causing a delay of from 24 to 48 hours between the shooting of the film and its transmission. By the early 1980s most television reporting had transferred from film to videotape, thus avoiding the need to process the film. Portable electronic cameras known as 'minocams' record pictures and sound on videotape, which is then edited on portable machines and transmitted directly via microwave or telephone lines. Satellite communications for sending and receiving sound pictures are now available in almost every country. One of the consequences of these technological innovations has been to substantially reduce the expense of story transmission.

Another consequence has been a tendency for news organisations to send home-based reporters to cover foreign crises and other events rather than to leave permanent correspondents abroad. Given the expense of having permanent correspondents abroad (£25,000 and upwards) this is not surprising. The weakness of using the visiting reporter, or 'fireman', is that he is unable to bring to his reporting the background knowledge and contacts which a reporter based in a foreign capital builds up over a period of time. Some news organisations, including the BBC and quality newspapers, have resisted the tendency to reduce permanent correspondents. The 'stringer' correspondent, who is likely to have been in a place for many years, often has the background knowledge and political and military contacts. The problem with leaving a permanent correspondent in a place for some time, as well as of relying on the 'stringer', is that the journalist may develop 'localitis' or no longer observe events as the objective outsider.

Foreign news, in the form of agency tapes and correspondents' reports, is processed by a news organisation's 'foreign desk'. Its size and structure varies with each organisation. Thus, the *Daily Mirror* has a foreign editor but no desk separate from the main news desk to handle foreign copy alone. The *Sun* has neither a foreign desk nor a foreign editor. At *The Times*, where overall charge for foreign coverage lies with the foreign editor, day-by-day, hour-by-hour responsibility for the flow of copy is in the hands of the foreign news editor and four assistants, at least one of whom is in the foreign newsroom from 10 am to 2.30 am. Copy is 'subbed' or edited at a foreign sub-editor's desk, which is staffed in shifts from 1 pm until 4.30 am. The quantity of space available for foreign news consists of about 16 columns and half the front page, and a little less space on Saturdays and Mondays.[5] The largest foreign news-gathering operation in Britain, apart from Reuters, is at the BBC. BBC Radio, BBC TV, and the BBC External Services have separate newsrooms. Each branch of the BBC has its own foreign correspondents – BBC Radio has the highest number of them – although in practice each can use the reports of the entire pool of BBC correspondents. At BBC Radio the foreign news editor and his deputy are assisted by

MD–D

five foreign duty editors. The duty editors are either former foreign correspondents or journalists being groomed to become correspondents. Each newsroom receives about a million words a day, 90 per cent of which comes from the international news agencies. They also receive a teleprinter service from the BBC Monitoring Service. An important part of the operation is the 'futures' meeting where representatives of the different newsrooms discuss likely foreign developments and arrangements for their coverage. When a major crisis breaks, such as a war, a special crisis team is formed under the editor of radio news, which is manned 24 hours a day by journalists with a specialist knowledge of the countries concerned including former foreign correspondents in the region.

CREATING THE IMAGE

Access to a place where news is being made and to news sources is often a problem in all types of news reporting, but in foreign reporting it can be acute. The degree of freedom of access which foreign reporters have influences the flow of information about international affairs. Thus, reporters' lack of access to Afghanistan has resulted in the Soviet invasion receiving only sporadic coverage. In many developing countries foreign reporters face difficulty – for instance, in attempting to enter Black Africa countries such as Nigeria, Tanzania, Malawi, Somalia, Angola and Mozambique. In 1983 Black states neighbouring South Africa prohibited foreign reporters based in South Africa from entering their countries on the grounds that by being based in South Africa their reporting of African affairs was biased.

This contrasts with the United States where foreign reporters are an integral part of Washington's political scene. They have regular contact with senior US officials. Henry Brandon, the former Washington correspondent of the *Sunday Times*, had known Henry Kissinger from when the latter was an unknown Harvard academic:

I was able to get him on the telephone up to a dozen times a year. I have known Cyrus Vance for 20 years and he knew that the *Sunday Times* is an important medium. I saw a great deal of Kennedy, Johnson, and Nixon during their periods in office. I would see Johnson myself every six months. I saw Nixon three times between 1968 and 1973.

Restrictions may be introduced by governments for a number of reasons. First, a government may be sensitive about information regarding the internal situation reaching the outside world. The unwelcome reporter will be faced with obstacles and distractions ranging from censorship to expulsion. Reporters who arrived in Afghanistan following the seizure of power by the Communist Revolutionary Council in 1978 were unable to send out their dispatches. The *Daily Telegraph*'s reporter wrote that 'phone calls have suddenly gone dead in the middle of conversations ... the rather absurd routine reached its climax when with colleagues I submitted material for transmission at the telex office which was returned later to me with a scrawl reading "Notice: We can't send your messages for a week due to heavy traffic"'.[6] During the Cultural Revolution in China the foreign press corps in Peking lived in the segregated foreign quarter of the city and required permission to travel more than 15 miles outside the city. Interviews with knowledgeable Chinese were difficult to arrange. As a result the correspondent based in Hong Kong was often better informed about internal Chinese politics.

The South African Government introduced restrictions on foreign press reporting in November 1985 including a ban on television journalists, still photographers and radio recordists from 38 districts covered by the state of emergency imposed in July, where about a third of the country's Black population lives, and a rule by which newspaper correspondents would need police escorts in these areas. South African officials believed that the intensive coverage of the troubles in the Black townships during the previous 15 months – particularly heavy since the declaration of the state of emergency – was a key factor in the collapse of international confidence in the country's economy. Things came to a head with dramatic footage, shown around the world, by the American network CBS of the 'Trojan Horse' incident in Capetown in October in which police marksmen who were concealed in a police lorry which drove through a coloured district, on being stoned by demonstrators, opened fire killing three youths. The foreign press corps totalled 170 in November, having doubled in the previous 12 months; this does not include an estimated additional 150 journalists whose accreditation was questionable. Even before the new regulations, the South African Government, in vetting applications from foreign reporters for visas to report from the country, took into account the past record of a particular news organisation in reporting the country's affairs and the journalist's personal record.[7] Notwithstanding this, South Africa was at that time regarded as the freest country to report from in the continent, according to one BBC executive.[8]

Second, governments impose restrictions on foreign reporters because they fear that their reports will filter back to the population at home. One reason why the Indian government refused to permit the BBC's Delhi correspondent, Mark Tully, to return to India after he left in 1975 following the introduction of emergency measures was that the BBC, via the External Services, was an important source of news to many Indians. In the South African case the ban on television journalists from black townships was partly stimulated by the belief that their presence encouraged rioting. In rejecting the restrictions on reporting the South African Foreign Correspondents' Association argued that it was absurd to hold a small group of journalists responsible for a profound political conflict.

Third, governments bar access, or limit it, if they take exception to a particular news organisation's record in reporting the country and the journalist's own record. The Iranian Embassy in London sends the Iranian Foreign Ministry a digest of reports and editorial comment in the British press, and British reporters in Teheran have been called in and questioned about these. The Maltese prime minister, Dom Mintoff, vented his anger at the BBC's failure to broadcast an interview with him in 1978 by banning all British reporters from the island.

The BBC's attempts to reinstate their India correspondent illustrate the trouble news organisations face in gaining access to some foreign countries. When Mrs Gandhi introduced the emergency measures which set down guidelines regarding those types of news which could not be reported, Tully, the BBC correspondent, left the country voluntarily. Other reporters, who had refused to sign acceptance of the new regulations, were expelled. The BBC, faced with no early prospect of India returning to its previously uncensored state, had to decide whether it should resume reporting from India as a 'closed country' or not. Opting for the former, BBC executives recognised the need to convey to their audiences the changed circumstances for reporting the country. The Indian government, however, objected to the return of Tully and other correspondents; in some respects no media coverage suited the government more than a bad media.[9]

BBC executives discussed ways in which the Indian government could be encouraged to reverse this decision. A programme plan was drawn up. One suggestion was to take up an option still outstanding for Mark Tully and Michael Charlton to interview Mrs Gandhi. If it went ahead Tully might be able to stay on in Delhi, some executives thought. But the head of the BBC's International Relations Department argued that a more cautious approach should be adopted, such as a feature programme without a political flavour. The ice was broken in April 1976 with a BBC 2 film portrait entitled 'Mrs Gandhi's India'. Also, the Indian high commissioner took part in a Radio 4 'Analysis' programme. None of these, however, involved visits by BBC journalists to India. In June 1976 the Indian minister of information, V. H. Shukla, visited London to discuss with editors the subject of British correspondents reporting from India. He accused British news organisations of hostility towards India. Anyone who reported that Mrs Gandhi had overturned democracy was 'acting in a unconstitutional manner'. If British journalists wanted to be allowed back they had to prove they were friends of the country. The BBC director-general dined with Shukla but emerged with little hope of Tully's early return. It was only in 1977, some months after censorship had been lifted, that Tully and other British correspondents returned.[10]

Governments which limit access to foreign reporters need to balance the benefit accrued, namely reducing the quantity of bad news reaching the outside world, with the cost of cutting off also the good or neutral news about their country. International understanding about a people, its government and policies is achieved through a flow of information reaching the outside world. International prestige, and therefore influence, is gained by a government regularly appearing in the media limelight. The foreign press corps in a country gives a government means to achieve this. A country from which the foreign media are banned is perceived in the West as a closed, backward, undemocratic society. These considerations notwithstanding, there is no indication that governments will decide that the benefits to be gained from getting one's message across outweigh the benefits of banning the media.

In the long term, advanced technology such as satellites and reconnaissance flights may contribute to weakening the government censor. Ironically, many of the governments which ban foreign reporters are at the forefront of the UNESCO campaign for better media coverage of the developing world. For editors there is a need to find ways and means to overcome the danger of distortion from not covering some countries. This is particularly true with television, where availability of 'actuality' or film footage of an event influences whether a story gets included in a news bulletin. One means, albeit a non-visual one, is to have a reporter sit in the studio to give the background to a particular event.

If governments can influence the flow of international news, so may editors through their definition of what is news and what is not. The value judgements of journalists about what constitutes news may be examined under a number of headings. First, it is sometimes argued that the media emphasise and sensationalise crises and dramatic events. A survey of the British press in 1975 found that only 20 per cent of news reports were 'dramatic', 'exciting', or 'violent' and 73 per cent were not. However, 36 per cent of reports in the survey were unexpected items in terms of being unpredictable events or statements.[11] Longer-term positive events, such as economic and scientific developments, failed to be defined as news. Further, aid and development stories accounted for only one per cent, social welfare abroad 3 per cent, and medical news from abroad 2 per cent, in contrast to international political and diplomatic stories which accounted for 20 per cent, non-violent or violent change, 9 per cent and crime and legal matters, 16 per cent.[12] The more similar the frequency of an event to the frequency of the news medium, the more likely that it will be defined as news by that medium. While murder takes little time and as an event occurs between two successive issues of a newspaper, or two successive news bulletins, longer-term developments go unrecorded unless they reach some climax, such as a scientific discovery.

Second, it is said that editors emphasise personalities and elites. If an action can be seen as having been caused by specific individuals it has a greater likelihood of being defined as news. The same survey found that news which concerned personalities ranged from 61 per cent (*Daily Mirror*) to 36 per cent (*Morning Star*). The same hypothesis may be applied to 'elite countries'. The country figuring most prominently was the United States, followed, after Britain, by the Soviet Union. Fourteen per cent of all reports concerned an official, a diplomat, or foreign minister, 7 per cent a prime minister, 5 per cent a head of state or representative, 4 per cent a celebrity, star, or 'personality', 3 per cent an opposition leader or politician, 2 per cent a military leader, 2 per cent a business leader, and 1 per cent each for artists/intellectuals and for religious leaders. In terms of elite institutions, 21 per cent concerned the executive or legislature, 7 per cent the police or army, 3 per cent business firms, 2 per cent a political party, 2 per cent a trade union, 2 per cent a legal body, and 1 per cent a city or town.[13] In British press coverage of the British government's decision to impose an embargo on arms deliveries to the Middle East following the outbreak of the 1973 Arab–Israeli war, the embargo only became news when it became a subject of debate in Parliament, when it was reported in party political terms. Thus, for the first week after the embargo was announced, and before Parliament had debated it, the embargo went unreported by the media; but once it became the subject of controversy in both houses of Parliament it became a prominent item in news reporting and editorial comment.

Third, there is a tendency for culturally proximate countries to make the news and culturally distant ones not to. Or, as sociologists Galtung and Ruge have put it, 'the more meaningful the signal, the more probable that it will be regarded as worth listening to'. This leads to inevitable distortion. The 1975 British press survey found that 40 per cent of news reports were located in Europe (excluding the Soviet Union) and 18 per cent in North America, while only 12 per cent were located in Africa, 11 per cent in Asia, 10 per cent in the Middle East, 3 per cent in Latin America, and 3 per cent in Australasia.[14] A survey of British broadcasting found a similar dominance in news from Europe and North America.[15] A 1978 study of British press coverage of the war between Black African nationalist groups and Ian Smith's government in Rhodesia found that much greater coverage was given to white civilian casualties than Black African casualties even though Black casualties were higher. For example, the murder of 12 Elim Pentecostal missionaries in June 1978 was the lead story in every national daily newspaper, while news of the deaths of several hundred African civilians a month earlier was figured less prominently — in the popular papers, coverage was limited to a single sentence.[16] Related to this is the tendency for the media in covering international meetings to emphasise those aspects concerning the government or country of the media. This was confirmed by a study of British press reporting of the Eighteen Nation Disarmament Committee meeting in Geneva in July 1968.[17]

The immediate cause for the geographical distortion of international news is a similar imbalance in the flow of news agency copy. A survey of the copy of Reuters, UPI, and AFP found that the region which was most covered was Western Europe (37–38 per cent). The most covered region on AP's tapes was North America.[18] There was a similar geographical imbalance in the case of news organisations' stationing of their own foreign correspondents. A 1976 survey found that over 80 per cent of staff correspondents of British national daily newspapers were based in North America and Western Europe. There were, then, no British staff correspondents in the Soviet Union, Latin America, or Australasia. The remaining fifth were distributed evenly in Africa, the Far East, and the Middle East. The popular papers had no correspondents outside Western Europe and North America.[19] Public interest in, and ability to identify with, West European countries, the United States, and ex-British colonies has resulted in correspondents being posted there. The large flow of material from these culturally proximate places stimulates even greater audience interest in them, while the lack of coverage from other places only makes them more culturally distant.[20]

With television the public's fastest source of news, the popular press have had to redefine their role. The 'our man in the Seychelles' story, which used to make for good copy in these papers, has made way for more investigative, feature material in Britain. Yet surveys point to considerable public interest in foreign affairs. One survey found that 87 per cent of newspaper readers were either very or fairly interested in foreign affairs. This included 23 per cent and 84 per cent (very or fairly interested) in the skilled manual occupational category and 22 per cent and 81 per cent in the semi-skilled manual category.[21] But when some of the popular papers, such as the *Daily Mirror*, attempted to go 'up market', market competition forced them to lower their goals. Of Britain's popular national daily press – the *Daily Mail, Daily Express, Daily Mirror, Sun, Daily Star,* and *Daily Record* – only the first succeeds in providing readers with comprehensive coverage of international events. Some reader interest can be stimulated by explaining foreign news, including the EEC, nuclear weapons, and oil supplies, in terms of their domestic implications. Foreign news with a human angle or involving Britain or British citizens, including a war involving Britain or a Briton arrested abroad, is also saleable. The disjointed character of foreign affairs coverage by the popular media means that when a *coup d'état* in a distant country occurs or a foreign economic crisis breaks, the reader, exposed to a sudden torrent of facts after years of not reading about the area, is at a loss in understanding the significance of the event. A study of British broadcasting coverage of the Soviet invasion of Afghanistan found that editors had to explain it less in terms of Russo–Afghanistan relations and more in general East–West terms.[22]

Notwithstanding all this, there are trends in the media against the cultural proximity thesis. Television news now reports and analyses the complexities of culturally distant conflict zones like Chad and Central America when years ago a conflict had to involve Britain such as Aden, Cyprus, and ex-colonies in Africa. In redefining their role in the television age, the serious press provide more background and analysis to international developments, which broadcasting may not have the time for. Greater public awareness, particularly among serious newspaper readers, of international developments has certain ramifications for policymakers because as soon as a foreign crisis breaks, informed public opinion is already alerted and the public agenda is fixed in terms of a likely public reaction, thus limiting the options open to policymakers in their reaction to the crisis.

Another factor influencing the media's image of the world is the inclusion of political values by reporters and editors. Descriptions of foreign leaders or governments as being conservative, moderate, extreme, revolutionary, populist, or radical may be meaningful to a western audience but may be inaccurate or meaningless in describing them. Bias may also be intentional by an editor or proprietor. A study of press coverage during the period before the EEC referendum in June 1975 found that the printed media were markedly biased. In the period from December 1974 to February 1975, 53 per cent of *The Times'* coverage was pro-EEC, 12 per cent anti-, and 35 per cent neutral. Feature and editorial matter was more biased; at the extreme was the *Daily Telegraph* with 98 per cent pro-EEC and 2 per cent anti-. Yet the

bias was not recognised by readers: a survey of reader satisfaction with
the coverage of the press before the referendum found that 'rather
dissatisfied' and 'very dissatisfied' with the non-bias of press coverage
varied from 10 per cent to 6 per cent, contrasted with 41 per cent to
52 per cent who thought the media were not biased.[23] Press coverage
contrasted with broadcasting where scrupulous efforts were made to
achieve fairness in covering the referendum campaign. The BBC adopted
a 50–50 division between the pro- and anti-Marketeers, with the amount
of time given to both sides in current affairs programmes logged in
minutes and seconds.[24]

A study of news with East–West ramifications concluded that the
news was presented and discussed in a way favourable to the West.
According to the Glasgow Media Group, the rise of the Solidarity
trade union and of democracy in Poland has been portrayed in the
media as a good thing because it upset the Soviet Union, whereas the
fall of democracy in Turkey was not shown as being such a bad
development.[25] An example of proprietorial pressure occurred when
the editor of *The Observer*, Donald Trelford, reported in April 1984
about atrocities by the Zimbabwe government in the province of
Matebeleland. The paper's proprietor, Roland 'Tiny' Rowland, who
has commercial interests in the country, wrote to Mr Mugabe, the prime
minister, dismissing the allegations made in Trelford's report.

Distortion also occurs in a different sense. The separation of fact
from comments means that much traditional news gathering lacks
context and meaning to its audience. Birt and Jay have argued that
since all facts are value laden it is justified to remove the barrier
between fact and comment in favour of a contextual journalism in
which analysis would be mingled with 'fact'.[26] The BBC has argued
that while explanation is important, 'it is the task of the reporter to
report what is happening *in* the world, and not to shape his report
to convey to the "citizenry" a personal interpretation of what is
happening *to* the world'. The greater use of background and feature
articles and programmes is a movement towards breaking out of
what Birt and Jay call 'the atomised presentation of events'.[27] But
Schlesinger does not expect this trend to continue towards the ultimate
disintegration of the barrier between fact and comment because he
believes that when honestly applied it is likely to cover in greater depth
the suppressed interests in society, and thus be resisted by the
establishment.[28]

An additional factor influencing the media's image is the financial
cost of news coverage. Over half of BBC Radio News' budget is spent
on foreign coverage. In 1982, after two major wars, the Falklands and
Lebanon, and the conflict in El Salvador, BBC Radio had overspent

on its budget by £½ million. The BBC estimates that each staff foreign correspondent costs £30,000 per annum. Owing to the cost involved, the number of foreign correspondents of British national newspapers fell by 30 per cent from 103 in spring 1974 to 76 in spring 1976.[29] Inevitably, the first posts to close are the culturally distant ones. In order to overcome the high cost some news organisations have created a third category of foreign correspondent between staff and stringer, known as 'contract' correspondent, in which the correspondent receives a guaranteed minimum fee and has to report first to that organisation before freelancing for other organisations. The BBC correspondents in Rome, Geneva, Harare and Islamabad, for example, are in this category, and cost the corporation about £5000 per correspondent each year. To send to Europe a film unit, comprising a reporter, a producer, a cameraman and assistant, a soundman and an electrician cost the BBC in 1978 about £600 for a day's filming or £4000 a week. Further afield the costs multiply. As a result of exhausting the budget, BBC TV current affairs producers were in 1978 forced to cancel further film coverage for the remainder of the fiscal year until April 1979. Foreign film footage was imported and programme controllers hoped to 'get over' the lack of foreign coverage with the concentrated coverage of the 1979 general election.

DIPLOMACY AND THE IMAGE

Given that the image of the world conveyed by the media is not a mirror image of the real world, it has to be asked whether the media's construction of reality has implications for diplomacy. In diplomacy as well, the image does not amount to an objective reality. Foreign policy involves an image of a desired reality, with goals and strategies to achieve it. Media and diplomacy are therefore two subjective images of a reality which meet and influence one another. By playing up or playing down an issue, the media influence the diplomatic process. A member of the 1970 Conservative Cabinet noted:

Our government was desperately anxious to sell more arms to South Africa and Sir Alec Douglas Home was unable to because of the vigilance of the media. You would very frequently get in cabinet the comment 'We must be very careful about doing this because the media will be largely hostile and this will cause more trouble than we can handle at the UN and in Black Africa'.

The media's image inspires reactions and counter-reactions from governments and publics. An investigation by Adam Raphael in *The Guardian* in March 1973 into the wages and working conditions of Africans who work for British firms in South Africa resulted in a House of Commons Select Committee investigating the matter, and drawing up guidelines for British employers in South Africa. The government's White Paper which followed said that British firms should be encouraged to give evidence that they are treating their employees satisfactorily. In preparing ministers with answers to likely oral questions in Parliament, the FCO's Parliamentary Unit follow the British media for news reports which may stimulate lines of thinking among MPs. The FCO News Department prepare for their briefings with journalists by looking at the media as a guide to the questions journalists will ask. Often the FCO makes an off-the-record comment to the media, not because it itself wishes to make an issue of a particular matter, but in response to journalists' questions. Such comments, quoting 'informed sources', have an impact on the flow of diplomatic communication between Britain and other governments.

Media coverage of an international conference may arouse unrealistic expectations, which brings pressure on the participants to produce results. Sometimes this pressure 'helps' the participants to reach a compromise agreement. In other cases it produces an artificial agreement. Time will be spent by the respective parties planning whom to blame publicly if the negotiations fail; the apportionment of blame will, in turn, influence the future state of relations between the parties. The media's image may also have an effect in the bureaucratic process of policymaking. 'A recent television series on India, showing the attempts made to evolve an industrial economy suitable for that country, will no doubt help our high commissioner in Delhi in his representations to London for more aid', an official suggested.

The heavy media coverage of some events may become so intensive that millions of spectators become participants in the historical drama. Certain types of images are aggrandized beyond their normal size. The intensity which television in particular can give an event was illustrated in the siege at the Libyan diplomatic mission in London in 1984. The emotional impact of the instantaneous and continuous coverage of the siege gave the affair greater political significance than it would have received before the age of television. Yet for all the media's attention, people understood little about what was happening inside Libya. The scant coverage of Libya over the years, caused partly by a lack of access to foreign reporters, resulted in the siege and its news coverage lacking perspective.

This is not to argue that the media necessarily create the event. The Vietnam War began irrespective of the media; the media, however, may have influenced the progress and outcome of the war. Katz defines a 'media event' as one not initiated by the media. A media event, he suggests, is an event which is broadcast live, framed in time and space, features a historic personality, and has the force of a social norm, making television viewing compulsory. Few foreign issues involving Britain fall into this category. For example, the Falklands War was not broadcast, let alone broadcast live and limited in time and space. President Sadat's trip to Jerusalem in 1977, however, offers a good example. The visit aroused euphoria in both countries. There was a dramatic shift in the perceptions of Israelis and Egyptians about each other. Sadat's image in the USA improved significantly. The event liberated Sadat and Mr Begin for a time from the restraints of their own bureaucracies and political parties. The media, though not causing the visit, were instrumental in causing these effects. 'News events', by contrast, concern conflict, whether institutionalised such as a debate in Parliament or non-institutionalised such as a war. News comprises news events much more than media events.[30]

In certain cases the media not only mobilise public involvement in an event but are themselves engulfed in a socio-psychological atmosphere which they have created. McLuhan has explained how in the information age the media possess their own dynamics.[31] In these cases the media are swept away by a psychosis, losing their objectivity. 'Pack journalism' defines which issues a journalist will report and which he will not. The individual journalist can break out of the momentum only incrementally. The media give meaning to events, a rational pattern, even when one might not exist. This is not to suggest that society or the media have deliberately planned an ideological role for news. Rather, the image of news is, as has been argued, the consequence of various factors in the organisation and performance of news gathering, selection, and presentation.

Nor should the impact of the media's image on diplomacy be exaggerated. Diplomacy does not comprise only those issues which form part of the media's image of reality. Most diplomatic negotiations are not publicised. As has been shown, international economic and commercial matters, and bilateral relations, for example, tend to go unreported until a crisis breaks or a climax is reached. Only with those diplomatic issues which the media deem to be 'news' is there usually the potential for Parliament and the public to react and become participants. And in many of these cases 'perhaps TV can make friends and influence people in a generalised sort of way, can affect the mood, but in the last resort what is said across the table between the ambassador and foreign secretary is what counts', an ambassador argued.

CONCLUSION

Compared with citizens of other countries, Britons are well supplied with foreign news, some news organisations possessing their own considerable networks of foreign correspondents. Nevertheless, the image conveyed is limited both by inbuilt mechanisms in the media – an interest in crises, and in news from culturally proximate societies with little information from culturally distant ones – as well as by such external factors as financial budgets and foreign governmental controls over the movement of foreign correspondents in their country. Given the role of the media as a major source of information, this image must have an effect on policymakers. But it most strongly affects the wider public, which usually has no major alternative source of information about up-to-date developments.

CHAPTER FIVE

PUBLIC OPINION

'The media are not an entity of their own. They are really reflecting what people are saying in Parliament and what public opinion is. Only in rare cases, such as in the United States where you have a pundit like Walter Lippman, do the media affect foreign policy. The question really is what is the effect of public opinion on a minister.'

— Permanent under-secretary

'Few decisions are changed by the media. The influence is futuristic. When planning policy one takes what the media are likely to say into account.'

— Deputy under-secretary

Apart from the media having an effect on foreign policy in terms of their image of the world and in terms of their being a source of information, their influence is also to be found in relation to their audiences — MPs, interest groups, and the wider public — and the extent to which ministers are receptive to pressure from these. Parliament, public opinion, interest groups, and the media form an interdependent system sometimes called in the literature on foreign policymaking the 'domestic environment'. This contrasts with the 'international environment' or the pressures from abroad which face a government. The media are dependent on these other elements in the domestic environment — notably Parliament and public opinion — in changing foreign policy. If Parliament and public opinion were to cease to exist, the influence of the media would also cease because the media are dependent on their audiences for any pressure on government to succeed. A British government is answerable to the public and to Parliament, not to the media. Parliament is the chief means by which the media exert influence because in most cases only pressure on a government from its own supporters in Parliament produces a policy change. 'I can't think of a case where press clamour made us change our point of view. The way it works is the impact of the media on Parliament which then comes to ministers', a prime minister said.

The reverse hypothesis also illustrates the interdependence. If the media cease to function, the work of Parliament and interest groups is made more difficult. Parliament, interest groups and the wider public are dependent on the media for information about foreign affairs. Interest groups and, to a lesser extent, MPs use the media as a channel to communicate and a means to bring pressure on the government. Additionally, the media often reflect public opinion. Beyond this inter-dependence, there is also an overlap of individuals among these entities. There are MPs who engage in journalistic activities and are leading members of interest groups. There are journalists who are members of, or identify with, interest groups. Many participate in the activities of the Royal Institute of International Affairs (Chatham House) and the International Institute of Strategic Studies. Pall Mall clubs are a meeting point for these, though to a lesser extent than they were. That the British media, press and broadcasting, are London-based in terms of being available to all these elements of informed opinion and written or pro-duced by people in the capital adds to the overlap. 'You can't compart-mentalise it. The chances are that a person who is passionately interested is involved in all these areas', an official remarked.

Some claim that it is at this level of personal relationships, of senior ministers and officials, rather than the influence of public opinion in con-junction with Parliament where the domestic pressure on foreign policy is to be felt. 'Not by public demonstrations in Downing Street or Trafalgar Square, or by marches from and to Aldermarston, but over lunch at the Reform Club or the Travellers, by means of letters to *The Times*, and its countless other miniature, latter-day agorae. It is in secure, private conversation that those directly involved in the making of policy can talk and listen without commitment and without record', Vital argues.[1]

For example, during the First World War, the editor of the liberal *Manchester Guardian*, C.P. Scott, became an advocate of the Zionist cause for a Jewish home in Palestine, which Britain had captured from the Ottoman Turks. A friend of Lloyd George, the Liberal prime minister, Scott introduced to him Chaim Weizmann, a leading Zionist who became the first president of the Jewish state. Scott regularly advised Weizmann on views about Palestine in government circles, as well as occasionally addressing the Zionist cause to government ministers.[2] The degree of overlap should not, however, be exaggerated. Few, if any, appointments in the diplomatic service are made from the media or academia, unlike in France. Nor do the media make great use of academics or ex-diplomats.

This chapter will first examine the role of the media in connecting interest groups and MPs to officialdom, with one another, and with the wider public. It will then assess the overall influence of the media on ministers and on officials.

FROM SPEAKER'S CORNER AND WESTMINSTER
TO FLEET STREET AND WHITEHALL

The different goals of interest groups, their activity, size and type of membership, and relationship to Whitehall, make any generalisation about their use of the media arbitrary. Some groups have as a primary objective the explanation of their views to the wider public, and the media therefore play an important role. Others, such as Indian, Pakistani and West Indian associations, are less concerned with achieving wide public support and more with developing bonds among members of their own community; Asian and Black media provide this linkage. Other groups aim to alter the course of British foreign policy in a particular direction. Some of these, such as the Confederation of British Industry and the Trades Union Congress are, depending on the government of the day, in regular contact with the FCO. The majority of interest groups on foreign affairs do not have regular contact. This contrasts with foreign policy formulation in the United States where over three hundred interest groups are formally represented in the Department of State on advisory committees attached to the different regional bureaux and to liaison offices for groups concerned with business and labour. Although Question Time in Parliament and the back bench committees give the MP friendly to a particular cause the opportunity to promote it, the absence of regular debates on foreign policy issues in Parliament means that the quality press and broadcasting have become major forums for debate.

The degree of accessibility which interest groups have to the media varies according to the newsworthiness of the objectives or tactics of the groups. Trade associations and those groups fostering friendly relations with another country tend not to be newsworthy in contrast to the more politically motivated groups, such as pro-Black African and pro-South African groups, pro- and anti-European Community groups, and groups campaigning on behalf of political dissidents in Eastern Europe and Latin America, all of which may expect a certain amount of publicity for their views. But, with the exception of the Common Market issue, even these issues are of little permanent relevance or interest to the wider public and once the crisis is no longer in the news headlines the media cease to report the views of such groups. The plight of the Ethiopian, Kampuchean, Vietnamese and Biafran refugees aroused wide public concern, but once the crises were seen to subside only the quality press, notably *The Times, The Guardian* and *The Observer*, took a continued interest.

Some interest groups maintain full-time information personnel. Others, without the financial resources, leave the public relations work to the group's director or another official. This work includes monitoring

how the media cover and comment on the news, responding to cases
of perceived bias or misrepresentation, developing contact with individual journalists, preparing press releases, and advising the group on
publicity matters. Some groups encourage their members to monitor
press and broadcasting and to inform the executive of cases of bias or
misrepresentation, or to respond to such cases by writing to the editor.
An interest group requires some finesse in dealing with news organisations. Chittick's classification of the relationship of American interest
groups and the media in terms of 'antagonism' and 'community of
interest' is also relevant to Britain.[3] Material sent by interest groups to
journalists is generally regarded as propaganda. Complaints about an
individual journalist to his editor can sometimes cause greater damage
than good in the long term. On the other hand, a successful interest
group will be a good source of reliable news.

While interest groups lacking direct access to Whitehall must use the
media, MPs have direct access to ministers. There is, nevertheless, a
close connection between Westminster and Fleet Street. As an institution
Parliament is assured media coverage, in contrast to interest groups
which often have to lobby to receive the media's attention. The involvement of MPs with the media includes appearances on TV and radio,
writing newspaper articles, and contacts with individual journalists.
A survey of ten MPs who take an active interest in foreign policy
showed that each wrote from five to ten letters to the editor a year on
foreign affairs, and that most were accepted for publication: three out
of four or four out of five.[4] Given the access MPs have to ministers
and to their party hierarchy, the value of using the media lies in bringing
additional pressure to bear. 'I write to ministers on particular cases
affecting my constituents. But on major issues you cannot influence
a minister by writing to him. You need to create a pressure group and
whip up support in the press', an MP said. Another said, 'I can get more
coverage from a letter in *The Times* than from a parliamentary question'.
'A good foreign affairs question in the House can lead to appearances
on TV and to newspaper articles. It is a factor – not the only factor –
but it does dawn on one that one might be biting gold', another
remarked. While *The Times* was recognised by some MPs as the best
newspaper through which to reach the front bench, others preferred
the *Daily Telegraph* and *The Guardian* for reaching the Conservative
and Labour front benches, respectively.[5] Less use appears to be made
of the political weeklies.

An additional media technique used by both interest groups and MPs
is the political advertisement. Such advertisements are sometimes used
when a group fails to get its views published through other means. But
the high expense restricts the use of advertising to groups able to receive

financial support from outside sources such as a foreign government. Political advertising on foreign issues tends to be restricted to the quality press, notably *The Guardian, The Times, The New Statesman,* and *The Observer*, suggesting that groups using advertising may be aiming to influence not so much the wider public as informed opinion and policy-makers. Like all advertising, its potential to change public attitudes is questionable. 'On the whole I have an emotional prejudice against signed adverts. But gaining signatures across the spectrum – from politicians to writers to academics – may have an effect', an MP remarked. One advertisement which may have had considerable effect was a full-page one in *The Guardian*, in May 1971, signed by 100 pro-European Labour MPs calling on the Labour leadership to back European entry. At the time Harold Wilson had not publicly committed himself to support or oppose entry. The trade unions were hostile and James Callaghan was competing for the Labour leadership on a 'Get Britain Out' ticket. The advertisement, which included eight members of the Shadow Cabinet and 23 other MPs on the opposition front bench, together with leading European socialists including Willy Brandt, Gaetano Martino, Guy Mollet, and Pietro Nenni, brought the issue to a head and Wilson sub-sequently decided to back entry.

The United Nations Association, the British Section of Solidarity, and the Council for the Advancement of Arab–British Understanding The relationship between three interest groups and the media may be contrasted regarding their publicity goals and their access to Whitehall. The UNA has two major objectives: to influence government policy, and to win greater public support for the United Nations Organisation. The symmetry between the UNA's raison d'être and successive British governments' support for the UNO – as a founding member Britain has a permanent seat on the Security Council – has resulted in the UNA having a consultative status with the FCO. It involves the UNA director participating in the twice-yearly conference of the FCO advisory com-mittee on UN matters where they discuss British UN policy and strategy, a small government grant to the association, and access to ministers. It was therefore unnecessary for the UNA to build support outside Whitehall in order to influence government policy. Moreover, the UNA would be concerned lest its public relations upset its contacts with Whitehall. 'We would be careful in not issuing a press statement which could harm our relations with the minister', a UNA officer commented.

In contrast the Council for the Advancement of Arab–British Understanding found itself, in the early years after its establishment following the 1967 Middle East war, on the fringes of respectability in Whitehall. Both pro-Arab and pro-Israeli groups are a hindrance to

Whitehall, with government policy satisfying neither side, and while both groups are given hearings by the FCO and their lobbying activities are followed by the Near East Department, the initiative has not come from Whitehall. By the end of the seventies, with an inclination of British policy towards the Arabs, CAABU's image in Whitehall had improved somewhat, and its headquarters had been visited by the foreign secretary.

The UNA has been less successful in gaining public support. The association reaches its 25,000 members, who are divided into sixty local branches throughout the country, through its monthly newsletter. With more than double this membership 30 years ago, it has been anxious to enlarge its membership, but attempts to publicise the UN cause in the national media have mostly been unproductive. The UNO's economic and social achievements lack newsworthiness and the growing hostility towards the western world in the General Assembly has produced resentment against the UNO in the media. The UNA used to have a full-time press officer, but owing to financial restrictions the post no longer exists and the UNA director does most of the publicity work. Out of a dozen letters sent to newspapers only one on average was published; even letters signed by MPs who were patrons of the association would often not be published unless they had the signature of a privy counsellor. 'The main function of the press is that it gives us something to moan about. It is no good cursing – the fault is that we don't have the resources to maintain contacts with individual journalists', a UNA official said.

CAABU, on the other hand, has been more successful in gaining media support. It was founded in order to 'waken British public opinion not only to the injustice that has taken place in the Middle East but also to the dangers that were likely to overtake Britain and its Western allies if the injustice was not checked and, if possible, reversed'.[6] To achieve this, CAABU has a full-time assistant director of information. In their book, *Publish It Not ... The Middle East Cover-Up*, CAABU's co-founders blame the media for the public's misunderstanding of the Arabs. Some of this, they argued, was caused by news organisations employing Jews as correspondents in Israel. In the BBC's case, CAABU campaigned for the removal of Michael Elkins, the BBC's Jerusalem correspondent, on the grounds that his Jewishness coloured his reporting. The BBC replied that it was irrelevant whether a BBC person is Jewish or a supporter of Zionism as long as in his capacity as a professional journalist he operated objectively. Subsequently, the BBC appointed as a Beirut correspondent a freelance journalist who had been a member of CAABU's general committee. The book, *Publish It Not...The Middle East Cover-Up*, was the subject of controversial litigation in a Jerusalem district court in 1979.

Since the mid-1970s there has been greater coverage of the Palestinian Arab refugee issue in the British media. How much of this has been due to CAABU's efforts, or to the diplomatic support which the Palestinian Arab groups have received from Arab governments, or to the publicity from acts of terrorism, is difficult to say. But the council's efforts have played at least a supportive role to the situation in the Middle East.

An example of the association's lobbying efforts, one that illustrates the antagonism which can develop between an interest group and a news organisation, occurred following the UN resolution of November 1974 equating Zionism with racism. *The Times* carried four feature articles criticising the UN resolution but only one in favour. In a letter to the then editor of the newspaper, which was clearly not intended for publication, CAABU complained that *The Times* had been unfair both in its feature coverage as well as on its letters page where 97½ inches had been given to pro-Zionist letters and only 50 inches to anti-Zionist ones. The editor, William Rees-Mogg, took the unusual step of publishing the letter on the centre feature page with an accompanying editorial entitled 'Is *The Times* fair to the Arab lobby?' *The Times* said that it had published the letter because 'we think it is better that an argument of this kind should be conducted in the open'. The paper had given more space to the pro-Zionist case because 'in our view it was a foolish resolution and, from the point of view of making peace, a bad one'.[7]

The British chapter of Solidarity contrasts with both organisations. While there is broad public support for Solidarity's goals, this support is qualified in some sections of informed opinion. While approving the emergence of Solidarity some newspapers and commentators have argued that repression is less brutal in Poland than in other East European countries, that it is unrealistic to hope that Poland will opt out unilaterally from the post-war division of Europe, and that strong expressions of support for the movement upset dialogue with the Soviet Union. The British chapter's goals include, first, redressing misinformation released by the Polish government about Solidarity. Second, while, unlike the UNO, it has few official links with the FCO, it supplies its specialists with information about the internal situation in Poland. Third, being integrally involved in the survival of Solidarity in Poland, the British chapter has set up friendship branches in the British trade union movement.

The group keeps in close touch with the media by supplying journalists with information about the situation in Poland, and by appearances on radio and television (with a higher success rate than either UNO or CAABU). In this sense the British chapter is an establishment-oriented group. In another sense, however, it is a grass roots one, organising demonstrations and leaving the business of contacting MPs at Westminster to another group, the British Friends of Solidarity, whose members include lords and MPs. Unlike UNO and CAABU, the British chapter is run on a shoestring budget, with a staff of two Poles who are paid a minimal wage. It monitors the media for errors and instances of misrepresentation, but owing to the shortage of funds much of this is done in the public library and by a volunteer who uses a video to record television programmes on Poland.

How do ministers and officials react to interest groups and MPs using the media? Are the media recognised as legitimate channels for reaching policymakers? 'If you had six of your backbenchers writing to a newspaper — and it would depend who — you might laugh, you might change policy, or you might see them', a minister said. Another said, 'You can't generalise whether one listens to pressure groups which write to *The Times*. It depends on the issue, who supports them, on how strong their influence is, on whether your information coincides with the information they are presenting'. In one sense, then, the media are as legitimate a channel of communication as the parliamentary process. In a different sense, media exposure enables the sender to apply pressure which a privately sent letter to a minister does not. On the other hand, as one minister put it, 'If they write to the papers that is the end of it. It is much better for MPs to go to the minister and go on and on until they get what they want'.

INFLUENCING POLICY

At the beginning of the chapter it was suggested that the media play an important role in reflecting public opinion. Although public opinion polls, sponsored by news organisations and other companies, offer a guide to public thinking between elections, only a small number of polls deal with foreign policy. In their absence — and in the absence of governments carrying out their own polls — the views expressed in the media are equated with public opinion. Through reading the press, FCO officials gauge public reaction to foreign issues. A function of the FCO's News Department, aside from explaining foreign policy to the media, is to advise the office about public attitudes. During the siege of the Libyan diplomatic mission in London in March 1984, one of the officials in COBRA, the special interdepartmental unit handling the affair, had the task of analysing public opinion trends as expressed in the media.

The equation of editorial opinion with public opinion is, however, questionable. In the 1975 EEC referendum, for example, all the national press, with the exception of the *Morning Star*, favoured remaining in the EEC but only half the population voted likewise in the referendum.

Especially prone to this inaccurate equation are officials, because their major exposure to domestic opinion is from the media. Ministers are also exposed to public thinking via Parliament, their party hierarchy and other public contact. 'In measuring what public opinion is you have to take what the newspapers report to be public opinion, though you apply such checks as you can – after all one is in close touch with the public and one assesses whether the public feeling is right or wrong', a prime minister said. But Kenneth Younger, a former Foreign Office minister, has argued:

The popular press is an unreliable guide. Its viewpoint is often that of the proprietor rather than of the readers it is addressing. Moreover its intervention tends to be spasmodic. Far more effective is the weekly flow of questions in Parliament.[8]

In assessing the media's influence on policy it should be noted that although according to constitutional theory policy is made by ministers while officials implement their political masters' instructions, in practice election manifestos do not cover the entire spectrum of foreign policy, and international developments often necessitate policy changes. A minister is dependent on his officials for advice and information. In his submission a civil servant presents his minister with all the policy options, including those which are likely to arouse a strong reaction from Parliament, the media, and the public. It is for the minister to weigh the strength of the reaction and decide whether he can carry parliamentary and public opinion. A permanent under-secretary said:

I think myself that Britain should do something on the Falkland Islands totally different from what public, parliamentary, and media opinion would consider. But it is not for officials to judge what the minister can or cannot do in relation to public opinion. Their job is to make recommendations.

Nevertheless, officials tend to de-emphasise domestic pressures in preference for the longer-term 'national interest', advising the minister that what the media are preaching, for example, does not necessarily coincide with the national interest and that something else will be occupying the media's attention tomorrow. An official said:

Officials try to maintain a policy which is detached from domestic opinion, and which is what they consider to be the national interest, and they try not to be affected by immediate currents of public opinion. If a minister feels a policy has to be adjusted in the light of a current of opinion at home he will give the necessary instructions.

Given the need in modern administration for the minister to delegate responsibility to his officials, the barrier between him and the most senior civil servants – the permanent under-secretary and deputy under-secretaries – has become less clear. While one permanent under-secretary, on saying to his foreign secretary, 'Of course this policy will be unpopular with public opinion', was told 'You stick to the policy and I'll tell you about public opinion', the relationship is often easier, resulting sometimes in the permanent under-secretary being considered as almost a junior minister. 'If it was in the country's interest to recognise a new regime but all the press were up against it, one would say to the foreign secretary that despite public opinion the best thing to do is to recognise now rather than later because of x, y, or z; the foreign secretary might then say, "Well, I would have a terrible time in the House"', a permanent under-secretary said.

The media and such other non-official actors as public opinion and interest groups affect only a small number of foreign policy issues. Wallace has divided policy issues into high policy, sectoral policy, and low policy.[9] Low policy issues involve few political values and few domestic interests; they are detailed technical agreements between governments. The majority of issues fall into this category. In sectoral policy, MPs and interest groups exercise pressure on the government. The government's task is less to find a common policy agreeable to all and more a compromise between conflicting national and international interests. High policy includes not only official policymakers and informed opinion, but also mass public opinion and the media. The former identify the issues at stake and create the initial climate of opinion, and the latter play a negative role of limiting the options open to the policymaker. With the possible exception of wartime, only a small number of high policy issues can be considered at any one time because the number of issues which can be debated at any one time in Parliament and in the media is itself limited. Further, the attention span of Parliament and the media for any one issue is usually limited, resulting in the issue quickly moving from high policy to sectoral policy.

Under which conditions may the media cause a change in policy? First of all, their editorial comment and coverage must be critical of government policy. 'Only a single solid line by all the press would have an influence upon the minister. But on, for example, South Africa most of the press are in agreement and support the Labour government', a Labour minister said. A single outlook among the media can be said to influence policy in another sense. 'When a parliamentary democracy is working efficiently, the government tends to identify itself almost unconsciously with a vaguely sensed general will', Younger wrote.[10]

The influence of the media on foreign policy really comprises two questions: the influence of the media on the public, and the influence of public opinion on foreign policy. The first question has been keenly debated in mass communications research, with some scholars arguing that the media change public attitudes and others that the media focus public attention but confirm existing attitudes.[11] One survey of the impact of broadcasting on public attitudes during the 1975 EEC referendum found that four out of five people did not change their minds on which way to vote, and that those who did change their view and attributed it to the (pro-EEC) media amounted to about 5 per cent.[12] Regarding the second question, an indication of wide public interest in news about foreign affairs is found in a 1977 survey showing that 27 per cent of newspaper readers were very interested in it, 60 per cent were fairly interested, and only 13 per cent were not interested at all.[13] If an increase of interest has occurred it is partly due to so many 'foreign' policies having domestic implications, and domestic policies external implications, leading to a greater interdependence between the internal situation in a country, in particular the economy, and the international situation. Lord Carrington said:

Issues which can be classified as pure foreign policy, of no immediate interest to any other government department, are now the exception rather than the rule. On most important matters of policy, our decisions need to reflect the balance between international and domestic considerations: a Foreign Minister needs to talk to, and listen to, his colleagues in other government departments, in order to do his job.[14]

The greater involvement of home departments in 'foreign' policy produces a greater weighting by policymakers to domestic pressures including the media. Also partly responsible is the broader public exposure which television gives to foreign affairs than do the printed media. While people reading newspapers select the material that interests them, few television viewers turn off the set if particular news stories do not interest them. Television creates opinions where there were formerly none. Further, while newspapers through their editorials tell the reader what to think about an event, the footage on television allows the image to speak for itself and this often has a stronger rather than a lesser effect. And whereas popular papers tended to concentrate on conflicts in those regions of British concern – Aden, Cyprus, Suez – television documentaries have covered other conflicts including Chad and El Salvador. Conversely, while television may arouse a strong reaction on certain subjects such as human suffering or war, others, including policy issues, economic issues, or the significance of a political revolution, which can be explained in print, are conveyed less easily by television. The time span of the visual image is shorter because it is succeeded by other images.

Although it has increased, the public's interest remains passive and generally fails to develop into an active pressure on government.[15] While the media not only shape the audience's perception of events but also the events themselves in one or two cases a year, in most cases the media's influence is limited to shaping the audience's perception. The influence of public opinion is as a negating force in terms of the social acceptability of foreign policy, limiting the options open to policymakers. 'If anyone had wanted to be nice to Idi Amin public opinion would have reacted', a minister suggested. A prime minister thought that 'by and large questions of foreign policy don't take up much of the public's mind. The prime minister's interest is in informing the public and getting them to understand the foreign situation as he sees it rather than to listen to what they say because they seldom say anything really'. Since Suez no British government has been faced with the kind of pressure from public opinion which the Nixon government faced over Vietnam. The danger of the argument that the influence of public opinion is in terms of what the country will or will not stand for is that it allows the policymaker to believe that his policy is democratic when it may not be, Hill argues.[16] In the Falklands War there was public support at the outset for not leaving the Falkland Islands in Argentinian hands. Had the war become a lengthy one with heavy losses, and if television film reporting the losses had reached Britain, a grounds-well of opinion might have forced the government to bring the troops home.

A difference needs to be drawn between the influence of the media on existing policy decisions and on future policy. In the case of an existing policy decision, only when a government faces strong pressure from among its own members in Parliament is a substantive alteration in a decision likely. A minister said:

If both press and the Commons took a similar tune we would have to take it into account. We have to be aware when public opinion plus our party plus the constituencies plus the press take a particular line, but this is very rare and we make our policy on what we think is right and we try to influence the press on the correctness of our view.

And the constitutional principle requiring that Parliament be the first to be publicly informed precludes early investigation and discussion, for Parliament cannot be informed until the government is ready to press its proposals to legislation. If the government is challenged, it must protect itself by defending its policy. In America, Waltz notes, deliberation takes place as part of the effort to find a policy or to form a new one.[17]

The Biafran civil war illustrated the difficulties for domestic opinion to change an existing policy. The media turned the forgotten bush war into a major foreign issue. It aroused public opinion and Parliament to demand that Harold Wilson's Labour government stop supplying arms to the Nigerian federal government under General Gowan. Despite the pressure, there was no policy change:

It was a terrible problem for a government in a democracy. Within the parliamentary party we were under persistent and bitter attack from young and idealistic members and from privy counsellors .... The head of government has to face these problems not singly but simultaneously against a background of a hundred other issues, economic, financial, diplomatic, and political.[18]

In certain other countries, including Belgium and the Netherlands, where the strength of domestic pressure was less, governments reduced the arms supplies to Gowan's side.

The number of instances when all the elements – the media, Parliament, interest groups, and public opinion – have linked up to oppose an existing foreign policy decision is small. The media, first, have to identify a particular issue as news. The chain can already break down given the public's propensity to be only passively interested in foreign affairs and not aroused enough so that any opposition becomes, in the words of one minister, 'a deafening chorus'. This assumes that enough of the government's supporters in Parliament are similarly aroused. During all this time officials may be advising their minister that the views of these domestic critics do not coincide with the longer-term national interest. The cost which a change in an existing policy would entail in terms of Britain's international interests – including relations with 160 other governments – is, they may argue, too high. In domestic policy, such as industrial relations, it is much easier for a government to alter course without too much concern for international reaction. Despite strong public pressure the Attlee government in 1949 signed the Atlantic Pact. The Heath government joined the European Economic Community despite the opposition. Similarly, cruise missiles did arrive in Britain. And in most cases public pressure tends to concern 'individual cases or episodes rather than involving an entire policy. Then you have to react quickly', a permanent under-secretary said. The heavy publicity over the case of Timothy Davey, a British boy jailed in Turkey on drug charges in November 1972, resulted in the foreign secretary, Sir Alec Douglas-Home, taking up the issue with his Turkish counterpart.

The influence of the media is more to be felt at the planning stage when policy options are decided. In considering which policy to adopt in a particular situation the likely reaction of the media will be taken into account, and it will be in the domestic interest of the government not to decide on a policy which will produce a negative reaction. An FCO minister in Heath's 1970–74 government noted:

there was the question of an official visit by the Czechs in the early seventies. Officials in the FCO wanted to see a Czech visit but I was opposed to it. Bernard Levin was writing these articles in *The Times* against it and these articles had some type of effect on me. When the visit of Emperor Hirohito of Japan was planned we had quite a lot of discussion about domestic reaction, yet we went ahead with that. On the other hand we refused to have the Greeks here.

Yet even at the policy planning stage, external factors tend to influence policymaking in most cases. The desire to avoid a negative domestic reaction to a policy will be overcome less by changing the policy and more by presenting it in a different way. 'When you are thinking of doing something which you know will produce a political or press reaction you need at the same time to ask what is going to be the criticism, and how are we going to justify and sell the policy', an official said. The anti-nuclear movement caused considerable concern among ministers, particularly before the 1983 general election. A ministerial team was set up to decide on how to respond to the groups concerned, but the policy itself remained unchanged. In NATO itself there was an awareness that the western case was being weakened by the public dissension, and this came up at most inter-ministerial NATO meetings in 1982–83. Levi has argued that the compelling need to guarantee a nation's survival makes social norms irrelevant in international relations, and that the general and abstract formulation of moral norms subjects them to the most varied interpretation to suit a given situation.[19]

'The Times' and Mozambique

On July 10, 1973, *The Times* disclosed evidence collected by Father Adrian Hastings and other church missionaries in Mozambique, then a Portuguese colony, that Portuguese troops had committed a massacre at a village, Wiriyamu, in which 400 people died. The report was published six days before a visit to Britain by the Portuguese prime minister, Dr Caetano, marking the six hundredth anniversary of Anglo-Portuguese relations. The report aroused substantial criticism of the Portuguese regime and there was pressure on the Conservative government to call off the visit.

This case illustrates the general inability of the media to influence a foreign policy decision once it has been made. The opposition leader, Harold Wilson, called on the prime minister, Edward Heath, 'to inform the prime minister of Portugal that his proposed visit to the country is unacceptable to the British people unless he can clearly and convincingly show that the report is false'. Heath rejected the call. Although African matters were an issue of disagreement between Britain and Portugal, it did not prevent Britain from maintaining friendly relations. There was, however, to be an adjournment debate on the report in the House of Commons. The furore which the disclosure sparked was the main news in the British media before and during Dr Caetano's visit. On *The Times'* letters page the subject of the massacre was the lead story in all but one of ten issues after the original disclosure, and on three days correspondence was spread across four columns. Defenders of Portugal, including the *Daily Telegraph*, questioned the authenticity of the disclosure, noting that foreign correspondents visiting the area of the alleged massacre failed to find any trace of a village called Wiriyamu.

In the House of Commons debate, Mr Wilson criticised the government for not calling off the visit. The foreign secretary, Sir Alec Douglas-Home, questioned the authenticity of the report of the massacre, and quoted statements which Mr Wilson had made when he was prime minister to the effect that while Britain disagreed with Portuguese policies in Africa this did not necessarily mean there should be no diplomatic ties.

Although the report in *The Times*, and the debate it aroused in Britain embarrassed the Portuguese, they had little effect upon Dr Caetano's talks with British leaders. An FCO minister said that

all that *The Times*' report worried us was that there would be a row in the House of Commons. As to whether it was an embarrassment during his visit he didn't raise. In fact they were very happy with the way we handled it. We went back to them before the visit and asked them whether they still wanted to come in view of the uproar, and they asked us do you advise us to come.

Whether a Labour government in the same position would have ignored the criticism and gone ahead with the visit is questionable. The disclosure of the massacre would probably have had greater effect if it had come when the government was planning to invite Dr Caetano. In the event, while the disclosure failed to affect Anglo-Portuguese relations, it did affect Portugal's international standing. The pope spoke out, as did foreign trade unionists and other interested groups. Ten days after its publication Father Hastings was giving evidence before the United Nations Committee on Decolonisation. The UN set up a special commission to investigate the Wiriyamu massacre and other massacres in Mozambique, which reported that Portuguese and Rhodesian troops had been responsible for the torture and massacre of at least a thousand Africans in Mozambique.

CONCLUSION

The media's influence on foreign policy is both horizontal and vertical. In horizontal terms, the media connect interest groups, MPs, and concerned individuals by creating a forum for the exchange of information and for discussion, in which attitudes towards foreign policy are crystallised. In vertical terms, the media's influence on policy is part of the complex process of policymaking involving a considerable number of factors. Among domestic factors, usually only party and parliamentary pressures are likely to produce a change in existing foreign policy. These have to be reconciled with pressures from foreign governments. More broadly, however, the media create a climate of opinion on international matters. This climate limits the opinions available to policymakers.

The media's influence on policy has been examined according to three aspects:

1. Which media are seen and read by whom?
2. What image of the world is conveyed by the media?
3. What effect do the media have on policymakers?

Before considering the reverse process, i.e. the influence of government on the media, it is necessary to consider an intermediate stage: the use of the media by policymakers to signal to one another and to disclose sensitive information.

CHAPTER SIX

INTERNATIONAL NEGOTIATION

'Leaks, negotiating manoeuvres? No. I can't imagine how one would work it.'

— British ambassador

Communication is a key element in international negotiation. One government communicates to another in the hope of persuading it to behave in a way which is in the interest of the first state. They communicate through various channels. These include the formal diplomatic framework involving diplomats presenting their government's messages to their counterparts in other countries, and less formal means like statements and speeches by ministers in Parliament and at political rallies.

Among these informal channels are news media, the audiences of which include foreign governments. 'When you get an ambassador in London writing to *The Times* you know the message is for you. It is meant to be read by the Foreign Office', a diplomat said. Other ways of communicating via the media, apart from letters to the editor, include articles by officials and ministers; press, radio, and television interviews; and off-the-record leaks to journalists.

The wide use of the media in international negotiation today makes a mockery of the diplomatic convention of confidentiality. By revealing publicly information previously known only to the two sides involved in a diplomatic negotiation, one party wishes that the other will be forced towards or away from a particular decision. The use of news media rather than, say, formal diplomatic contacts is not just a choice between one channel of communication and another. There is a real difference in the outcome of the communication exposed to the public and that not exposed. It may not be a media event itself, but the journalists carry the spotlights, thus heralding the event. They bring the focus on personality, on suspense, and on the negotiation's success. Most important, the presence of the media is an additional pressure on the parties to yield.

One of the features of the use of news media in international negotiation is that diplomats deny its very existence. 'If the local government wants the story put out they can put the message on.... We? We don't leak. We are in touch with the leading journalists and express our view', said one diplomat.

Apart from the intentional use of news media as channels of communication by diplomats, information is sometimes published in the media at their own initiative which has unintended effects in international relations. During the 1956 Suez War the British ambassador in Cairo complained, 'I could never persuade Nasser that every remark by a BBC commentator or backbencher was not directly inspired by the Prime Minister and represented the British Government's policy'.[1] In the years preceding the Second World War *The Times* was seen by Hitler as being the voice of the British government, and on several occasions the British ambassador in Germany complained to the Foreign Office that the press was worsening Anglo-German relations.[2]

The exposure to the public − including foreign governments − of diplomatic communication via the media helps to explain why diplomats have in the past been reticent to use this form of diplomacy. For example, in July 1944 the American newspaper columnist Drew Pearson published a State Department telegram from the US special representative in India, William Phillips, which advocated US support for the growing nationalist campaign in India for independence from Britain. The refusal of the US government to dissociate itself publicly from the contents of the cable led to some unpleasantness in the Anglo-American relationship, and the refusal, on the other hand, to publicly endorse Phillips' recommendation resulted in the US continuing to be perceived by Indians as collaborating with Britain.[3]

The increase in this century in the use of news media in negotiation has been caused by a number of factors. The benefits to be gained from using the media became more apparent and attractive. In the case of the Phillips cable which had been given to Pearson by a State Department official who supported the campaign for Indian nationalism, the facts that no public disavowal by the US government was forthcoming, and that privately the US government told the British government that it backed Phillips' recommendation, meant that whatever the costs in terms of 'fallout' among unintended audiences, the leak had been successful in pushing the US government further towards the nationalist position.[4] In addition, the decline after the First World War of secret diplomacy, which came with the growing need to keep public opinion informed and to avoid speculation about secret agreements and commitments, has further strengthened the link between negotiation and the media. Additional factors include the rise of new states and communist states and the concomitant decline of the European states' system with its respect for diplomatic confidentiality, and the large number of mass media, widening the opportunities for the diplomatic use of the media.

FORMULATING FOREIGN POLICY

The use of news media as a channel of communication occurs not only when governments are involved in negotiation but already when ministers and diplomats are planning policy. Differences among them, resulting from different perceptions of the national interest or from opposing interests of different government departments, are not always resolved within the formal governmental structure. Information is disclosed in the media with the desired aim of manoeuvring a minister or the cabinet as a whole towards or away from a particular course of action. Given that ministers and officials are unable to express in public their disagreement with government policy, this is usually expressed in the form of off-the-record leaks, which give no clues as to the identity of the speaker.

Leaks to the media have, until recently, been less a feature of British government than in some other countries. In the United States the large number of individuals involved in foreign policy – in the State Department, the National Security Council, the Pentagon, the Central Intelligence Agency, and Congress – creates more opportunities for leaks to occur. In Britain sensitive information has often been confined to a handful of people: the minister, the under-secretary, and the ambassador. The greater involvement of home government departments in foreign policy, partly as a result of British membership in the EEC, has challenged this. When one includes copies of a particular document sent to other ministers and officials for their background knowledge, the number of copies in circulation and thus potentially leakable runs easily into double figures.[5] When clerical officers, in the offices of these ministers and officials, are included the number can go into three figures. A remaining difference between the United States and Britain is that in the US many senior officials are political appointees who have an interest in pursuing particular policy objectives, whereas in Britain the FCO is staffed by career diplomats who are less willing to risk opportunities for advancement by going outside the official machinery to promote policy. British officials who previously served in the United States saw this system at work, dealt themselves with the media, and on returning home felt more comfortable in speaking to journalists.

When ministers are served by a permanent, professional, non-political bureaucracy, there is always the possibility of differences or even tension between the two sides in defining the national interest. As a result of frequent postings abroad and an absence from the domestic pressures of Parliament and the wider public which ministers face, diplomats develop their own perceptions about the national interest. And politicians find that once they are elected to office the realities of world politics frequently necessitate a modification of their policy goals as stated while in opposition. Yet it is argued by some that few of these differences find their way to the outside world. 'The influence of the Civil Service on British foreign policymaking is certainly very powerful, but what chiefly characterises its relations with the political component of the hierarchy is nevertheless its fundamental and ultimate docility', Vital argues.[6] 'There is cohesion in the Foreign Office – but it is not quite as monolithic as it may appear. There are strong differences of opinion on foreign policy but nobody would prevent a policy being effected by talking to the press', a foreign secretary said. An official said that 'if the foreign secretary says this is our policy everybody does it, and if you disagree you try and implement it as well as possible'.

Although the British civil servant is more docile than his American counterpart, there are examples of the use of the media by officials against ministers.

- On the eve of the 1976 Italian general election when there was a real possibility that Communists would win, some West European governments said Italy might have to leave the EEC. Anthony Crosland, the foreign secretary, refused to think along these lines, but senior officials did, and in order to get this known in European capitals they leaked to the media that the FCO was considering such a possibility.
- In 1974 senior officials disagreed with Mr Callaghan, the foreign secretary, about the line to be taken at the Conference on Security and Cooperation, which led up to the Helsinki accords. These officials, who took a more hardline attitude, indicated so to journalists. With the News Department headed by a Callaghan appointee rather than a career diplomat, a situation was created in which the official spokesman was telling the media one thing and senior diplomats were saying another.
- The Thatcher government, implementing policies which failed to receive the blessing of the entire cabinet, let alone the civil servants, sometimes met and took decisions as an inner group of ministers in order to prevent leaks. To improve security, the government introduced in 1983 a 'super secret' classification for the most sensitive cabinet documents.

It is partly the difficulty of tracing leaks which encourages them. A minister remarked:

No 10 orders a witch hunt. Great circulars come round asking everybody from the minister downwards whether they have spoken to Journalist X in the last Y days. These invariably produce a blank. I'm always on my ministry's side rather than No 10's because you never get any results.

After an internal Whitehall inquiry failed to trace a leak to *The Guardian* in October 1983 of a Ministry of Defence document discussing publicity and the arrival of cruise missiles in Britain, in an unprecedented move Scotland Yard's serious crime squad was brought in, which resulted in the prosecution and imprisonment of an FCO clerical officer, Sarah Tisdall. Those leaks that occur, whether by ministers or officials, fall into a number of categories.

1. Leaks by officials to get the attention of ministers, in the hope that a minister will order a brief on the subject that has appeared in the press, or in the hope of getting a minister to think again about a particular decision. Or, having failed to persuade the minister towards a particular line of thought, officials leak in the hope that the daily reading of the press by the prime minister and other ministers will lead them to adopting that position. After the minister of defence, Duncan Sandys, announced in 1957 that protection for Britain against nuclear attack was impossible and that defence policy must therefore be in the form of deterrence, the service chiefs, deploring the planned economies in each of their services, used newspapers to get their views to the prime minister and the cabinet, bypassing their minister.[7]

2. Leaks that occur when a particular minister or official favours a policy which lacks the support of other ministers and officials.

3. Leaks that occur when individual cabinet ministers disagree with a decision but cannot say so publicly because of the conventions of collective responsibility and the secrecy of cabinet meetings; instead, they leak to journalists.

4. Leaks to create the impression that the government made a decision it in fact had not; if the news is well received by the public, the prime minister might feel obliged to go along with the announced decision or appear in the unwelcome role of reversing a decision popular with party supporters or the wider public. When the Labour government was considering whether to resume arms sales to South Africa in 1967 because of the poor economic situation after sterling was devalued in the same year, the FCO News Department and the foreign secretary, George Brown, attempted to precipitate a decision by informing the press that the embargo had been reversed. But Harold Wilson, the prime minister, who called the leak 'the most blatant and inaccurate briefing of the press I have ever known, damaging alike to the coherence of the Cabinet and to our standing in the party', was not pushed on the issue, and the embargo remained.[8]

IMPLEMENTING FOREIGN POLICY

Once policy options are hammered out, other government departments are consulted, a decision is made, and the guidelines for the implementation of the decision are drawn up, the policy must be communicated to the relevant governments. Whereas most contacts between governments take place within the official diplomatic framework of ambassadors and other diplomats, a small number of contacts and negotiations take place through informal conduits including news media. An examination of Anglo-American relations from 1943 to 1947 in the *Foreign Relations of the United States* shows that of 37 effects which the media had on bilateral relations 17 concerned leaks. The remaining 20 effects included the use by diplomats in their cables of press opinion in order to reflect public opinion.[9] Events leading to the 1947 European Recovery Programme, the 'Marshall Plan', illustrate the efficacy as well as the pitfalls of the media as a channel of diplomatic communication.

The Marshall Plan

In the period following the Second World War the thinking of the US State Department was that the unity of Germany could be achieved through the unity of Europe. And this could best be achieved through technical cooperation in economic matters rather than through diplomatic negotiation. It was therefore imperative to rescue Western Europe from its economic malaise.

In developing some of these ideas, the under-secretary of state, Dean Acheson, said in a speech in May 1947 that since there would be difficulty in obtaining congressional approval for further economic aid for Europe (Congress had already approved a loan to Britain), the initiative for the loan would have to come from Western Europe rather than the United States. But in order to give these ideas on economic aid the stamp of official policy – and thus stimulate feedback from West European governments – the US secretary of state, George Marshall, would have to speak about them.[10] Given the fear of reaction developing in Congress against the aid programme, it was important that Marshall present his ideas in a low-key fashion and for the response from West European governments to come quickly.

Marshall took the opportunity of a degree ceremony at Harvard University on 5 June to make his speech. Two days beforehand, on 3 June, Acheson happened to be lunching with three British correspondents in Washington – Malcolm Muggeridge of the *Daily Telegraph*, Rene MacColl of the *Daily Express*, and Leonard Miall of the BBC – who held lunches with notable Americans at frequent intervals. MacColl later wrote:

Dean Acheson 'laid it on the line'. He told us about the whole magnitude of the contemplated plan. Then he looked at us gravely and added that it was essential – 'absolutely essential' – for some prominent European statesman to pick up the American offer and publicly, quickly, announce acceptance when the next sign was given.[11]

When Marshall made his speech two days later it failed to get a mention in news bulletins in America and the news agencies gave it only a few lines. It seemed to them an innocuous speech at a university gathering. 'Miall, Muggeridge and I, hovering about the tickers in our offices, saw the scanty agency references coming in, got the general idea, nipped round to the State Department and secured full texts. This was the "sign" Acheson had been talking about. Back to Britain roared the stories. Big stuff. Hot. Give it the works', wrote MacColl.[12]

But the 'sign' failed to get sent back to London by the British embassy in Washington. According to a State Department memorandum by Charles P. Kindleberger which attempted to reconstruct the events leading to the Marshall Plan, the press officer at the British Embassy, Philip Jordan, a trained journalist, read the text of the speech underlining the important sections, and took it to the chargé d'affaires who told Jordan, 'Oh, this doesn't justify cable charges. Send it by sea-bag. It's just another commencement speech.'[13] However, the author Andrew Boyle, who named Anthony Blunt as the fourth man in the Burgess–Maclean–Philby spy ring and suggested that up to 25 people were involved in the ring, has hinted strongly that Jordan, who was in the Washington embassy at the same time as Burgess, was one of these.[14] Did the 'sign' fail to reach the Foreign Office in London owing to Jordan's doing, or was its significance simply not registered?

Whatever the reason, the sign reached London via the three British correspondents. The *Daily Telegraph* and *Daily Express* printed prominent reports of the Harvard speech, and it led the BBC's news bulletins. It also featured in the BBC's 'Atlantic Commentary' later that evening which, Miall wrote, 'I happened to be giving.... I devoted almost all of it to the importance of Marshall's overture, and to the American Administration's desire for a dramatic response from the European side'.[15] When Ernest Bevin, the British foreign secretary, heard the BBC news, 'I grabbed it as a lifeline. I grabbed the lifeline with both hands.'[16] To the surprise of the Foreign Office, Bevin called an immediate meeting in Paris with the foreign ministers of France and the Soviet Union to decide on a response to the USA.

The role which the media plays in international negotiation varies with each case. The media may be used by one government to state its objectives to another government, for instance where no formal diplomatic channels exist between the two. After Ian Smith declared Rhodesia's unilateral independence in 1964, and diplomatic ties between London and Salisbury were severed, the media were sometimes used to send messages. Other cases, not concerning Britain, include the use of the American correspondents in Teheran during the seizure of the US embassy by Iranian students in 1979 to send ultimatums to Washington; and Sadat's statement in a CBS interview, following behind-the-scenes diplomacy by third parties, that he would like to address the Israeli parliament, followed by Begin's reply, also through CBS, which heralded the era of peaceful relations between Egypt and Israel.

Often, too, governments will use the media as additional or faster channels than the formal diplomatic ones. The US military action in Grenada in 1983, which followed a Marxist takeover of the island's government, received considerable criticism in western countries. There was even a temporary crisis in Anglo-American relations. The absence of foreign correspondents in the military operation added to the lack of understanding of, and credibility about, US goals. To show that the USA had intervened in response to a request from other governments in the East Caribbean, the US State Department leaked to the media cables from these governments requesting US assistance. In another case, at one stage during the negotiations between Britain and Uganda to obtain the release of the British teacher Denis Hills, who had been arrested by President Idi Amin, Anthony Crosland, the foreign secretary, interrupted a House of Commons debate to make a special statement about the Hills affair. Crosland was not then speaking primarily to Parliament but was using a forum that would be reported by the BBC World and African Services to communicate the government's position to Amin.

Nevertheless, even where there are no formal diplomatic relations two governments may prefer to use a third country which has diplomatic relations with both in order to avoid the message being distorted if transmitted by the media, a problem to be discussed at greater length in the chapter, as well as in order to respect the convention of diplomatic confidentiality. In a wider sense, a clearer understanding of a government's objectives is achieved by media coverage since through communication misperceptions may sometimes be reduced and conflicts brought nearer to resolution. But to argue that all conflicts will disappear through better communication between the two sides involved is an exaggeration, since a clash of real interests usually lies at the source of a conflict. In addition, full communication of the opposing objectives of two sides may often deepen an existing conflict.

Apart from a government using the media to make a statement of its objectives, another type of diplomatic communication is conveying the impression to the media that a government is seriously interested in bargaining with another even though it really desires no agreement. During war, for example, a government may agree to negotiations either to assuage public opinion or to give itself time to reorganise the army or acquire new weaponry. Alternatively, a government may enter into diplomatic negotiations for the purpose of making propaganda. A conference is used not so much to reach an agreement over a range of issues as to make broad appeals to the outside public. A conference extensively covered by the media is an excellent forum for influencing public attitudes; the best example of this is the United Nations General Assembly. An experienced diplomat can easily discern when a government involved in a diplomatic negotiation is using it primarily to influence attitudes of the general public rather than to reach a diplomatic agreement. These signs include the persistent use of slogans, epithets, vague phraseology, and the repetition of totally unacceptable positions.

If and when serious negotiations begin, an agreement has first to be made regarding the status of the media. Will the talks be closed to the media, thereby avoiding the pressures and slow progress which public exposure causes, or will the talks be open, thereby avoiding undue speculation and alarm? A compromise is sometimes struck namely that the negotiations will be confidential and that agreed communiqués will be issued. But opportunities to win gains in the negotiations sometimes result in these preliminary agreements being abandoned, and delegates from one or both sides begin to hold their own press briefings. At first only the contents of their own positions will be disclosed, but later so will the positions of the other parties. Whether a preliminary agreement to limit contacts with the media to agreed communiqués is adhered to depends on a number of factors. These include the extent to which the interests and objectives of the parties concerned are compatible or incompatible, the relationship so far between the parties, and whether there are other elements directly or indirectly involved in the topic of the negotiations such as public opinion and interest groups. Where there is considerable agreement between the two sides, negotiations may involve only working out the details. But where objectives are irreconcilable, with both sides maintaining a strong commitment to their respective positions, there is a need to influence the behaviour of the parties through diplomatic bargaining. Two stages of diplomatic bargaining are involved: getting an agreement in principle, and working out the details of the agreement. The media are involved in both.

The strategies for using the media are manifold. These include a government 'playing' to its audience at home to show that it is not giving away too much to the other side; or raising the hopes of their public so as to tell the other side that their public will not 'allow' them to compromise; or 'preparing the ground' among their public for compromise. Similarly, the public in the other country, or international audiences, may be played to in order to lower, or raise, their expectations. Another strategy is getting issues, or parties, included or dropped from the agenda of the negotiations. When in 1945 the Montreux Convention on the Dardanelles came up for renewal the United States wanted the consent of a number of governments involved, including Turkey, Bulgaria, and Roumania, but the British government wanted to settle the matter with the US alone. In an attempt to force the US position, the Foreign Office told the London correspondent of the *New York Times* that Britain and the US were seeking a joint policy 'in order to create a solid front to face the Soviet Union and wanted to settle the issue above Turkey's head'. As it happened the manoeuvre failed to change the US position and its secretary of state, Byrnes, said at a press conference that the US had no information on a joint British plan and was in contact with Turkey on the whole subject of the renewal of the convention.[17]

Another strategy is to use the media to create the impression that an agreement has already been reached, after which a form of pressure is applied on the other party to agree or find itself in the unpopular role either of being the party obstructing the agreement or of encouraging pressure, at home or abroad, to develop in the meantime against an agreement. During the discussions about the future of Rhodesia at the Commonwealth Conference in Lusaka in 1979, the Australian delegation leaked a copy of the draft agreement to the media. The fear of a hostile reaction from among Conservative backbenchers to the proposed deal encouraged Mrs Thatcher and her foreign secretary, Lord Carrington, to reach a quick agreement.[18]

Still another strategy is for interested groups against the negotiations to disrupt them by leaking. When secret negotiations were held in London in 1978 between Britain and the prime minister of the then British colony of Belize, George Price, which would have resulted in the colony's division, with the northern and southern areas being given to Mexico and Guatemala which had long-standing claims on them, opponents leaked the information to *The Guardian*'s diplomatic correspondent. The disclosures were reported back to the colony where strong hostility developed and Price, whose domestic political position was not strong, was forced to leave the London talks.[19]

The use of the media in international negotiations varies from government to government. Communist states regard propaganda as an end in itself; western governments regard it more as a means to achieving a diplomatic objective. If a line were drawn starting with states using propaganda as an indiscriminate objective in negotiation and ending with states which respect the convention of confidentiality in negoti- ations, Britain would lie nearer the latter extreme. The British style in using the media is less to leak during negotiations, as is usual with the USA, and more to give their own definitions of international matters by giving prominence to British interests. Press conferences are held (at UNO in New York the British delegation was the sole mission to give a daily briefing to the press corps until, due to expenditure cuts, it was ended) and announcements timed. Most leaks are made by the minister or the under-secretary rather than lower-ranking officials. Given the limited contact between ministers and diplomatic correspondents, which will be described in Chapter 8, these occur less than, for example, in the United States where contacts are much greater. The use of disclosure varies with each diplomatic setting. In the EEC context all governments, including Britain, take the initiative in using the media, whereas in the European security discussions diplomatic confidentiality is respected. There is an element of diplomatic reciprocity. 'A lot depends on what type of diplomatic ballgame you're playing. Once one party breaks the rules then it's a different ballgame', an ambassador said.

As a form of communication, the news media play an integral role in negotiation. Bargaining, ultimately, concerns one party com- municating to another its wishes and intentions. Other means through which a message may be communicated include military postures, economic measures, and changes of personnel. The media's role extends to creating a veil of partial truthfulness. Ikle has argued that bargaining is incompatible with completely truthful information. If a completely truthful government said that it would not withdraw from some par- ticular territory, even if the other side gave in to its demands, no with- drawal would take place. Likewise, if, on the other hand, a party became known to give only false information, its threats and commitments would lose credibility and its offers to sign an agreement would lose all value.[20] By the media willingly publishing conflicting leaks, scoops, and other disclosures – which are monitored by the other side – a situation is created of ambiguity and expectations of high demands. Before the Argentinian invasion of the Falkland Islands, but after Argentinian intentions became clear, it became 'known', incorrectly, that a nuclear-powered submarine, HMS *Superb*, had left for the South Atlantic. The Ministry of Defence did not officially deny the rumour because it wanted the story published in the vain hope of discouraging Argentina from its invasion plans.[21]

In using media, diplomats have to fit into their framework and agenda. This involves not only timetables and deadlines but also making the contents of the leak fit the media's definition of newsworthiness. Only if the leak is newsworthy will it be published by the media, and the process involving reaction from different publics begun. As was suggested in Chapter 4, in order to meet the criteria of news the subject of the leak should be dramatic, or involve personalities rather than issues, and concern 'newsworthy' regions of the world like Western Europe and the United States.

When a government does not use the media as a whole but gives the information it wants publicised to a particular journalist, its choice of journalists will be determined by a number of factors. The quality newspaper is 'recognised' as the primary news medium through which a government sends a diplomatic communication to another. *The Times* is regarded by foreign diplomats, wrongly or correctly, as reflecting British government thinking. In countries with a controlled media the media do reflect government thinking; thus *Pravda* and *Izvestia* are voices of the Soviet government. In a country with a language not widely known outside, if there is an English- or French-language newspaper for the foreign population it will be used by governments to communicate. A key distinction is that the state-controlled media are one-way media open only to the host government and closed to foreign governments, in contrast to free media which can be used by all parties.

The newspaper is used more than other forms of news media. It is impractical to communicate via the news agency because the nuances of the information will not usually be included in the brief news agency story. The journalist on a quality newspaper has greater latitude to not only report news but also interpret it. Radio and television reports are similarly shorter than in a quality newspaper; the main reports in a radio or television news bulletin rarely extend to more than two minutes of air time, or 250 words, in contrast to those in a quality newspaper which may often extend to over 1000 words. Nor are radio, television, or the news agency as easy to monitor for a foreign diplomat as the newspaper. In many cases a diplomat may want to direct the information to a distinct group of policymakers and to avoid the message being picked up by the population at large; a small circulation newspaper read by the intended group of decisionmakers is then the best medium. But in cases when as large a public audience as possible is desired, the best media are popular newspapers with large circulations or even international news magazines. Whether the diplomat desires to limit his audience or not, if the information is significant it will be picked up by other news media and communicated to a much larger audience than intended.

There are two types of location for use of the media: the foreign ministry in the capital, and the diplomatic post abroad situated in the capital of the other party involved in negotiations. Similarly, there are two types of media: that of the country using the media and that of the other party. Schematically, if the British government uses the media to communicate to the US government, there are four channels:

1. A communication in the form of a press statement, leak, or interview by the FCO in London to the British media to be picked up by the US Embassy in London.
2. A communication by the FCO in London to the US press corps to be picked up in Washington by the US State Department.
3. A communication by the British Embassy in Washington to the American media to be picked up in Washington by the State Department.
4. A communication by the British Embassy in Washington to the British press corps to be picked up by the US Embassy in London and sent back to Washington.

The choice of which channel a British diplomat would make is determined by a number of factors. Channel 1 is a more direct one to reach policymakers in Washington, and has greater certainty of being picked up by its intended recipients. This channel is recognised in diplomacy as the official one through which a government would communicate. Channel 4, in contrast, is clumsy and indirect. The choice between Channels 1, 2, and 3 depends on the diplomat's intended audience. If it is the State Department he would use Channel 1, whereas if the American public he would use Channels 2 or 3. If his intended audience is the British public he would use Channel 1. Channel 2 is used much more than Channel 3, i.e. the information is given to American correspondents in London rather than by the embassy in Washington because, first, as one diplomat said, 'the foreign correspondent is preferred to a local journalist — after all he is the one who writes the story', and second, as another said, 'embassies don't usually have the kind of information to leak to journalists'.

The use of the media in international negotiation is not as Machiavellian as it may sound. There are no fixed rules limiting which media should be used and where. Although a diplomat may want to use a particular news medium or journalist to reach a specific audience, in practice he usually does not say 'I am going to leak X, Y, and Z to correspondent P of news organisation A', but will take an opportunity in meeting journalists to get across his message.

Is it ethical for the free media to be used as channels of communication by governments and others? A difference must be drawn between inaccurate messages sent via the media and accurate ones. An inaccurate message not only deceives its intended party but also results in the public being misinformed. Thus, given the legitimacy of the free media in a democracy, the use of the media for sending inaccurate messages is unethical. There are other means available for deception besides the media. There can be little objection, however, to sending accurate messages through the media. Some citizens may object that their elected leaders use the media given the practical danger that a message sent via the media is liable to distortion.

Is the message received by the other side? One of the reasons why diplomats read the media is in order to pick up messages. A number of problems in picking up messages are evident, however. Does the correct message get picked up by the intended government? The fact that over 160 other governments, as well as other entities, listen to a message remains a problem in diplomacy. There are occasions when a government needs to say something in public which it knows will be received badly by another government. 'If I have to say something which is going to scare Government X, I will send them a telegram explaining to them why we are addressing ourselves in this way. This is not insulting in public and apologising in private, but showing that I am at great pains to explain why we are taking this attitude', an ambassador said.

Will the other side attribute an unattributed message in the media to its correct source? Does its passage through news processing distort its meaning? And is the meaning of the message correctly interpreted by the other side? In the case of the Marshall Plan, George Marshall admitted later that he was worried about whether the signal to European leaders would be picked up. The State Department's Press Office had issued the speech in the normal way but its importance had been played down lest American journalists, in reporting reaction to the speech, would contact Congressmen who were opposed to further aid for Europe. Marshall had wanted to tip off Mr Bevin about the significance of the speech, but decided against it because he would also have had to inform the French foreign minister at a time when US ties with France were cool.[22]

The problems facing the other side in deciphering a non-attributable message are not helped by journalists not revealing their sources. The foreign ministry may indicate that a change of policy has taken place, or, if it is simply 'flying a kite' in order to test likely reactions to a particular move, may not. 'If I go to the foreign ministry and say "Have you gone and leaked something to the newspapers?", they will say "You are insulting us. Of course we didn't leak it. What do you mean?"' said an ambassador. The diplomats who used the media are themselves in doubt whether the message has got through. But they can soon tell from whether they get feedback from the other side that the message was or was not received. If it was not, then 'if we repeat the message to enough people it will catch on', said an official.

CONCLUSION

The media are channels for signalling and causing disclosures among policymakers. They are intended to affect either other policymakers in the foreign policy bureaucracy or other governments. Disclosures, as distinct from signalling, necessarily involve the public in the process because it is the public disclosure of sensitive information which, it is hoped, will have a desired public impact on policymakers and governments. In the types of disclosures discussed in this chapter, the public serve as means, and the 'ends' are the policymakers. As we shall see in the next chapter, the public can also serve as 'ends', that is the target of British government attempts to build public support abroad through the media.

CHAPTER SEVEN

MOULDING OPINION ABROAD

'There is to be a defence debate in the House of Commons and matters of great importance to the US are to be revealed. I get telegraphic instructions from London: "You will wish to know we are going to do A, B, and C in the next few days. Prepare the ground. Sow the seed. Create the right climate for events to follow". You might reorganise your social plans and decide the night before the debate to invite two or three newspaper editors to dinner and surprise, surprise. It's rather fortunate you are here tonight because there's some information that there will be an announcement during a debate in Parliament and as far as I know the main points are A, B, and C ...'
                        – Information attaché, New York

Implementing foreign policy involves negotiating with another government or a non-state actor. A secondary aspect of foreign policy is gaining the support of publics abroad. The challenge which an unfriendly public can pose to a government in achieving its policy objective varies with each case, but increasingly over the last 60 years British ministers and officials have come to recognise the importance of explaining foreign policy. With foreign governments and other actors using public opinion in order to influence international relations, there has remained no choice for a British government but to interpret and persuasively present its policies to publics abroad. The British approach to propaganda is that it remains an adjunct to diplomacy. The Soviet government, by contrast, perceives propaganda as an end rather than a means to conducting diplomacy. The British approach shows an appreciation that subtle indirect projection is often more successful than more explicit attempts. Like other governments, the British government defines international developments and policy objectives in terms conducive to the country's interest, including the image that the country still wields considerable influence in international affairs. 'Although since the war Britain has not been terribly involved in international transactions, the British press officer managed to inject Britain into the regular briefing', a foreign correspondent at the United Nations in New York observed.

In explaining British policies – not only foreign policy but all government policies – to the public abroad, the media play a major role because public support is best achieved through channels of communication which are recognised by their audience as unbiased and as independent of government. 'The whole point of using the media is to get somebody else to sing the song. A preacher standing on a street corner for twenty-four hours doesn't rate very much attention but if a man who is known to be uncommitted starts evangelising your song your work is complete', an official said. In practical terms the media's roles in information work include:

1. Getting to know local editors and directors of radio and television stations abroad in order to brief them about British policies.
2. Translating and placing publicity material prepared by the Central Office of Information (COI) in London.
3. Placing and selling television and video material.
4. Explaining policy and giving assistance to foreign correspondents in London and to visiting journalists.
5. The broadcasts of the BBC External Services.

There are other means to build public support apart from the media, including cultural promotion through the British Council, and encouraging tourism to Britain. But the media remain key means for building overseas support.

The media's role in image building has two sides to it. The media's image of Britain is not solely determined by the efforts of British officials. These can do little, for example, to combat the bad image of the British economy, and the consequent decline of confidence in Britain as a country to invest in. The task for the official engaged in image building is to get a word in edgeways. Some of Britain's image abroad is influenced by British media seen abroad. Twenty-three per cent, or 45,000 copies, of the *Financial Times* are sold abroad. A survey of Arab investors found that 23 per cent listened to the BBC World Service, 69 per cent to the BBC Arabic Service, 13 per cent read *The Economist*, and 5 per cent read the *Financial Times*.[1] In the US administration, for example, both the American and British media are read by policymakers responsible for US–British relations. The British media are followed closely by the US Embassy in London and by relevant desk officers in the State Department, and important extracts are included in a daily summary of foreign press reaction produced for the White House and other US government agencies.

Unlike the Soviet official engaged in information work inside his country, who is working in a vacuum without competing hostile forces, the British official doing information work abroad faces a number of competing forces. First he has to present his message in newsworthy terms. While a speech by the US president commands a ready audience overseas, the reduction in Britain's imperial red on the world map means that, as one ambassador said, 'the British embassy has to try to get into the game and prove it is useful to the media'. The problem was alluded to by an Indian foreign correspondent at the UN:

I used to go to the British briefing but now that Britain's role is minimal I don't. I don't see much of the British mission nowadays – once every six months I see the British ambassador in the corridor and we say Hallo and I don't ask anything.

A second problem is whether the local media are free or state-controlled; in other words, accessible to the foreign diplomat or not. The mass circulation press in the communist world is virtually inaccessible to the foreign diplomat. But the technical and trade press in a number of these countries, including Czechoslovakia, Hungary, and Yugoslavia, have published material prepared by the COI. The signing of the Helsinki Agreement in 1975, allowing for a greater flow of ideas between East and West, has meant that some official publications, including *Anglia, Brytania,* and *Panoramic Brittanic,* are distributed by British diplomatic posts in the Soviet Union, Bulgaria, and Poland.

Another problem concerns the level of development of the free media. In Western countries, where the press and broadcasting are financially strong, a foreign government has little opportunity to get its material accepted; but in the developing world where news organisations are much poorer a foreign government can often place its material with little difficulty in the local media. The BBC's Topical Tapes and Transcription Services, comprising programmes broadcast on the BBC, are widely received by radio stations in the developing countries. In the Western countries there are, however, opportunities for foreign governments to get material on new products and scientific developments accepted in the technical and trade press. 'While it is difficult in Toronto to get your material used by the national media which has little need for it, you have a large trade and technical press – McLean Hunters alone has 600 journals – and here you have a large market for export promotion publicity', said an information official in Toronto. Given the British government's priority of export promotion in the developed world, there is a happy coincidence between the information official's goals and the readiness of specialised trade and technical media to accept government-sponsored material for publication.

FROM PROJECTING BRITAIN TO PRODUCT PUBLICITY

The information priorities vary from place to place according to the nature of the bilateral relationship. In a parliamentary capital, a foreign diplomat's main efforts will be directed towards parliamentarians rather than journalists. In a commercial centre the information effort largely consists of holding trade fairs. The overall trend over the last ten years in Britain's information policy has been a major streamlining of work from a general projection of British policies and life towards commercial information work. The Plowden Report was 'sceptical of the value of information work of a generalised character such as "projection of Britain". It should be clearly and consciously linked to specific policy objectives. Information campaigns should do more than simply convey the idea that Britain is a fine country, with a fine past and a promising future'.[2]

The Duncan Report said that information work should focus on projecting British commerce.[3] While only 30 per cent of publicity material prepared by the COI in the mid-1950s comprised commercial publicity, by the 1970s this figure had risen to 70 per cent. Key aspects of the commercial publicity include information about positive economic developments in Britain, British participants at overseas trade fairs, and new and improved products. About 20 radio and television programmes are regularly produced, some weekly, others monthly, by the COI radio and film divisions. A major series is 13 14-minute television programmes 'Living Tomorrow', featuring new ideas in science, medicine, technology, and industry. The programme has editions in English, French, Spanish, Brazilian, and Arabic, and is transmitted by over 100 television stations in 40 countries including the US, Canada, Latin America, some European countries, Australasia, Africa and the Arabic world. This, and other commercial publicity efforts, are said by the COI to generate thousands of inquiries from industries and individuals.

The change has occurred as a result of a number of factors. There is a greater emphasis in external policy on export promotion. There has been a reassessment of the value of generalised image projection. Britain's international position has declined, resulting in a seemingly lesser need for information work. And this has caused less media interest in Britain with the British spokesman less looked to as a source of information by journalists. But the most persistent factor has been cuts in public expenditure. The percentage of expenditure allocated to the FCO information departments and to the COI out of the total budget for information and cultural work (including external broadcasting and the cultural work of the British Council) has been halved in the last fifteen years.* The focus on commercial publicity means that the general media are less important to the information officer as a channel than they used to be, and that the technical and trade media are more important. Some requirement for information work to support particular policy objectives nevertheless remains. The situation in Ulster, for example, is closely followed in countries with Catholic populations. The information officer has to demonstrate the complexities of the problem and to explain that Britain is not simply in a colonial situation. In the United States British officials, at both the informational and political levels, are involved, and are assisted by officials seconded from the Northern Ireland Office.

The change in information priorities is reflected in the number of information officers and in the places to which they are posted. While in 1964 there were 235 full-time UK-based information attachés abroad,[4] this had decreased by 1980 to 60.[5] The 1977 Berrill Report's recommendation that the number of full-time information attachés be reduced to 25 was rejected by the government. However, by July 1983 this number had indeed gone down to 27. Responsibility for information work is held by commercial and other attachés, or by the British Council representative. In 1983, 123 UK-based diplomats abroad had partial information responsibilities. They were assisted by 399 local engaged staff. The change has been most noticeable in Commonwealth countries. Canada, which until the 1960s had 15 to 20 full-time UK-based officials, now has only one in Toronto, the centre of Canadian publishing; in Ottawa and Edmonton there are diplomats who combine information work with other responsibilities. Today, there are few full-time UK-based information officials in the developing world; in Pakistan, Tanzania, Egypt, Argentina, and with two exceptions all other posts in South America, there are no full-time officials. In contrast, important markets for British exports, including such oil-producing countries as Norway, Nigeria, Kuwait, and Venezuela, each have one.**

---

*Comparison of expenditure on overseas information work, excluding aid aspects of the British Council:

	1968/69 %	1982/3 %
FCO information services (including ⅔ of the COI)	£9.1m (31.5)	£20.2m (14.4)
BBC External Services	£12.0m (41.5)	£81.0m (57.6)
British Council	£7.8m (27.0)	£39.5m (28.1)
	£28.9m	£140.7m

(*Source:* Foreign and Commonwealth Office)

** The dominance of the western developed world in information priorities may be seen from the fact that in 1983 there were 13 full-time UK-based information attachés in Europe, five in the Americas, five in Asia/Australasia, and five in Africa/Middle East. The numbers of UK-based attachés spending over 50 per cent of their time in information work were eight in Europe, 10 in the Americas, five in Asia/Australasia, and two in Africa/Middle East.

The major posts in terms of expenditure and staff are New York, Washington, Bonn, Johannesburg, Paris, New Delhi, Brussels, Tokyo, and Ottawa.

Whatever the merits of a highly targeted information strategy, there is nevertheless a need to create the right climate of opinion about Britain. Unless there is a high regard for the country the information machinery cannot perform its function when specific cases arise. Thus, efforts to sell British products are nullified if there is a negative picture abroad about the state of the British economy. Articles and programmes in the overseas media in the 1970s suggested Britain was in the throes of a political and social revolution, with the political parties losing effective power to the trade unions. A CBS programme in 1976 by Morley Safer, for example, asked whether Britain was in danger of a Marxist revolution. There is little which official information efforts can do to disguise this image, or any other negative image, particularly when generalised projection has been abandoned as a policy.

One area where a lot can be achieved at a relatively small cost, however, is that of the foreign press correspondents in London. Until recently few officials recognised the fact that much of the image about Britain in the foreign media is created not abroad but by the correspondents in London. Information work used to be considered the responsibility of the diplomatic post abroad rather than that of the FCO, the functions of which are to plan and coordinate policy rather than implement it. This is a reversal of the attitude established during World War I when the official wireless service was used to transmit material to overseas posts for inclusion in the local media rather than relying on the whims of the correspondents in London to include the British view. Only since the mid-1970s has the FCO recognised the importance of the foreign press corps in London and had an official in the News Department with special responsibility for liaison with them. The initiative for briefings lies with the correspondents. The American and European correspondents each come weekly to the FCO. At different periods the Europeans have come all together and at other times according to country with French, German, Dutch, and other country groups each receiving a separate briefing. In 1983 the Arabs and Indians each came weekly, and the Israelis, Australians/New Zealanders, and the Japanese each came regularly but less frequently.

No 10 Downing Street has for some time also had regular briefings for the Americans, for the Europeans, and for the Foreign Press Association. The COI distributes material to the foreign press corps, runs a film library, and organises tours for them. But until the late 1970s the home government departments failed to recognise the importance of the foreign media. Some improvement has occurred with the appointment in each home government department of an official with special responsibility for liaison with the foreign press corps. But in terms of journalists' access to ministers the old attitude still prevails. In the Falklands War the foreign press were very critical of the lack of facilities given to them both in the South Atlantic and in London.

The foreign press corps in Britain comprises about 400 journalists. Fifty-five per cent of them represent West European media, 17.5 per cent United States media, 10 per cent each from East Europe and from Africa, five per cent the Middle East, and from two to five per cent each from the media in Australasia, Latin America and the Far East. Many news organisations post correspondents to London because it is a convenient place from which to cover the rest of Europe and because English is the language rather than because Britain is today a source of diplomatic news. The presence of a large press corps thus gives Britain an audience it might not otherwise have. Another factor for the large press corps is the interest and affinity for British culture and life. 'Britain is a kind of political and social laboratory in which we can speculate on the impact of the welfare state and on other topics', an American correspondent said. But the presence of a large press corps also means that bad news is given greater foreign coverage than in a country with fewer correspondents.

The one area of overseas information work which has not been brought into line with the new priorities favouring commercial publicity is external broadcasting. Only a very small part of the output of the BBC External Services comprises new products and scientific developments. The BBC contributes to creating the right climate of opinion about Britain needed in order that specific information programmes, such as product publicity, will be successful. The BBC has escaped government rationalisation more because of its very success as one of the world's leading external broadcasters, as well as its visibility, which has, in turn, won it many supporters in Parliament and elsewhere. It owes its success to its perceived impartiality and to the credibility thereby created. In contrast to most other external broadcasters, the BBC presents mostly factual news accounts and critiques of British policies. Within these confines certain topics and themes are played up or played down. It has nevertheless not received from successive governments all the capital investment it has required to maintain good audibility, and individual language services have been reduced or closed.

Successive government inquiries have examined the priorities of external broadcasting. The 1968 Duncan Report was in favour of concentrating on moulding élite opinion abroad rather than foreign public opinion at large, and recommended that the BBC concentrate on its English-language World Service and reduce foreign language broadcasting with the exception of Eastern Europe and the Middle East. The BBC replied that in many parts of the world influential people did not understand English at all or had an insufficient command to listen profitably. The Berrill Report recommended concentrating on countries denied information, reductions in foreign language broadcasting, and an eight-hour shutdown of broadcasting from 20.00 to 04.00 hours. The BBC replied that in addition to losing breakfast-time listeners in many parts of the globe, and expensive transmitters lying unused for a considerable part of the day, the cuts involving 40 per cent of output would produce no more than 10 per cent of operational costs. Except for the proposal to increase capital investment, the government rejected the Berrill Report's proposals on broadcasting.

It could be argued that with the loss of territorial possessions Britain, rather than reduce external broadcasting in line with this degree of international power, needs to exploit other forms of international influence including external broadcasting. Given that 'the nation benefits from the unique reputation of the BBC's External Services as a well-informed and unbiased source of world news and comment', as the 1978 White Paper on Britain's Overseas Representation put it,[6] a British government could do worse than maintaining and expanding the BBC's role as the world's provider of information about international affairs rather as Switzerland has a key role in the International Red Cross.

Irrespective of the national interest, the BBC fulfils another function, namely, of being a source of unbiased news about world affairs to those deprived of it. The provision of information to those who lack it is an extension of a society based on democratic ideals. A survey of external radio listening by Poles, before the introduction of martial law in December 1981, estimated that 6.7 million Poles, or more than a quarter of the population listen at least once a week to the BBC.[7] After the introduction of martial law, broadcasting by the BBC Polish Service was increased by 45 minutes to 3¾ hours a day. This function, however, not infrequently clashes with the objective of maintaining positive diplomatic relationships because governments, particularly totalitarian ones, perceive foreign broadcasting as a threat to internal stability. 'You would get the Shah or Gromyko saying to you, "Well, how do you explain this sort of thing when you want friendly relations with us" and it was very simple — you explain that "you must understand that unlike your country our press have freedom",' a Prime Minister said. There is on average one protest a month about the BBC from a foreign government.

Another function of external broadcasting, related to that of broadcasting to areas of political and economic importance, is as a tool of psychological warfare. An analysis of the patterns of broadcasting to those countries where the population is deprived of unbiased information shows some inconsistencies. While the BBC broadcasts 34¾ hours weekly to the Soviet Union it broadcasts to China in Standard Chinese and Cantonese for only 10¼ hours and 5½ hours, respectively. Is this simply a case of the BBC resisting government attempts to reorganise the pattern of broadcasting, or is it the government using one of its resources in fighting the Soviet Union? The BBC is aware, and concerned, that increases in the amount of broadcasting hours at times of crisis, such as broadcasting to Poland after the military clampdown, or the increase in broadcasting to Afghanistan that occurred after the Soviet invasion, may be construed as continuations of the Cold War. Another example of the political use of broadcasting occurred after the Rhodesian government's unilateral declaration of independence in 1965, when the British government asked the BBC to undertake a special broadcasting operation directed at white Rhodesians to stress their isolation and vulnerability as a result of the Smith regime's illegal action. A transmitter set up in Francistown, in neighbouring Botswana, was inaudible. Some BBC officials opposed the operation fearing that it would raise doubts about BBC credibility.[8]

In considering as a whole the gravitation in information policy from general projection of Britain to promoting its products it could be argued that if instead of being a nation-state Britain were a commercial enterprise its public relations policy would be highly targeted publicity for its products in key markets like the USA, Western Europe, and Japan. As a nation-state, however, Britain's objectives are much wider. They include, among others, (1) promoting Britain's prosperity, (2) upholding and extending the basic values and freedoms of democracy, and (3) working for a peaceful and just world. Each of these objectives entails information work for the media. At present each of these goals is achieved despite the narrow definition of information work as being almost solely about commercial publicity. The first goal is the aim of information work; the second is achieved by the BBC and the British Council's cultural relations work; and the third is contributed to by the BBC through its supplying world news. The second and third goals are also contributed to by British media seen abroad, such as Reuters and *The Economist*, and via the foreign press corps in London.

Whether these goals will continue to be achieved in their informational terms depends on various factors. Will Reuters continue to be a key agency dominating the flow of international news, or will the developing world strengthen their own news agencies? Will London still be a base for foreign correspondents, offering the British government a means to express its policies and gain a favourable image? Will the official agencies like the BBC still have their audience, or will they have to adapt to newer media patterns such as external television? Given the changing state of the media and their audiences, those planning information policy require to ensure that these wider national goals are achieved by the information structure or by other means.

COORDINATION AND CONTROL

With the exception of the two world wars when responsibility for overseas information work lay with the Ministry of Information, it has always been the preserve of the Foreign Office. Given that overseas information constitutes part of a country's overseas representation, and given that in job terms it takes up a significant part of this representation, it is not surprising that the FCO insists on being the lead department. At the same time, there has been, and to some extent remains, a disdain among diplomats for information work. People enter the diplomatic service in order to deal with other governments rather than to become involved in public relations – an attitude not peculiar to diplomats from Britain. The 1954 Drogheda Report spoke of 'the need to break down any prejudice there might be against information work and to offer good prospects of promotion to those who prove themselves capable of it'.[9]

Today, it is more accepted by diplomats that the hat of spokesman is worn by all of them. 'Information work in its very broadest sense is the function of the whole Embassy and not just a section of it. The Information Officer, if anybody could be called that, is the Ambassador himself', an under-secretary responsible for information wrote.[10] In certain countries, including the United States, the personnel policy is to have a class of public relations officials in the State Department rather than career diplomats handling information work. The need for the information officer to understand the growing sophistication of mass communications gives this attitude particular validity today. But the counter-argument is that a career diplomat doing a stint as an information officer can bring his experience in diplomacy to his new job.

The Plowden Report argued that 'information officers are not primarily technical. What an information officer needs first and foremost is close collaboration with political and commercial colleagues, an appreciation of what they are trying to achieve and the personality to put this over at his particular post.'[11] Journalists find they gain more from a briefing given by a career diplomat than by a public relations man. As one said, 'While public relations people are on the side of the press they don't have the perspective of international affairs'. To compensate for any absence of technical knowhow among diplomats about the workings of the media, the COI used to run three-week courses for diplomats but these have been discontinued with the reduction in information work. In 1982 the COI began short courses for ambassadors on such media techniques as how best to appear before the television camera. The growing technological sophistication of mass communications would argue for COI officials to be seconded to major posts such as in the US to work with career diplomats.

Given the changed nature of information work, with over 70 per cent of COI's work being commercial publicity, it could be argued that the Ministry of Trade, which is responsible for export promotion, should become the lead department in determining policy on commercial publicity instead of the present system where the FCO remains the lead department with the Department of Trade and the British Overseas Trade Board (BOTB) being consulted. Under this new arrangement commercial publicity could be more closely tied to changes in the economy and developments in different industrial sectors. In addition, information officers in countries where Britain's bilateral relationship is largely commercial, such as Japan, should come from the Department of Trade rather than from the FCO because the former are better informed about the economy and equipped to do trade promotion.

Further, it is surprising to find that the current administrative structure of the FCO for information work is almost identical to that planned at the end of the Second World War. Today there are three departments doing information work: the News Department, which is responsible for relations with the foreign press in London; the Information Policy Department, responsible for overseas information work including drawing up information priorities, liaison with the BBC External Services, preparing publicity material, and appointing information officers; and the Cultural Relations Department, responsible for liaison with the British Council. The Information Policy Department has had a history of splits and mergers between two departments, one responsible for information policy, expenditure, and the hours and languages in which the BBC External Services broadcasts, and another for preparing guidance material for overseas posts. This suggests that the correct relationship between those who prepare material and those who decide on information priorities has still to be achieved.[12] There is also a clash of interest between the Information Policy Department, which is wholly in the business of propaganda, and News Department, which is the intermediary between the FCO and the media in London and has the function of drawing up the Foreign Office line. There is considerable need for interdepartmental coordination between the FCO's Information Policy Department and other agencies of government including the COI and the British Overseas Trade Board. A tripartite committee comprising the FCO, the COI and the BOTB meets quarterly to review informational aspects of Britain's trade position. Within the COI, an Exports Information Group, under the chairmanship of the director-general and comprising the home and overseas controllers and the relevant divisional heads, meets quarterly to review planning and progress on export publicity. There is also some inter-governmental discussion and co-ordination between Britain and the EEC governments and certain Commonwealth countries including Canada.

Fig. 7.1

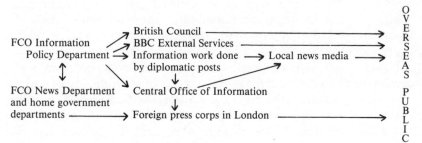

In one sense a network of linkages between the FCO, the official information agencies, and the media affords the FCO considerable control over the process of building up Britain's image abroad. The News Department, and home government departments, explain British policies to the foreign press corps in London. The Information Policy Department determines the flow of information material produced by the COI which diplomatic posts receive for local distribution, and the patterns of external broadcasting. The Cultural Relations Department oversees the work of the British Council. But in another sense the relationship between the FCO and the various agencies is not ideal. The BBC External Services are concerned with objectivity. The British Council stands apart from active governmental intervention. The COI is both without direct ministerial supervision and serving many government departments.

The relationship between the FCO and the BBC External Services is one of particular sophistication. The nature of the relationship, as officially depicted, is that in addition to financing the services through a parliamentary grant-in-aid, the government allots the hours, languages, and areas to broadcast and, as the BBC puts it, beyond this point the BBC is completely independent in determining the content of programmes.[13] Thus, the logic goes, the BBC, in contrast to most other external broadcasting organisations, is editorially independent of governmental control.

The government, however, exercises control over the BBC's output in a number of ways. First, under the License and Agreement, the BBC, according to Section 13.5, is obliged to 'obtain and accept from the Government such information regarding conditions in, and the policies of Her Majesty's Government towards, the countries so prescribed ... enabling the BBC to prepare programmes in the national interest'. But being obliged to include information about policies and life in Britain sometimes leads to editorial decisions not being made on purely newsworthy grounds. Thus, happenings involving Britain, such as a foreign visit by a British minister are included in world news bulletins and current affairs programmes when if the same matter involved another country it would not warrant editorial inclusion. This can be self-defeating because particularly during crises involving Britain, such as the Falklands War, much more attention is given to including information presenting Britain in a more positive light than the other side, and this can result in the committed listener tuning to another station for news at just the time when Britain most requires a wide audience.

Second, there is considerable informal contact at all levels between the FCO and the External Services. This is most clearly seen in the relationship between the heads of the various language services and the corresponding regional desk officers in the Information Policy Department. These may meet once a week or more. The extent of contacts will vary according to the area involved, how controversial it is, and how many crises develop. BBC controllers, heads of language sections, and current affairs producers receive a selection of telegrams from the FCO which it has received from diplomatic posts.[14] Although journalists may ignore the information they get from these contacts, which may or may not be counter-balanced by confidential information from other sources in a similar or different quantity, the exposure of journalists to the flow of information from the FCO leads more or less to an interpretation of diplomatic developments not too distant from FCO thinking. While an appearance of balance is preserved, outside contributors to current affairs programmes who are ideologically at odds with FCO thinking are used less than those more proximate with Whitehall thinking.

A third type of influence of the FCO on the BBC which has usually not occurred would be pressure by the government on the BBC to broadcast or not to broadcast certain information. The absence of any overt pressure is the basis of the BBC's claim to independence from governmental control. There have, however, been instances when the government has attempted to apply pressure. In one instance, during the 1956 Suez War, there was conflict between Bush House and Whitehall when the former broadcast in 'Review of the British Press' and in other programmes details about the domestic opposition in Britain to government plans to invade Suez and subsequently to the invasion itself. Concerned that an image of disunity in Britain was being conveyed to Egyptian President Nasser, Anthony Eden, the Prime Minister, attempted to bring pressure on the BBC. A Foreign Office official sat in Bush House ostensibly to liaise with the BBC, but since he had no editorial function or powers, he could intervene only intermittently. The BBC was told that the parliamentary grant-in-aid would be cut and the External Services reorganised, but neither of these threats was carried out.[15] Suggestions that Eden actually instructed the lord chancellor to draw up powers to take over the BBC[16] have been denied[17] on the ground that the Licensing Agreement already made provisions for this.

A lesser instance of an attempt at governmental pressure occurred during the final months of the reign of the Shah of Iran. The Foreign Office was among various bodies and individuals which told the BBC about the effects on the Shah's opponents in Iran which its Farsi Service was having by broadcasting the statements of the Ayatollah Khomeini who was in exile in France.

'While there have been discussions and differences of opinion as to the advisability or otherwise of transmitting a certain programme item, and there have been occasions when the BBC has, in fact, heeded the government's remonstrances on the subject, but of its own accord', a managing director of the External Services said, there have not been occasions when the government has 'actually instructed the BBC'.[18] When the Soviet Union threatened to call off diplomatic discussions with Britain, designed to cool tension in the Middle East in the weeks before the 1967 Arab–Israeli war, Sir Hugh Greene, the then director-general of the BBC, agreed to postpone for 24 hours the broadcast of Svetlana Stalin's 'Letter to a Friend'. Similarly, when during the regime of Idi Amin of Uganda the BBC planned to interview the author of a book on Amin, it postponed the broadcast in response to a Foreign Office plea that the lives of British nationals in Uganda would be put at risk.[19]

The number of occasions when the government has asked the BBC to broadcast or not broadcast something is said to be small. Rather, the influence has to be seen in macro-terms, i.e. in terms of the government determining the hours, languages, or areas to which to broadcast, and in terms of the confidential guidance telegrams to which BBC journalists are privy. The technique is that of the subtle propagandist: by presenting newsworthy information through channels perceived by their audience as editorially impartial, the government succeeds in getting its message across.

ASSESSING INFORMATION WORK

A key problem in information work, as in many other areas of policy-making, is to evaluate effectiveness. Since much information work is gradual – reinforcing attitudes, imparting factual information, and building new attitudes – it is difficult to prove causality between policy achievement and information programme. Only where the objective of an information programme is precisely defined, such as to sell a particular product, or, in wartime, to encourage surrender among enemy military forces, is it possible to prove causality between a policy's achievement and the information programme. But most information programmes do not have such specific objectives.

There are a number of means of assessing the effects of information work. In certain countries the BBC commissions surveys of their listening audience. In others, such as communist countries, it is not possible to carry out such surveys. Diplomatic posts reply to an annual questionnaire sent by the COI asking them about the usefulness of the material they receive from London for their local needs. In addition, posts send the COI periodic reports about the COI material accepted by the local media for publication. Another form of assessment is a system, begun in the late 1970s, by which diplomatic posts send the FCO News Department details of inaccurate reporting by foreign correspondents in London, which are examined and where appropriate taken up with the particular correspondent.

The weakness with all these types of assessment is that they do not measure the actual impact of an information programme on decision-makers or the wider public. Thus, a BBC survey of listeners can indicate the size of an audience and which programmes listeners like most, but it cannot measure to what extent that public or its government adopts a more favourable attitude to Britain. Even knowledge about what key policymakers read and listen to is unsatisfactory unless it is also known whether policymakers are influenced by it in their decisions regarding Britain. It is the difficulty of measuring success in information work which often results in its being one of the first areas of overseas representation to be axed when public expenditure cuts are made.

CONCLUSION

The media are channels – legitimised by their audience – for the British government to gain foreign public understanding and support for Britain and its policies. Such problems as an increase in state-controlled media have, to some extent, lost significance in Whitehall with, in a world of shrinking public expenditure resources, the increasing centrality of promoting British exports and technological innovation. Britain's information policy is characterised by the lack of a master plan. On the one hand, the generalised image projection by overseas posts and the COI has been slashed. On the other hand, the BBC External Services remains a pillar of support. If a balance is lacking in explaining policy abroad, at home a certain balance has emerged, as will be seen in the next chapter, in the form of a combination of secrecy in foreign policy, FCO promotion of policy, and responding to media inquiries.

CHAPTER EIGHT

MOULDING OPINION AT HOME

'We do not seem to learn very much on these routine occasions and there was not very much to do with that little − protocol denied us the right to say "The Foreign Office view is" and our usual formula was the obscure one "informed sources close to Whitehall". The Foreign Office is one other section of government bureaucracy with the usual reservations and inhibitions, the usual constipated habits of mind, the usual unattractive mixture of smugness and lack of real self-confidence.'
                              − Diplomatic correspondent.[1]

The moulding of opinion abroad, discussed in chapter 7, is characterised by a single objective: the projection of Britain abroad. The FCO's relationship with the British media has two main characteristics: the projection of foreign policy at home, and sometimes satisfying but at other times deflecting pressure from journalists. The latter is illustrated by what an under-secretary described as 'the inbuilt and natural defence mechanism which all civil servants have in relation to the media'.

Secrecy in the FCO is caused by a number of factors. In legislative terms, the 1911 Official Secrets Act forbids an official to disclose official information unauthorisedly. The 1972 Franks Report, while arguing that the 'catch-all' element of the act should be nullified, favoured the continuation of the act for security, defence, and foreign affairs. 'The field of international questions is full of difficult, sensitive and contentious issues. It is a fact of international life that the resolution of such issues without resort to force, and the maintenance of our national position and interests, often depend upon a measure of secrecy.'[2]

The chief legislative means for preventing the publication of sensitive defence and foreign affairs information are the 'D Notices', which delineate categories of information which editors should not publish. Although voluntary and not legally binding, the 'D Notices' generally are adhered to. But secrecy is more than legislative in character.

It reflects an underlying mood in the governance of Britain. 'Part of the culture of the British bureaucracy is being secretive', a journalist commented. Expediency, and a belief that publicity of policy will upset the implementation of the best policy as civil servants define it, and will challenge the principle of ministerial responsibility, the political neutrality of civil servants, and their relations to ministers, are some of the reasons given by bureaucrats to justify secrecy. There are also, however, reasons specifically associated with diplomacy. There is a requirement in international relations for confidentiality in governmental negotiations. Further, any statement made by the FCO has a potential audience of 160 foreign governments, the international financial markets, overseas public opinion, the British Parliament, and British public opinion. All of these may react differently to a particular statement. Logic dictates, therefore, an ultra-discreet approach. There is thus a basic contradiction between a foreign ministry's function as propagandist and that of not upsetting relations with other governments.

Yet a lack of information leads to public speculation and suspicion that secret deals have been made. To overcome this dichotomy a system of unofficial relationships has evolved – as it has in cases of other government departments and other democratic governments – in which information is given to journalists on condition that the source is not revealed. 'The basic defence of non-attributability is that you can say a great deal more than you could if things were "on record", in quotation marks, which are liable to be thrown back at you', the FCO spokesman said.[3] Other reasons include that if an official statement is made it gives the matter that much extra weight and suggests that the FCO is giving it importance – which it may wish to. If, on the other hand, 'sources close to Whitehall' are used it is understood that the government does not want to make a straight statement either because the particular matter is not its direct business, or because the time is not right for it to make an official statement.

Information or comment which is released by the FCO falls under a number of categories.

1. 'On the record' is a statement which a journalist can attribute to the FCO.
2. The bulk of information is 'off the record' or 'non-attributable'; while a journalist cannot attribute it by name to the FCO, he may indicate its source by such phraseology as 'informed sources close to Whitehall' or 'the government thinks'.
3. 'For background only' is information which may be used but cannot be attributed in any way to Whitehall.
4. 'Not for use' is information given to journalists for their background use only. In practice journalists do not recognise the validity of this category and leave the briefing lest they discover the same information later from another source.

The phraseology is well known to the diplomatic community as referring to the FCO. A diplomatic correspondent found 'this evasiveness both pointless and irritating; what could "informed sources" be save the Foreign Office itself? Whom was this formula designed to fool?'[4] As the spokesman indicated, the evasiveness allows the FCO the option of denying later what the FCO is indicated to have said, as well as, more importantly from the media's perspective, giving the media access to a great deal more information than they would get if everything had to be given a source. For the journalists' audience, however, terms like 'sources say' and 'informed sources' raise questions about the credibility of the statements or the vested interests of the sources. The audience is often not alerted to the source's reasons for speaking to the media or for wanting (and being granted) anonymity. It does not even know whether the use of unidentified sources is just a journalistic ruse enabling the reporter to promulgate his personal view.

The nature of the briefing itself is secretive. Instead of the FCO taking the initiative to issue information, most of it comes in response to journalists' questions: 'Anything new from Peking?' or 'Is it true that Country X is developing a nuclear reactor?' A briefing thus becomes a guessing game. That the initiative comes from journalists also means that the flow of information from the FCO is largely determined by subjects in which journalists are interested.

The FCO are nevertheless aware of the opportunities to gain public support for foreign policy through the media. Although public opinion and interest groups in Britain are generally less crucial to the policy-maker than the views of foreign governments, and few general elections have been fought principally on foreign issues, ministers are anxious to avoid arousing hostile reaction from Parliament and from the public. 'It is very important when something happens which receives press criticism to try to respond to it quickly so that it does not become an explosive issue', a permanent under-secretary said. The public element enters into the policymaking process already at the planning stage because many policy reviews in the FCO are attended by an official from the News Department. He is able to inject advice on the likely reactions from the public and the media to different policy options, and on the best way in which to present policy. 'Information policy does not exist separately from policy. You don't get a situation where policy is decided and then turned over, as it were, to the packaging men and told "Okay, here you are, go off and present it" ', an under-secretary for information remarked.

The FCO's ability to influence the media is limited by the number of foreign affairs subjects in which the media are interested. It is difficult to arouse interest in international economic policy. The reduction in

Britain's international role means that foreign policy is less relevant to the media. A skilled PR man, however, can often find a media angle to a 'non-media story'. Yet even the US State Department cannot assume it has a ready audience. On completing a two-week tour of Asia in July 1983, Secretary of State George Shultz bemoaned the lack of press coverage his tour received in the US media, due mainly to the Democratic National Convention being held at the same time. Apart from the serious papers the rest of the media virtually ignored the tour. The Associated Press and United Press International did not assign reporters to the Shultz plane, leaving coverage to reporters in various capitals visited.

No longer, given Britain's reduced role in diplomacy, is the FCO privy to the same type of confidential diplomatic information as at one time. 'For a long time the Foreign Office briefing was useful but in recent years I hardly bothered to go; I sometimes got the impression that I knew a lot more than they did', said a diplomatic correspondent. Its remaining usefulness lies in the interpretation of events. Another correspondent said:

I find it extremely valuable to turn to the Foreign Office people who have read their own independent intelligence, and have enormous experience of a given country, and say 'Well, we all know what is going on, and frankly we don't expect you to tell us more information, but what do you think is going to happen, what does this mean?' – their thoughts and judgements are very valuable.

Information is power. The FCO's influence in the past lay in its very secretiveness. By monopolising much of the information on foreign affairs the FCO was able to manipulate journalists into not being too critical to British foreign policy. Diplomatic correspondents were known as 'trusties', which in prison parlance refers to those prisoners used by warders to do menial jobs and who can be trusted with certain prison keys; a 'trusty' was therefore a journalist whom an official could trust not to disclose his source of information. Certain journalists whose newspapers were supportive of the government, like *The Times* during different periods, had close ties with the FCO while others, notably the *Daily Worker* (predecessor of the *Morning Star*), the organ of the British Communist Party, had none. Today this control remains, but is less firm. The increase in the number of diplomatic correspondents, caused mainly by the increase in broadcasting, and the large number of foreign embassies in London which give journalists an alternative source of information, has made the trusty system less tightly controlled.

The distinctions made by spokesmen in the type of information they disclose to the highly trusted correspondents of the inner circle and those on the fringes are also less than they used to be. 'With certain exceptions and certain nuances, what you can say to one person you can say to everybody. The faster our communications system works and the smaller the world gets the more true this is', the spokesman claimed.[5] In addition, most foreign news is collected abroad rather than in London and concerns international crises and superpower diplomacy rather than British foreign policy. The exposure of a news organisation to FCO thinking is somewhat limited to the diplomatic correspondent because few editors are in regular contact with the FCO or its ministers. On the other hand, in defining British foreign policy interests and goals, ministers and their officials remain major moulders of public and media attitudes on international questions. To the extent that the information given by the FCO to journalists both enhances the government's position and meets the criteria of newsworthiness – which is not always the case given that crisis rather than achievement is a key determinant of 'news' – and to the extent that information which is likely to harm the government or the country is held back, the FCO's influence remains. Disquiet among the media over the diplomatic correspondents' relationship with the FCO, like that about the lobby system, also remains. As editor of *The Guardian*, Alastair Hetherington wanted to withdraw his paper's diplomatic correspondent from the FCO's system of briefings; yet the facility of gaining information, particularly useful during international crises, convinced him not to.[6]

THE SPOKESMAN

The News Department is the authorised point of contact between the media and the FCO. It owes its origin to the need to centralise the media's inquiries about foreign policy in order to ensure that the FCO speaks with a single voice. A former foreign secretary was in favour of reducing its size from ten spokesmen to about four so that the emphases and gloss of the foreign secretary should more clearly reach the media. To be sure, heads of department rather than the foreign secretary are the ones who interpret policy. Each official in the News Department specialises in particular areas and subjects, including the Common Market, Western Europe (apart from the EEC), East–West relations, the Middle East, Africa, Asia, Latin America, economics, energy, and terrorism, and they are each responsible for maintaining close contact with the relevant geographical, functional, and administrative departments of the FCO and for briefing the rest of News Department on these areas and subjects. Before the Second World War the News Department was, like the press office in other government departments, staffed by specialist information officials, but since then career diplomats have been used. The advantage of using these is that they are able to bring to their work as spokesmen a diplomatic background. The disadvantage is that initially the new member of News Department does not understand the needs of journalists or the business of news gathering. Some learn quite quickly about these needs and some never do. In the aftermath of the Soames affair, Harold Wilson favoured appointing an information officer to head the News Department in the hope that he would be more politically sensitive. Thus, Tom McAffrey, a deputy press officer at No 10 Downing Street, was appointed to the FCO. But when the foreign secretary, James Callaghan, became prime minister, he took McAffrey with him to become his spokesman, and the FCO machine succeeded in getting the post of head of News Department returned to a career diplomat.

The head of the News Department, the spokesman of the FCO, is usually a senior diplomat with the rank of counsellor, and at least 15 years of diplomatic experience behind him. In contrast to other departments in the FCO which have to submit their papers to under-secretaries, who in turn, if necessary, submit them to junior ministers, the exigencies of news deadlines necessitate that the spokesman has direct access to the foreign secretary. The need for an easy relationship between a minister and his spokesman is obvious and will influence the flow of information between the FCO and the media. With the exception of Mr Callaghan, who brought in a spokesman from outside the Office, it has been largely a matter of luck whether the two men see eye to eye; Sir Alec Douglas-Home and Michael Stewart left publicity matters in the hands of the News Department, in contrast to George Brown and Dr David Owen whose relationships with their spokesman were described by some officials as 'conflictual'. The relationship between the prime minister and the FCO is also important. Mrs Thatcher's antagonism to the FCO, and her antipathy to Francis Pym, meant that, in the words of one correspondent, 'the FCO were on the defensive, engaging little in moulding opinions'.

The daily work of the News Department begins at about 9 am when officials begin reading the cables which arrived overnight at the Office. At 10.30 the head of the department attends the 'morning prayers' meeting of the under-secretaries, chaired by the permanent under-secretary, where the main problems of the day are discussed. He takes the opportunity to clarify the positions he is to adopt with the media and to offer advice on the matters under discussion. At 11.30 the News Department holds an internal meeting where officials report on their contacts with the rest of the Office and where positions to be taken at the official briefing at 12.30 and at the off-the-record briefings in the afternoon are clarified. The need to ensure that the FCO speaks with a single voice is self-evident. As spokesman, McAffrey introduced a system by which the various spokesmen put down what they said on paper, which was then circulated in the department. Bernard Ingham, the No 10 spokesman, one of whose functions is to coordinate the government information service, proposed in 1983 to centralise government positions, on-the-record announcements, and ministerial speeches by having them fed into a computer at No 10. At weekends a duty spokesman is on duty in the News Department and at nights he may be contacted at home.

The extent to which the News Department is able to inform the media depends on the information they receive. It comes from their contacts with the rest of the Office, and from the flow of cables which the FCO receives from overseas diplomatic posts. Since the Suez crisis — when an information blackout occurred that lasted several days — it has been recognised inside the Office that the News Department can perform its function only if it is kept informed of diplomatic developments from their earliest stage as policy options. Because the various departments in the Office are not formally required to inform the News Department about all decisions taken, the flow of information to the latter is necessarily anarchic. The overseas cables help to fill the vacuum by providing background to the decisions taken by, and instructions sent from, these departments to the diplomatic posts. It is instructive to compare the structure of the FCO with the US State Department, where public affairs officials are formally attached to the regional bureaux and are therefore more involved in the policymaking. During crises, when the FCO sets up an emergency unit comprising relevant departments and which is manned 24 hours a day, an official from the News Department is invariably seconded to it. An important part of the work of the News Department is to predict events and prepare the necessary positions to be taken. The problem arises with events which could not be predicted and when it is essential for the government to declare its view before other agencies, including foreign governments and the media, create an undesirable impression about the event.

THE DECLINE OF THE DIPLOMATIC CORRESPONDENT

The main contact by the media with the FCO has been through the diplomatic correspondent. The majority of national daily newspapers have a journalist designated as the diplomatic correspondent. In addition, the three national Sunday quality newspapers have a diplomatic correspondent, the Press Association has one, Reuters has two, the BBC three, ITN two, and a handful of provincial newspapers have one. Other news organisations leave diplomatic reporting to the political correspondent.

Most diplomatic correspondents have been in their present position for more than ten years, and a couple of them for more than twenty.

A number had previous experience as foreign correspondents. While expertise is clearly an asset in specialist journalism and could conceivably act as a counterweight to the FCO's influence, the danger is that over a period of time the journalist comes to see things from the vantage point of the FCO and fails to question basic assumptions about policy goals and national interest. The correspondents have their own professional association, the Diplomatic and Commonwealth Writers' Association, founded in 1960 for Commonwealth correspondents and extended in 1967 to include diplomatic correspondents. Its chief objective is the improvement of facilities for obtaining information. The DCWA organises monthly luncheons which are addressed by politicians and visiting foreign statesmen.

The official press briefing of the FCO, at 12.30 daily, is limited to announcements of official statements, diplomatic appointments, and the Foreign Secretary's diary. It is attended mostly by the correspondents of the news agencies and evening newspapers because of their early news deadlines. The core of the News Department's work is the off-the-record briefings in the afternoon. For many years the correspondents divided themselves into two main groups, the 'trusties' and the 'circus'. The trusties comprised the correspondents from *The Guardian*, the *Daily Herald*, the BBC Home Service, and the BBC External Service. The circus comprised the popular papers: the *Daily Mirror, Daily Sketch*, and *Daily Express. The Times* and the *Daily Telegraph* had, due to their insistence, their own individual briefings.

On a number of occasions these groups have re-formed as a result of correspondents retiring and their successors not gaining admittance into the group, or of changes in the number of news organisations, or, as one of the trusties put it, because 'we have a stiff old customer and so we had to form our own group abandoning him to a group of his own'.[7] Up to the end of 1985 there were broadly three groups:

1. The correspondents of the national newspapers – *The Times, The Guardian*, the *Daily Telegraph*, the *Financial Times*, the *Daily Mail*, and the *Daily Express*.
2. The news agencies and broadcasters – Reuters, the Press Association, BBC Radio, BBC TV, the BBC External Services, ITN, and Independent Radio News.
3. The provincial papers. In 1986, a single group briefing was introduced for all diplomatic correspondents.

The 12.30 official, on-the-record briefing, which is also attended by the foreign press corps in London, attracts on a day of 'average news' about ten correspondents. All members of News Department attend this briefing. Attendance in the off-the-record group briefings varies from five to six on a 'newsworthy day' to one or two or sometimes no correspondents. Two officials usually attend these briefings. Journalists may make notes throughout. They used to be shown selected cables from diplomatic posts, but since the occasion when a journalist published a cable in its entirety these are now only read out.

No serious diplomatic correspondent can rely solely on News Department for information about British foreign policy. Contact between the correspondents and the rest of the FCO, including ministers, may be divided between briefings arranged by the News Department at the request of a journalist who wishes to write an article on a specific subject, briefings on specific subjects arranged by the department for all the correspondents, and those private contacts which correspondents have made with ministers and officials. The correspondents of popular newspapers and some of them from the broadcasting companies tend to find most of their needs satisfied by the daily briefings of the News Department, while those from the serious newspapers are more keen to develop contacts throughout the Office. 'What you want is not a minister's point of view but a detached, experienced view, a non-political view', said a television correspondent. 'If the paper is having an extremely important article and it is rather necessary to get the top-level opinion on it I try either for the foreign secretary or for a deputy or assistant under-secretary. They have probably seen the Cabinet Papers. He may not feel free to tell you but at least you know that he knows what he is talking about', said the correspondent of a Sunday quality newspaper.

Although it remains formally the point of liaison between the media and the FCO, the News Department had by the 1980s lost the prominent position it held before the mid-1960s. The geographical and functional departments have become more accessible, and the journalist known to a particular official there is able to make his own direct contact, instead of going via the News Department. This process began with the Wilson government in the 1960s when ministers kept their own journalistic contacts instead of leaving publicity in the hands of the News Department. Senior and departmental officials felt a resulting need to build their own contacts with the media. Political correspondents were also briefed by No 10 on foreign policy because of a belief that the FCO failed to explain the Labour government's nuances on foreign policy.

The decline of London as a diplomatic centre means that the FCO is no longer privy to the type of information which journalists want. With the exception of EEC gatherings, editors tend no longer to feel it worthwhile to send diplomatic correspondents to cover international conferences, including the UN General Assembly. The Group 2 diplomatic correspondents, comprising the news agencies and broadcasting companies, did not find it worthwhile to come for a daily off-the-record briefing, as they used to, but instead came weekly. The *Mirror, Sun*, and the *Daily Star* do not have diplomatic correspondents. The *Daily Express* representative attends infrequently. Thus, the FCO's conventional channel to the majority of newspaper readers is non-existent. The usefulness of the News Department has changed. 'Their operation has much diminished in quality and authority and is almost of no value. I get most of my information from talking to visitors to London and from my general experience of foreign affairs', a correspondent said. This has made the work of the diplomatic correspondent somewhat redundant. 'My job declined not simply because of Britain's reduced role but because the Foreign Office didn't take independent positions on many international issues', a former correspondent said. 'My impression is that the diplomatic correspondent has been downgraded', remarked a permanent under-secretary. Diplomatic correspondents lost their legitimacy because some of them came to be regarded by their editors as being in the pocket of the FCO. For the FCO there is a need to find alternative channels to reach the public.

A number of patterns have developed in diplomatic journalism as a response to these changes. In some organisations, including *The Times*, the *Financial Times*, and BBC domestic and external radio, the diplomatic correspondent continues to concentrate wholly on British diplomacy, leaving general foreign news to foreign correspondents and to London-based specialist correspondents who cover such regions as Africa, Eastern Europe, the Middle East, the Far East, and Latin America. Given his background in international affairs the diplomatic correspondent might be said to be suffering from a similar complaint to one levelled at the British diplomat: overqualification for the job. In other organisations, including the *Daily Telegraph*, which has three correspondents, BBC TV, ITN, and IRN, the diplomatic correspondent's brief has been redefined to embrace the entire spectrum of international news.

There remains a continuing need for a News Department to keep doors open for the non-frequent journalist visiting the FCO, to make official announcements, and to reduce remaining suspicions which may exist among some officials about the media. Some suggestions for restructuring the department are offered in the concluding chapter. At a time when the value of Britain's diplomats is being questioned, the FCO is looking for ways to promote not only policy but also itself as an institution. Unlike the US State Department, whose spokesman is well known on American television, the FCO spokesman is an unknown figure. The State Department gave permission to television correspondents to film the official briefing during the Iranian hostage crisis in order to counter the demoralising footage from Iran; the cameras have remained.

In one sense, the presence of television cameras has had a trivialising effect on briefings, with television correspondents looking for a juicy fifteen-second quote by the spokesman, but there would be little danger of this in the event of the FCO permitting cameras since they would be limited to the official 12.30 briefing, which is attended by the foreign, as well as the British, press.

Contact between diplomatic correspondents and ministers is much less than that with officials. A former correspondent of *The Times* said that he saw the foreign secretary 'very seldom' and junior ministers 'perhaps once in three months'. Ministers tend to see correspondents before or after a foreign trip. Apart from the group briefings, individual contacts varied with the personality of the minister, with some giving more importance to maintaining their own press relations than others. 'I have not been one who has sought publicity or estimated its value. It is one of the things which can be useful to a foreign secretary and sometimes which isn't', said a foreign secretary. Another minister said: 'I made it a practice not to seek out journalists but I have made it known that I am available. The fact that I don't worry the media means that I do as well as those who publicise themselves.'

One factor influencing the degree of contact between ministers and correspondents is that requests for meetings, group or individual, are vetted by officials, who are likely to be better disposed to supportive correspondents as well as to supportive ministers. Since the 1970s, ministers have been more accessible for interviews with television and radio, as a result of a growing awareness among both ministers and officials of the need to react quickly during events. For example, as minister of state at the FCO, Douglas Hurd, who performs well on the air, was regularly used to explain policy. The journalists whom ministers see most of are the political correspondents at Westminster rather than the diplomatic correspondents. This was regretted by one minister because 'the lobby man is not so well informed on foreign affairs as the specialist correspondent'.

In addition to the briefings, diplomatic correspondents and others with an interest in foreign policy are able to receive various non-attributable printed material prepared in the FCO. 'White Briefs', dealing with topical matters of international interest, and 'Background Briefs', covering issues of longer-term interest, were introduced by Dr David Owen in 1978 in order to widen public discussion of foreign policy. These replace material which had been produced by the defunct Information Research Department. Founded in 1947 to prepare publicity material, much with an anti-communist stance and mostly for overseas consumption, IRD's material was received by many leading foreign affairs journalists in Britain.

Few if any diplomatic correspondents look to Parliament as a source of news. 'In my business of quick diplomatic reaction to, say, a coup in Algeria there is little point in ringing up an MP', a correspondent commented. While there are few House of Commons debates on foreign policy, it is discussed, and formulated, among the foreign affairs committees of the political parties, and is reviewed by the Commons' Select Committee on Foreign Affairs. These are considered the territory of the political and parliamentary correspondents respectively. But, given that they usually possess neither expertise in international affairs nor, with the wide area of Westminster politics they have to cover, the time to devote to these parliamentary dimensions of foreign policy, it is regrettable that the diplomatic correspondent limits himself to covering foreign policy from the FCO. In Washington, by contrast, major news organisations assign a journalist with a suitable background to covering congressional business relating to external affairs.

Another, smaller, channel through which support for British foreign policy is gained in the British media is the contacts abroad between Britain's diplomatic posts and foreign correspondents. In some foreign capitals with a sizeable corps of British foreign correspondents, including Washington, Paris, and Bonn, the ambassador holds regular briefings for the correspondents. Journalists contrast the openness of British diplomats abroad with a tendency towards being inhibited once they return to London. But given that the correspondents write mostly about the countries to which they are assigned, rather than about Britain's bilateral relations, they do not look to the British post as their primary source of information. At the headquarters of the EEC in Brussels, and the UNO in New York, however, the British delegation is an important source. In Brussels in particular, British officials are keenly aware that the British correspondents are key determinants of the image of the EEC, and of British policy, and that correspondents are in close touch with other government delegations.[8] In countries like the Soviet Union where political conditions make it difficult for the foreign correspondent to gather news among the local population, contacts are frequent. The relationship, it should be noted, is often two-way, with the diplomat looking to the foreign correspondent for information. 'Some of the British correspondents here have an exceptional status because they have been here so long and because their contacts are so good. By meeting everybody of note in Washington they contribute to our information gathering', a counsellor at the British Embassy in Washington noted.

FOREIGN DIPLOMATIC MISSIONS IN LONDON

The relationship of foreign diplomatic missions and the British media – including the individual contacts between foreign diplomats and journalists, the flow of printed and visual material to news organisations, and political advertising – is a subject deserving its own study. Here it is worth examining the relationship to see whether it serves as a counter-weight to the influence of the FCO on diplomatic correspondents. Sampson, for example, has argued that

the most effective centralisation of news has been achieved in a quarter where I believe it is least desirable, the Foreign Office. The News Department of the Foreign Office provides daily or weekly briefings, and controls the doors to the Foreign Secretary's office, so that no diplomatic correspondents dare consistently offend the official channels.[9]

With over 140 foreign embassies, together with the offices of assorted regional and international organisations and liberation groups, it may be suggested that the challenge facing the journalist has less to do with a shortage of diplomatic contacts and more with maintaining contact with the important embassies. All correspondents maintain varying degrees of contact with the embassies of newsworthy countries including the United States, West European countries, India and Pakistan, Israel and different Arab states, and certain Black African countries and South Africa. 'What I always try to do is to make sure I know one man in each embassy. I can then ring him up if there is a crisis for a rundown on the situation', said one diplomatic correspondent.

Although the press attaché may be the formal point of contact at an embassy for a journalist, contacts in practice are at all levels of the embassy staff. An embassy's attitude to the media depends heavily upon whether there is a high-profile ambassador or whether he or she is un-interested in, or inhibited from, speaking to journalists. Some embassies, including many from the developing world, do not possess the budget or personnel to maintain regular contact with the media. Contact with the communist embassies is small. The United States embassy is popular among journalists because it is the only one to provide them with a regular service of supplying texts of key speeches and statements within 24 hours of their delivery. Many missions underestimate the intelligence of professional journalists by sending them propaganda-laden material, or information which is already available.

The foreign diplomatic mission does not usually possess exclusive information which is considered newsworthy. It is a good source of information about bilateral relations with the host country, Britain, but bilateral relations are rarely newsworthy. It is also a source of information and interpretation about internal developments inside the mission's own country which, depending on the country, may well possess newsworthiness. Thus, to the extent that a diplomatic correspondent keeps in regular contact with the FCO but not with a foreign diplomatic mission, the FCO is in a good position to influence the correspondent. To the extent that the FCO is a source of interpretation of events, the relevant foreign mission may provide a counter-view. To the extent that the FCO offers correspondents information which is not obtainable from foreign missions, less and less true today, the FCO is in a position to exert influence. Yet to the extent that the total flow of news which an audience gains – which is what ultimately matters – is not made up mostly of diplomatic correspondents' reports but of foreign correspondents' reports, themselves conveying the positions of, or based on sources in, foreign governments, the influence of the FCO is limited.

CONCLUSION

A key channel for the FCO to mould public attitudes about foreign policy lies in the system of briefings, off and on the record, given by the News Department to the diplomatic correspondents. The relationship is characterised by three elements: secrecy, propaganda and response to journalists' inquiries. Whereas the relationship has throughout the last 80 years possessed each of these elements, there has been a shift in emphasis from the element of secrecy, and more recently from the propaganda element, towards that of responding to media inquiries – thereby beginning to create a genuine sense of trust between the FCO and the media.

CASE STUDIES

CHAPTER NINE

REPORTING A HIJACKING

'Just as, with prickly independence, broadcasters and reporters
revolt against the smooth manipulation of image-conscious
politicians, so there is another land of manipulation to guard
against: the possibility – the mere possibility – that they are
by design players in a bloody piece of theatre written and directed
by someone the cameras will never see.'

    – Editorial in *The Guardian* on the TWA hijacking[1]

The hijacking of a TWA airliner to Beirut in June 1985 by an Islamic
Shiite group illustrates certain aspects of gathering foreign news
including journalists' access to the area, the availability and reliability
of news sources, and transmission of news reports to head offices. In
spite of Britain's lack of involvement, causing the media coverage not
to have any policy influence, criticism was voiced that by providing
publicity for those involved the media became a participant in the
hijacking. It raises fundamental questions about the roles which
journalists should play during terrorist incidents, where publicity is often
a key objective of terrorists.

GATHERING THE NEWS

Whereas Beirut's good communications and free media made it the
Middle Eastern capital most favoured by foreign journalists for covering
the region, the poor security situation during the Lebanon civil war
resulted in many foreign news organisations transferring their bureaux
to Cyprus, Israel or Egypt, with reporters flying in to Beirut for reporting
spells. In June 1980 Bernard Debusmann, Reuters bureau chief in Beirut,
was shot by gunmen after reporting political unrest in Syria. Several
weeks later, after receiving threats, following his disclosure of an
assassination attempt on President Hafez el-Assad at Damascus Airport,
Tim Llewellyn, BBC Radio's Middle East correspondent, together with
Jim Muir, a freelance journalist working for the BBC, moved from
Beirut to Nicosia. 'Journalists who have spent their working lives with
violence and the threat of death are abandoning Beirut, admitting that

it is no longer possible to live there. They have been told quite simply, but effectively, that if they stay they will be killed,' Keith Graves, BBC TV's Middle East correspondent noted.[2] By early 1985, following the kidnapping of Terry Anderson, the Associated Press bureau chief, most American, and many other western, journalists had left the city. One of the few British journalists not to leave was Robert Fisk of *The Times*, himself the target of an abortive kidnap attempt in October 1984.

There had been fierce battles in West Beirut between Shiite Muslims and Palestinian Arabs several weeks before the airliner hijacking, when reporting conditions for the foreign press proved particularly difficult. Normally in fierce competition with each other, journalists shared their sources and released stories simultaneously so that they would not find themselves isolated and the target of threats. Graves, Gerald Butt, BBC Radio's Middle East correspondent, and Muir, also filing for the *Sunday Times*, were among the first journalists to report the extent of the battles, detailing how Shiites pulled wounded Palestinian Arabs from hospital beds and shot them. Nabih Berri, leader of Amal, one of the main Shiite factions in Lebanon, complained to the British ambassador about the *Sunday Times* report, which had been included in the BBC Arabic Service's review of the British press. Graves and his film crew were held up and their car fired at by Shiites at the entrance of one of the Palestinian Arab camps. 'The local Arab press has been basically frightened to report what's been going on or to report all the details, and the international media has also faced the same problem to survive and be pragmatic on the ground,' Muir said.[3] 'We got various warnings and we decided that the risk outweighed the story. We baled out on the first plane, and let it cool for about a week before returning,' said a BBC man.

Within days of the TWA hijacking most major British news organisations had a staff reporter in Beirut. The international repercussions – Would it become a repetition of the seizure by Iranian students of the US embassy in Teheran? Would the Americans, or even the Israelis, intervene with a rescue mission? – made this hijacking a particularly newsworthy one. It was surprising that none of the popular newspapers, with the exception of the *Daily Mail* and its Sunday counterpart, thought it appropriate to send their own reporters, relying instead on the news agencies and, in certain cases, on local stringers. It confirms a trend among the popular press towards less coverage of international news, concentrating instead on home features.

Broadcasting is particularly suited to reporting terrorism given its fast-changing developments. It was initially unclear whether the plane, hijacked on Thursday night, would fly to Beirut or Algiers. It flew to Algeria but the authorities refused to allow the plane to stay on Algerian soil, and it flew to Beirut. Graves and Butt flew to Beirut from Nicosia on Monday. They were later joined during the seventeen-day crisis by Muir, and a reporter and five support staff from London. The support staff comprised a facilities engineer for servicing equipment and for monitoring local transmissions, an electronic gathering pictures editor, a field producer, a cameraman and a sound recordist. More than half of the BBC's output on the situation in Beirut came from NBC, with which the BBC has a sharing arrangement, and which had five TV crews in Beirut. The BBC also had access to video footage from ABC (Australia), CBC (Canada) and Visnews, of which the BBC is part-owner. On the ground these bureaux cooperated by leaving a TV crew on stand-by at Beirut airport throughout the crisis. London-based reporters with two-man crews were also sent to Algiers, Athens, and Jerusalem. ITN had a correspondent in Beirut, one in Tel Aviv and one in Algiers, and Channel 4 News had one in Beirut. Much of the ITN's output came from ABC with which it has a sharing arrangement. While the American networks carried special programmes and additional news bulletins about the American plane hijacking, apart from some extended news programmes and news flashes at such key moments as the release of the hostages, the BBC and ITN covered the crisis in their regular news and current affairs programmes.

In the absence of satellite facilities in Lebanon – the ground station at Abadier had been destroyed and the road to it mined – the BBC and ITN sent their video reports overland to the ground station in Syria, some three hours away. To make sure reports reached their destination, an additional copy was flown to the ground station outside Nicosia, Cyprus. Newspaper reporters staying at the Commodore Hotel had to book their calls to their head offices, sometimes having to wait three hours. Had it not been for the time difference between American and European newspaper deadlines the pressure would have been even greater. The BBC office in Beirut kept a telephone line open throughout the crisis.

In terms of finance, the BBC and ITN's budget was miniscule when compared to those of the three major American networks, ABC, CBS and NBC. The BBC's estimate of £35,000, of which £18,000 was accounted for by satellite costs, may be compared with the estimates of £2m to £8m for each of the three American networks. These had dozens of reporters. ABC, for example, had thirty reporters and producers in addition to assistants, translators and drivers. And whereas the three networks had between them six chartered aircraft plying between Beirut and Cyprus, the BBC hired a plane only once during the crisis.

Journalists in Beirut had over the years built up contacts with Berri,

Ali Hamdan, his spokesman, and Akef Haider, the head of Amal's political office. Fewer had contacts in Hezbellah, which hid some of the hostages, and none were thought to have contacts in Islamic Jihad, which carried out the hijacking. Berri's image during the crisis was complicated by his presenting himself as a mediator between the United States and 'the hijackers' and by the fact that members of Amal had replaced Islamic Jihad in guarding the plane at Beirut airport, and hidden most of the hostages at different locations in West Beirut. A success in getting the hijackers' demands met, the most notable of which was the release of Shiite detainees in Israel, would enhance his reputation within Amal and among the Shiite movement. And the release of the hostages would raise his prestige — badly needed after the battles for capture of the Palestinian Arab camps in West Beirut — at home and abroad as an actor on the Lebanese political arena.

In wooing, and in being wooed by, journalists Amal displayed some understanding of the workings of the western media. The human story was played up through a news conference in which those hostages likely to come over most favourably took part. Interviews with hostages, edited by Amal, were made available. Much of the chat was routine banality, messages to family and friends. But the underlying appeal, either direct or implied, was 'Get us home'. Several hundred Shiites demonstrated at Beirut airport. With outbursts from Kalashnikovs — women clad in black gowns and veils — and chants of 'Death to America!' it produced ideal terrorist theatre for the TV cameras. On the last night of the crisis a 'farewell party' was held for the hostages overlooking the swimming pool at the Summerland Hotel. Berri was available most days to the American TV networks for interviews. The BBC also had access to him. ABC achieved a number of scoops including being present at the farewell party, and interviewing the pilot from the cockpit of the hijacked plane. Through its sharing arrangement for video footage with ABC, ITN was at an advantage over the BBC which shared with NBC.

In another sense Amal's public relations was inept. In the absence of regular daily briefings by the Amal spokesman, journalists camped outside Berri's home and office waiting for news. 'Their PR office is a bit of a joke. It entails going round to Berri's home and being told to clear off, and then being telephoned to come back', one British reporter commented. Little regard for accuracy in Amal's statements was evidenced by frequent contradictions in details about numbers and the whereabouts of hostages. The news conference with the hostages was a chaotic affair. 'What started as a "tea party", to use the words of an Amal official, ended prematurely with pictures captured by television camera crews that were far from those intended by Amal officials with so shrewd an eye for publicity', Robert Fisk of *The Times* wrote. 'In a scramble of hundreds of photographers, journalists and cameramen Amal officials brought the press conference to an unscheduled end as gunmen, enraged by the noise and confusion, assaulted journalists at one end of the room.'[4]

Other sources of information included the airport where journalists could enter the control tower and speak over the intercom to the crew on the plane. However, when compared with the diplomatic negotiations to secure the release of the hostages, the airport proved somewhat of a sideshow. Foreign diplomats, including the ambassadors of Britain, France and Switzerland, who were involved in the negotiations, were useful secondary sources. With all statements being made in Washington DC, the US embassy was not a major source. Nor were the Lebanese Ministry of Interior or the police, neither of which were involved parties. Local radio stations, such newspapers as the English language *Daily Star* and the French language *L'Orient–Le Jour*, and the *Middle East Reporter*, a daily translation of the Arabic press, were additional sources to journalists.

TERRORISTS, PUBLICITY AND INFORMATION

The news media play a number of integral roles in Terrorism. First, the media have informational functions. When terrorists are planning their operations, the media is a source of information about targets. And during certain types of operations, such as sieges and hijackings, the media may provide the terrorists with valuable intelligence about the authorities' counter-terrorist plans. Second, in addition to such specific aims as the release of their comrades in gaol, many groups which engage in terrorist operations aim to gain media publicity for their cause which, given their numerical inferiority, they would not normally receive.

The media were a source of information to the plane's hijackers and those holding the hostages, to the hostages, and to Amal. Lebanese and other Middle Eastern television stations have access to foreign reporting through the Eurovision News Exchange, in addition to the reportage produced by their own staffs. Local radio stations, as well as foreign radio stations, including the BBC World and Arabic Services, were followed. So were Lebanese and foreign newspapers. The Pentagon criticised ABC and NBC for reporting within hours of the hijacking that US military units, including the Delta force anti-terrorist unit, had been deployed, NBC adding that they were heading for the Mediterranean. 'It may have been one of the reasons for the erratic movement of the TWA hijackers between Beirut and Algiers', the spokesman argued.

During the hijacking of a Lufthansa plane at Mogadishu in October 1977, an Israeli radio monitor picked up details of an anti-terrorist unit sent by the West German government to Somalia. After its broadcast in Israel the Bonn government asked the international media to keep silent. *The Times* and the *Daily Telegraph* ignored the plea, arguing that something would have happened by the time they appeared, and that the hijackers were unlikely to see the British press. This second argument ignores the possibility that the information could reach the hijackers via the BBC External Services' review of the British press. The BBC itself decided not to include in its domestic or external services' press reviews any reference to the reports.

In domestic terrorism the terrorist aims to disorientate the local population and to create the impression that the government is unable to provide such basic requirements as law and order. The theory is that ultimately the citizen, faced by repressive police measures such as detention of innocents, will turn to alternative leaders like the terrorists, in the hope of an end to the violence and of a return to political, social and economic stability. In international terrorism, by carrying out terrorist acts abroad, a foreign terrorist group aims to arouse international public and governmental pressure for a solution to its grievances. Moreover, the media's predilection for presenting violent and conflictual news means that a group using violence has a greater chance of making the news threshold than a group not using violence. The wide media coverage of terrorism was confirmed by a study of *The Times*. This found that a sample of 158 incidents of international terrorism, which occurred between 1968 and 1974, produced 281 articles and 95 photographs. These amounted to 13,846 square inches or approximately thirty full newspaper pages. One hundred-and-thirty-four of the articles appeared on the first page, including 35 which made the first story.[5]

A terrorist needs to gain attention. J. Bowyer Bell suggests that the 'terrorist script' requires three conditions to be fulfilled. First, it should be staged in a place with adequate facilities for the media to report it. Second, the drama must offer the reality or prospect of violence: at any stage in the ritualised cycle of seizure–demand–negotiation–denouement there may be violence, and as negotiations continue the prospects of violence are raised. While the use of violence is in the terrorists' hands, the security forces also have a role to play – as a chorus, if there is a concession, or as gunmen (actors) if there is a confrontation. Third, a terrorist spectacular requires movement – such as when a seized airliner with hostages flies from one destination to another in search of sanctuary.[6] The type of terrorist operation will also determine media exposure. *The Times*' study found that 68 incidents, or 43%, in the sample failed to make the news threshold. While bombing was the most used type, accounting for 41% (the others were aerial hijacking 26%, kidnapping 14%, murder 8%, armed attack 4%, vandalism 2%, and robbery 1%) only 41% of all bombings made the news threshold in contrast to 77% of kidnappings, 71% of hijackings, 71% of armed attacks, and 62% or murders. There was also a regional bias: Palestinian Arab terrorism, European terrorism, and South American terrorism were the most newsworthy – with the first category receiving seven times greater exposure than the second, and the second eleven times the exposure of the third.[7]

To a considerable degree the TWA hijacking satisfied these criteria. The terrorist act was an aerial hijacking. The prospect of violence was confirmed by the murder of one of the hostages, Robert Stethem, a US marine. There was 'movement' in the form of the two flights by the hijacked plane to Algiers at the outset of the crisis. Confusion and uncertainty were achieved by the poor security situation in Lebanon and the absence of formal government, and by the contradictory roles played by Amal as both hijacker and mediator. Although there was not a large press corps in Beirut at the beginning, it was not long before journalists en masse arrived there. However, in the absence of an operational ground satellite station, there was no live coverage. In addition to these criteria, the involvement of an American plane ensured wide public interest in the United States and in the West in general.

The relationship between terrorism and the news media has raised the question of limiting media coverage. There is a contradiction between the principles of the freedom of the press and of not assisting terrorists. Taken to its logical conclusion the freedom of the press means that the media should publish even that information which could help terrorists or endanger innocent lives. Some journalists argue that once limits are placed on news reporting the authorities can use censorship for other reasons. Most British editors probably oppose transmitting information which could directly endanger lives. 'You have to assume that the kidnappers, hijackers or whatever are watching TV or listening to the radio. You can stop newspapers going in to them but you can't stop the broadcasting,' David Nicholas, editor of ITN, said.[8] In 1976 guidelines for news blackouts in kidnappings were worked out between the police and editors. During the siege of the Iranian embassy in London in April 1980 the police briefed the media, giving reasons for not reporting certain locations near the embassy and certain police movements. When the Special Air Service charged the embassy neither the BBC nor ITN, which had broadcast units outside the embassy throughout the siege, broadcast the rescue live.[9] In 1982 a reference to terrorism was included in the guidelines of the 'D' Notice system, the arrangement between government officials and editors under which certain types of information detrimental to national security are not published.[10] Discussions between the Home Office and British news organisations were held in the first part of 1985 in an attempt to agree on the procedures for covering hijackings and sieges. In addition to police requests not to show police marksmen in position or to describe neighbouring buildings, the two sides discussed the kind of facilities which the authorities would make available to news organisations, and whether the media should speculate about negotiating tactics used by the authorities.

Other measures which should be discussed include the question of direct telephone calls between journalists and hostage-takers, in which the former may unwittingly add to the latters' information, and whether the media should use certain newsgathering technology such as high-intensivity TV lighting and obtrusive camera equipment, which can hinder police operations. Electronic news gathering techniques providing for live coverage reduce the power of the editor to control output. However, this problem has been partially overcome, since recent developments in video editing include a mechanism for such a control.

More controversial are police requests to the media to broadcast information knowing it to be false. In 1984 one ITV company transmitted a coded message to a hostage-taker to reassure him that his grievances were being investigated when, in fact, they were not. In the Iranian embassy siege, the BBC, on being asked, together with other news organisations, to report certain information which the police hoped would have a desired psychological impact on the terrorists, initially refused because this was tantamount to broadcasting directed messages. But eventually the BBC did broadcast them because the messages were newsworthy in themselves.[11]

In considering the second aspect of the media–terrorist connection, namely the use of the media by terrorists to gain publicity, three attitudes have emerged: first, that the media should ban publicising terrorist spectaculars and interviews with terrorists; second, that such a ban clashes with the principles of the freedom of the press and the public's right to know; third, that the media merely reflects the problem, and that a solution to terrorism lies in addressing the underlying social and economic grievances of the specific group. As will be seen, none of these attitudes offers a satisfactory answer to the question under discussion – made more difficult by the paucity of empirical data regarding the media as a factor in the decision-making process of terrorist groups.

According to the first approach, the large number of reporters at a siege or hijacking reinforces the terrorists' sense of power and may contribute to prolonging a terrorist incident. Intensive coverage contributes to heavy public pressure on a government to cede to the demands of terrorists in order to save the victims. It also has a contagion effect encouraging other groups to use terrorist techniques to gain publicity.[12]

In the aftermath of the TWA hijacking, Mrs Thatcher called for terrorists to be denied the 'oxygen of publicity', arguing for a voluntary code by which nothing would be said or shown on television which could assist either the morale or the cause of terrorists.

The BBC, in its coverage of Northern Ireland, has, according to one study, failed to provide adequate explanation of the economic and social causes of the troubles with coverage consisting of not much more than bomb and body counts.[13] The same is true of domestic media coverage of internal terrorism elsewhere. The demand to deny publicity to terrorists is, therefore, more relevant to foreign terrorism, where in general there is less public outrage at, and less public identity with the victims of, terrorism. Denying publicity to terrorists could be achieved in a number of ways including using a pool of reporters instead of the entire press corps, and not identifying a terrorist group with its name but referring to it as 'a terrorist group'.

Even if there is some preparedness among the journalist community regarding censoring information which may endanger lives, there is no sympathy for not publicising terrorist incidents and little sympathy for not interviewing terrorists. These conflict with the principles of the freedom of the press and the public's right to know. 'Journalists and the public are curious about such events. It would neither be possible nor desirable for events of such magnitude to be concealed from public knowledge,' an Independent Broadcasting Authority official argued.[14] Among the public there is in fact some sympathy for limiting publicity. A BBC audience research survey following the broadcasting in 1979 of an interview with a member of the Irish National Liberation Army (INLA) found that four-fifths of those asked thought it right to broadcast the item.[15] However, in August 1985, following government pressure on the BBC not to broadcast an interview with Martin McGuinness – an elected member of the Northern Ireland Assembly and, at the time when the interview was recorded, the IRA chief of staff – a poll found that 54% oppose interviews with the IRA and Palestine Liberation Organisation and 40% favour them. Fifty-five per cent favour such interviews when the BBC believes them to be in the public interest.[16] A US opinion poll found that half of those questioned thought that news coverage of terrorism was necessary.[17]

Yet if there is to be ban on terrorist publicity, it is logical to ban publicity not only for terrorist groups, but for all those entities which manipulate the media by using violence including governments which use state terrorism.

Media coverage sometimes plays a positive role. In the TWA hijacking the sight of the hostages on TV and assurances about their physical and mental state provided comfort for their families. The media were an important source of information for US policymakers dealing with the crisis. Further, the intensive media exposure gave Berri a degree of authority which he used to stabilise the situation, and it may have tempted President Assad to give the world a show of his statesmanship which proved decisive for the release of the hostages. Notwithstanding certain advantages of media coverage, these are, it may be argued, outweighed by the fact that publicity is a major stimulant of groups engaged in terrorism.

According to the second attitude – which is held by most journalists – the vast majority of media coverage of terrorism presents the perpetrators in a negative light which, together with public outrage, robs them of any benefit from the publicity. The hijacking of the Italian liner *Achille Lauro* in October 1985 by a PLO faction, the Palestine Liberation Front, is a good example. The terrorists were supposed to travel on the ship to the Israeli port of Ashdod where upon embarking they were to launch a terrorist attack. But after the terrorists got frightened they took the Italian ship hostage instead. This, together with the murder of a crippled American passenger and the subsequent interception by the US Air Force of the Egyptian plane carrying the terrorists to freedom, worsened the PLO's international image.

A two-year study of coverage by the three major American TV networks of the IRA, the Puerto Rican Armed Forces of National Liberation (FALN), and the Italian Red Brigade found that underlying social grievances were not mentioned in 94 per cent of reports and that goals went unmentioned in 90 per cent.[18] The BBC survey found that the interview with the INLA member had increased hostility towards the INLA and IRA and made respondents more sympathetic towards the security forces.[19] However, since the aim of a terrorist group is to attract publicity which in the long term may result in the group's objectives being given public, or even governmental, attention, even negative publicity is considered an achievement.

Nevertheless, by limiting excessive coverage of terrorist spectaculars it is possible to reduce the extent of such achievement. Limiting excessive coverage can be reconciled with the principles of the freedom of the press and the public's right to know because imbalanced media images caused through excessive coverage do not satisfy any societal goal.

A number of institutional controls limit broadcasting's portrayal of violence. In both the BBC and IBA the inclusion of violent scenes, and interviews with terrorists and hostages, is only valid when these add to the public's understanding of an event. In the BBC there is a system of referral to the senior management for live coverage of a terrorist siege or hijacking and for interviews with terrorists in Britain. For interviews with foreign terrorists referral is only to the level of editor. There is a similar system of referral in the IBA. The BBC guidelines also draw a distinction between those groups which do have a following and those which do not. Another means of limiting excessive coverage is to balance reports of terrorist statements with contrasting information from official sources.

According to the third attitude, there is no point in banning media coverage of terrorism because media coverage is considered to merely reflect underlying grievances. If one solves the grievances one solves the terrorist problem. In this view, if the media is involved at all, it is by its lack of coverage of the grievances in the first place, forcing people to resort to violence. Shiite complaints, that their community's share of political power under the existing Lebanese constitution fails to reflect the increase in its share of the country's population, were little heard of abroad until the TWA hijacking. And the nature of the competitive media, with editors believing that stories about political, social and economic grievances are not newsworthy, as well as a tendency for proprietors of many news organisations to identify with those in power, makes it unrealistic to expect that editors will widen their definition of news to give a significant amount of coverage to grievances.

The weakness with the equation that terrorism equals grievances is that by adept manipulation of the media through terrorism an individual or group is able to gain much publicity even though it may lack a following and valid grievances. The volume of news coverage of a terrorist incident reflects the extent to which the incident meets editorial criteria of newsworthiness, and not the extent to which a group's goals are legitimate.

CONCLUSION

British media coverage of the TWA hijacking illustrates how news organisations are able to rapidly arrange for intensive coverage of an international crisis, and shows the difficulties and dangers which journalists may face in gathering and transmitting the news.

But coverage was most noteworthy for its lack of perspective, and for journalists being manipulated by Amal. It showed the disparity between reality and the image of it constructed by the media. In contrast to other types of international news, in the case of terrorist spectaculars editors are aware of the disparity but feel unable to take self-corrective editorial action.

Even if a terrorist group achieves considerable publicity, and gains public support, whether its goals are satisfied at the governmental level is a separate consideration. As was argued in Chapter 5, the effects of the news media and public opinion upon governmental policy generally need to compete with numerous other international and domestic factors before a change in the substance of policy is achieved. Even if publicity-orientated terrorism were to decline, groups are still likely to resort to terrorism in order to bring pressure upon governments.

CHAPTER TEN

LEBANON: IMAGES AND INTEREST GROUPS

'Press convoys would frantically dash north from the Israeli
border shooting past incidents as they went arriving at noon in
Beirut. A correspondent would rush to deliver a piece to camera.
After being sent by fast car to Tel Aviv the cassettes would be
'birded' by satellite to the USA and London.'
                                                    – BBC TV reporter[1]

Foreign correspondents were able to cover the 1982 Lebanon war from
both sides of the conflict. As a case study of media diplomacy, the
intensive coverage contrasted with many other wars where access for
journalists to the battle zone was limited. The Lebanon case also
illustrates the interplay between pro-Israeli and pro-Arab interest groups
and news organisations. However, in contrast, for example, to the
Falklands war, the British government was not directly involved in 1982
in the conflict and, therefore, any media influence on government policy
would have had no impact on the conduct of the war itself.

The British media's performance in the Lebanon War needs to be
seen against the background of media coverage and editorial comment
on the Arab–Israeli conflict. While much of the British media supported
Israel during the 1967 war, admiring how Israel had defeated the combined threat from three of its four neighbours, the media had by the
1973 war become critical of the Israeli control of the West Bank. The
1973–74 Arab oil boycott produced a further shift in attitudes towards
the Arab side, as did the election of Menachem Begin as Israeli prime
minister, so that by the 1980s most editorial writers recognised the
Palestinian issue as a central element of any Arab–Israeli peace. This
was despite wide condemnation of terrorist attacks, including those at
Lod Airport and the Olympic Games in 1972. During the Falklands War,
which immediately preceded the Lebanon War, reports in the media,
based on British government leaks, that Israel had supplied Argentina
with Exocet missiles damaged Israel's image.

IMAGE OF THE WAR

Israel's image in the British media in this war was more negative than it had been since the fighting in Palestine in 1947–48 when the Jewish state was established. In terms of press editorial comment, the attempted murder of Israel's ambassador in Britain, Shlomo Argov, which precipitated Israel's Operation Peace for Galilee, produced wide condemnation. But when the full extent of the military operation became clear, with the original 40-kilometre objective being superseded and with Israeli forces on the outskirts of Beirut by the fifth day, the operation was questioned and criticised among editorial writers. The *Daily Express* said: 'Israel has gone too far. It might destroy Lebanon, but it will not destroy the Palestinians. It will do itself no long-term good at all among the friends upon whom it relies, by setting itself up as the thug of the Middle East.'[2]

After the ceasefire was agreed at the end of the first week of fighting, the general media criticism of Israel cooled. *The Guardian* criticised the PLO for antagonising most Arab states and noted that 'the PLO is fighting dirty by putting their gun positions next to civilian buildings'.[3] However, inflated claims of casualty figures made by the Palestine Red Crescent, and Israel's siege of Beirut, produced further press criticism. The pro-Israeli *Yorkshire Post* said Begin's actions were producing 'evidence of excessive paranoia. Begin has lost the war in the eyes of the outside world, has split the Israeli people and has given a spur to latent antisemitism.'[4] The *Daily Mirror* described the Beirut siege as 'a carnage that no cause can justify'. It was 'close to being an atrocity. Israel's bombardment has been so brutal, so sustained and so devastating as to be a crime against humanity.'[5]

Editorial criticism of Israel came to a peak with the Phalange massacres at the Sabra and Chatilla camps in September. Israeli denials of knowledge of, or responsibility for, the massacre were dismissed by most papers. The *Daily Mail* said:

Israel cannot escape blame or responsibility; the Minister of Defence has organised a bloodbath, for if he did not plan the atrocity, he certainly permitted it. And what started out as a legitimate crusade to drive the PLO terrorists from the Lebanon degenerated into a terror campaign of its own. In the Lebanon, Israel had achieved its military aims by abdicating its moral responsibility.[6]

However, when the Israeli government subsequently established the Kahan Commission of Inquiry into the massacres Israel's image improved. *The Guardian* compared Israel with Syria,

which has sought to keep its massacre of its own citizens in Hama secret. If a judicial commission sat in Damascus, its results have not yet been learned. That is the difference between the Israeli democracy and the totalitarian states which occupy so much of the Arab world.[7]

The war was very widely covered from both sides of the fighting. Two thousand journalists reported the war from the Israeli side alone, 400 at any one period. It contrasted with earlier Arab–Israeli wars when Arab governments imposed controls on the movement of foreign journalists. The heavy coverage produced a distorted and exaggerated image of certain aspects of war, such as refugees and bombings. There were additional reasons to explain Israel's negative image, including errors in reporting the war. The Palestine Red Crescent's claim that there were 15,000 dead, and the claim of the International Committee of the Red Cross that there were 600,000 homeless – subsequently shown to be very wild exaggerations – were accepted unquestioningly by some in the media, while Israeli figures issued some two weeks later received much less prominence. Another example of inaccurate reporting was an ITN film report during the Beirut siege showing children in an advanced state of malnutrition with the impression that this had been caused by the Israeli siege. Nutrition experts subsequently told the Independent Broadcasting Authority that the malnutrition shown in the film report could not have developed in the short period of six weeks. Scenes of destruction of Lebanese towns gave the impression that it had been caused by the Israelis when in fact much of it occurred during the previous seven years of civil war in the country.

These errors reflected the fact that the war was reported by journalists not permanently based in the region and lacking a good knowledge of the complexities of the Lebanese situation. The errors confirm the view, expressed in Chapter 4, that the trend among news organisations to using 'firemen' rather than permanently based foreign correspondents leads to a decline in the quality of news reporting. The BBC Israel correspondent, Michael Elkins, noted that

the fire brigade people who come smashing in whenever there's a war anywhere – TV leading the pack but others as well – don't have any historical knowledge. So they can broadcast from Damour and in all innocence say the place was just destroyed. They don't know that a very large part of the wreckage was caused when the Palestinians devastated Damour, although if you just use your eyes you can see some trees growing out of the rubble and figure out that it wasn't blasted twenty minutes ago.[8]

The lack of knowledge of some reporters was reflected in the lack of background reporting of Israel's reasons for the operation, or of the extent of the terrorist threat on Israel's northern border, and in an emphasis on reporting the human side of war. The lack of background explanation may also be explained in terms of the limited outlets for analysis and background in programmes and newspapers. 'We do three-minute pieces for US newscasts. We have one current affairs show a week. What's the point of messing about asking stupid questions?' an American correspondent said.[9]

There were also cases of reporters allowing ideological bias and the use of derogatory descriptions to intrude into news reporting. The *Daily Mirror* carried the headline 'The butcher of Lebanon' with a picture of 'Death-dealer Sharon with Begin'. This was not limited to the popular papers. Robert Fisk, Middle East correspondent of *The Times* reported on August 23 that 'I saw a guerrilla a few yards away kissing a small boy, its mother with her head in her hands, an older woman raising her arms towards the man's face, an El Greco of beseeching eyes and hands'. Reporting the Israeli siege of Beirut, Fisk wrote on August 7 that 'we turned our backs in something akin to shame and fled'. Some members of Britain's Jewish community detected signs of antisemitism, such as the application of double standards, among some journalists. Keith Waterhouse, the *Daily Mirror* columnist, wrote that

the insidious proposition – put around I would guess by people who never did like Jews very much but found it socially or politically expedient to keep quiet about it – goes like this. All right, they had a tough time with the death camps and all that. We've felt guilty about it for days. But now that they are blasting the living daylights out of women and children and chucking all that phosphorus around, surely that gets us off the hook?[10]

But intentional distortion was not the chief factor. The key factor was the general atmosphere which the war created. As with the cases of Biafra and Suez, the media's inbuilt dynamics of aggrandising such types of images as bombings and destruction beyond their normal size resulted in viewers and readers becoming participants in the event itself. The media thus not only reported the war but were overtaken by the socio-psychological atmosphere they created.[11] Moreover, there was a curious readiness to accept uncritically allegations from the Arab side coupled with disdain for counter-claims from the Israeli side.

What impact did the media and the war itself have? There was a noticeable shift in public attitudes. A MORI poll conducted in August 1982 found that 25 per cent described themselves as pro-Israeli while 16 per cent said they were pro-Palestinian. This contrasted with a MORI poll in 1976 in which 36 per cent of those questioned said they were pro-Israeli and 7 per cent pro-Palestinian. However, 48 per cent of those questioned in the 1982 poll felt the same about Israel as they had felt before the war, 34 per cent said they were less sympathetic to Israel, and 10 per cent said they were more sympathetic.[12] Whether the media's influence lay in changing attitudes or in confirming existing attitudes about Israel and the Palestinians is unclear from these figures. In terms of influencing British government policy the media's role was minimal given the lack of a direct British role in the war. But after Britain joined the multinational peacekeeping force in Lebanon with the US, France and Italy, there was some concern in Britain about the safety and function of the British battalion. Following the deaths of nearly 300 US and French troops in October 1983 in car bomb explosions at their barracks, together with continuing civil violence in Lebanon and a shift in US policy from being simply peacemakers to going on the offensive against Shiite Muslim groups and their Syrian backers, pressure increased in Parliament, including among Conservative backbenchers, and in the media to bring home the British contingent. Mrs Thatcher resisted the pressure, but by February 1984, following a further deterioration in the security situation in Lebanon, the contingent was withdrawn.

INTEREST GROUPS AND THE NEWS MEDIA

The media criticism of Israel resulted in the roles of the pro-Israeli and pro-Arab groups being reversed from those in earlier wars. In those wars pro-Arab groups criticised the coverage of the Palestinian case. More sympathetic treatment of the Palestinian issue in this war may be seen from one survey of letters to the press which found that between 60 and 80 per cent of those printed were critical of Israel.[14] The improved image may also be explained by the growth in the Arab lobby itself. From 1967, when support for the Arab case was limited to political fringe groups, the Arab lobby included by 1982 university groups, parliamentary groupings, and many on the Left. Further, the lobby was now looking towards Britain's Muslim community for grass roots support. On the tenth anniversary, in 1977, of the founding of the Council for the Advancement of Arab-British Understanding, the pro-Arab group most closely identified with the British establishment, one of its founders, Christopher Mayhew observed that 'we have come a long way in ten years. To begin with we were regarded as barely respectable: now we are part of the Establishment, officially visited by the Foreign Secretary.'[15]

When war broke out in 1982 the various Arab groups coordinated their activities through an Emergency Committee Against the Invasion of Lebanon (ECAIL). CAABU, Palestine Action, and the London office of the Palestine Liberation Organisation were in regular contact with news organisations. CAABU placed advertisements in *The Times* and *The Guardian*. Material sent to MPs, journalists, and opinion formers included special editions of 'The Palestine Report' showing photographs of Israel's alleged devastation of Lebanese towns. Cases of perceived bias were taken up with editors, including, for example, the impression during the Israeli siege of Beirut that the media were emphasising the need for the PLO's evacuation from Beirut rather than the need for Israel to withdraw from Lebanon.

Pro-Israeli groups, by contrast, found themselves in this war on the defensive, concerned about the perceived lack of balance and unfair editorial comment. Groups like the British-Israel Public Affairs Committee (BIPAC) made attempts to explain and justify Israel's actions in Lebanon, but given the climate of opinion these were often unsuccessful. Booklets such as 'Lebanon: The Facts' were distributed among the wider public and the Jewish community. A solidarity rally for Israel at the Albert Hall attracted 5000 people. The Zionist Federation placed advertisements in the national press. The Board of Deputies of British Jews met editors and journalists and the director general of the BBC to complain about the intensity of coverage and the disproportionate emphasis on certain aspects of war. Its president, MP Greville Janner described the media's coverage as 'one-sided'.[16] While the media were entitled to their views, to compare the Israeli operation to the Nazi Holocaust was not only inaccurate but also harmful to race relations and could arouse antisemitism in Britain, the Board said.

Editors replied that the Jewish community was too sensitive and that journalists had a duty to report what was happening, including the human story of war. Donald Trelford, editor of *The Observer*, said that since Jewish organisations had in the past turned the media's attention to Israel they had to expect wide coverage. He added that the world expected higher standards from Jews than from Syrians. A deputy editor of BBC Radio News argued that the BBC's newsroom structure of over 350 people militated against bias.[17] This argument is weak because if a critical or hostile mood about a country prevails among a significant section of the newsroom a negative image of that country will result. An editorial in *The Times* said that 'to suggest that it was Israel which was a greater victim than the thousands of innocents who died is to reveal on the part of the spokesmen in Jerusalem and their apologists in the West a reluctance to take criticism'.[18] But this evades the question of the media responsibility in providing accurate and balanced coverage.

The attempts by pro-Israeli groups to gain public support for Israel's case were hampered by individual Jews who expressed their opposition to Israel's actions. An advertisement in *The Guardian*, signed by 120 British Jewish academics, artists, and lawyers, expressed 'outrage at Prime Minister Menahem Begin's murderous efforts to "clear" Lebanon of the Palestinians'.[19] One Benedict Birnberg, in a letter to *The Times*, wrote that

the Israeli action in Lebanon had been chillingly reminiscent of the Nazi policy of collective punishment in occupied Europe and British Jewry does neither itself nor Israel a favour in showing solidarity with a government hellbent on a brutal, arrogant and vain policy of coercing the Palestinian people into action.[20]

While individual Jews may have had private misgivings about the wisdom of Israel's actions in Lebanon, only a small but vocal minority gave such views public expression. Publicly, Britain's Jews were more united than in some countries including the United States and France, where Jews protesting against the Begin government outside the Israel Embassy in Paris clashed with another Jewish demonstration supporting the government. The dilemma facing British Jews, the *Sunday Times* reported, was:

Should they criticise Israel and so provide ammunition for Israel's enemies? Or should they swallow their doubts and accept the explanation of the Israeli government that the Beirut policy is vital to Israel's long term security?[21]

The question for the Jewish establishment was what to do about the breach in communal ranks. The *Jewish Chronicle*, while opening its correspondence and feature columns to both protagonists and antagonists of the war, took an editorial line, until the Phalange massacres at Sabra and Chatilla in September, which sought to justify the war. The chief rabbi, Sir Immanuel Jakobovits, who had in the past criticised the Begin government, wrote 'a message to Anglo-Jewry' which was circumspect of any criticism:

What should be indisputable among Jews is that, in self-defence, Israel's action was morally as just as any war in history; that Israelis fought brilliantly and at heavy cost not only to protect their northern settlements from the constant threat of terror, but to save all Israel from what could have been a mighty onslaught from the vast PLO in Lebanon.[22]

In one sense the war coverage in the general media contributed to dividing the Jewish community. Partly in order to counter this the Zionist Federation introduced a telephone newscast service of news from Israel. In another sense, the media's criticism rallied support for Israel. With the end of Israel's siege of Beirut in August following the departure of PLO forces from the city, divisions within Anglo-Jewry began to heal. But the Sabra and Chatilla massacres in September reversed this trend. In a message to the Israeli prime minister, the Board of Deputies said it was 'appalled at the latest tragic events in the Lebanon, and expressed the hope that all responsible will be brought to justice'. The resolution, agreed at an emergency meeting held on the eve of Yom Kippur, was unusual in placing the security of Israel secondary to concern about the situation inside Lebanon. And the *Jewish Chronicle*, in an editorial entitled 'End of the line', called for the resignations of Mr Begin and Mr Sharon.[23]

CONCLUSION

The media's voluminous coverage of the Lebanon War aroused considerable interest in Britain, particularly among the pro-Israeli and pro-Arab lobbies. The relationships between the media and the lobbies became reversed with, for the first time, the Arab lobby finding considerable support for its views in the media, and with the pro-Israeli lobby isolated. Moreover, the intensive and biased coverage contributed to weakening the unity of the pro-Israeli lobby's support base, namely the Jewish community, a situation that peaked with the Sabra and Chatilla massacres.

CHAPTER ELEVEN

MEDIA DIPLOMACY IN THE FALKLANDS WAR

'Our pictures from the Falklands were being transmitted at
20 knots − coming back by sea.'

− The Press Association[1]

The Falklands War contrasted with some other modern wars, including
Vietnam and the Arab−Israeli wars, because journalists were entirely
dependent on the British authorities for gaining access to the South
Atlantic and the Falkland Islands. This was an important determinant
for the media's image of the war. Out of several hundred British and
foreign journalists who applied for permission to sail with Britain's
naval task force, only 29 representatives of news organisations in
Britain − 3 television reporters, 2 camera crews, 2 radio reporters,
2 photographers, and 15 newspaper reporters − got places in the ships.
And this largely as a result of the pressure which their editors and
proprietors applied on No 10 Downing Street, which overruled earlier
decisions by the Ministry of Defence (MOD) and the military not to
take as many, or even any, reporters with them to war. Foreign correspondents, lacking this influence at No 10, failed to gain places.
Before the task force sailed it was suggested that all the press be taken
to the South Atlantic on a single small ship in order to centralise facilities
for the media, and in order to reduce the competition between the
media's needs for access to the communication facilities to London and
those of the military. But this was rejected because the Navy required
all available ships, and instead journalists were divided principally among
three of the largest ships in the task forces, HMS *Canberra, Hermes*
and *Invincible.* Given the access journalists were afforded to some
commanding officers, the former were in a good position to follow the
progress of the war. The journalists were accompanied on board by
MOD civilian information officials, but with little or no previous war
experience, these failed to gain the respect of either journalists or military
officers. Once a bridgehead on the Falklands was achieved by troops,
journalists were allowed to join a particular military unit.

REPORTING THE WAR

In order to send their copy to London journalists had to rely on the ships' communication facilities. The inevitable delays were even greater for television film and video reports, which, lacking access to a satellite, had to be flown to London. The 11 reports which Independent Television News received from their reporters during the ten-week war took a minimum of 11 days and a maximum of 23 to reach London and be cleared by censorship.[2] The Falklands War thus became a radio war.

In London an emergency press centre was opened by the Ministry of Defence. Open from 10 a.m. to 10 p.m., and for a short period for 24 hours, the centre provided access for press inquiries, briefings for journalists, studios, and facilities for relaying material to head offices. Attendance on the press briefings was highest during the first days of the conflict; on one day the number of journalists exceeded 260. But the quantity of information which journalists gleaned from these briefings was small. The off-the-record briefings which had existed for accredited British defence correspondents broke down a short time before the Argentine invasion and were not re-convened.

The media's image of the war was further limited by the introduction of military censorship for journalists with the task force. Press guidelines had been given out to commanding officers not to indulge in speculation with journalists about future possible military action, readiness state and details about the capabilities of individual units, military movements and development, intelligence about Argentine forces, and communications. A second level of vetting was introduced for copy once it reached London in order to act as a long stop. Double vetting was necessary, MOD officials argued, because only London could take an overall view of security concerns and only the task force could assess local security needs. The system proved controversial because there were occasions when journalists in London were permitted or refused permission to publish a certain piece of information while an opposite decision was taken in the South Atlantic. Notwithstanding this, journalists accepted the principle that some form of censorship was necessary. The government thought that the voluntary system of censorship, the 'D Notice' system, which exists in peacetime and consists of guidelines for editors about categories of sensitive information which may not be published, was inappropriate in the war because only military officers could judge whether publication of a specific piece of information posed a danger to security.

In the eyes of the media, the handling of information by the government showed some lack of awareness among the military of the media's needs for information and for meeting news deadlines. The chaotic manner in which journalists joined the task force, and only as a result of the pressure which their bosses exerted, and the exclusion of foreign reporters despite the importance of overseas opinion, are symptomatic of the military's amateurism in accommodating the media in modern war.[3] The Army, which had had experience of the media in Northern Ireland, had drawn up contingency plans for information handling in 1977. These, however, had not yet been approved by the chiefs of staff. In any case, the existence of these plans was forgotten when the naval task was assembled. Yet in the eyes of some military, any journalists taken along were bound to get in the way. Indeed, it was one of the few occasions when journalists were allowed to join in a strictly sea operation.

The limited flow of information for journalists was also experienced on the Argentinian side. Foreign reporters in Argentina had no access to the Falklands themselves. The only pictures available from the islands were censored footage from a government station, which was of marginal quality and without specific dates or locations. Foreign reporters were forbidden to travel to the southern part of the country where the military bases are situated. What news there was came in the form of communiqués by the Argentine joint chiefs of staff, public statements by members of the junta, television reports by Argentine journalists on the Falklands, and the wire services of the two official, and two semi-official, Argentine news agencies.

On the one hand, the Argentinians, like the British, were anxious not to let the war become a media war. On the other hand, their lack of credibility which resulted from their own exaggerated claims and lost opportunities to gain public sympathy, such as by not letting the foreign media interview survivors of the *General Belgrano* which was hit by the British force, showed the Argentinians to be even more inept in handling the media. British reporters in Buenos Aires were given the same facilities as other foreign reporters – as were the Argentinian reporters in London – with the exception that BBC and ITN crews were denied satellite facilities. Similar incidents to those involving British reporters, including the arrest of three on charges of photographing military installations, the abduction of an ITN crew, and the beating up of a reporter, occurred with other foreign reporters. Although the limited flow of information from the British side was balanced by an even more limited one from the Argentinians, there were occasions when information or film footage was available in Buenos Aires which was not available in London, resulting in the British public receiving the Argentinian version of events.

Other factors influencing the media's image of the war lay less with the government and more with news organisations themselves. Some of the reporters sent lacked any previous war experience, either as journalists or as soldiers. They were unprepared physically and psychologically for being confined to a ship for a journey of 8000 miles. Partly, this was due to news organisations having only a couple of hours before the task force sailed in which to select and despatch their representative. In London, while some defence correspondents are well respected – the BBC's Peter Snow and Christopher Wain and *The Economist*'s Jim Meacham have a military background – the quality of others is, according to one senior MOD official, 'low in the sense of preparing to do the work of reading the open sources about military capabilities and international politics'. A decision, made by the Army in the aftermath of the Falklands War, to take reporters on future military exercises is likely to make the media better prepared for reporting any future conflict, as well as to make the military more aware of the needs of the media.

Another factor was intentional distortion by the media. Journalists were divided about the balance to strike between their professional obligation to report objectively and critically and their obligation as British citizens to be patriotic. Popular papers which were closer to the second, notably *The Sun*, were necessarily selective in the image they conveyed of the war. The *Sun* reported the sinking of the ship *General Belgrano* with the headline 'Gotcha!',[4] and it reacted to reports of a negotiated settlement between the two sides with the headline 'Stick it up your Junta'.[5] The BBC, on the other hand, took to describing British casualties as 'British' rather than as 'our' casualties. 'Panorama' devoted a programme to dissent about the war among MPs, including Conservatives. Notwithstanding this, there were few detailed examinations of British claims to the Falklands until after the end of the war in June, when detailed articles appeared in *The Economist, The Guardian*, and the *Sunday Times*. At one point in the war, a *Sun* editorial attacked the BBC, as well as the *Daily Mirror* and *The Guardian*, which also took a more objective standpoint, for treason by not wholly supporting the British side.[6] The *Daily Mirror* replied by calling the *Sun* 'The Harlot of Fleet Street'.[7] The dilemma brought back memories of the 1956 Suez War when *The Guardian* and *The Observer*, which were critical of the Eden government, lost significant numbers of readers. This did not occur in the Falklands case. Rather, one survey found that 39 per cent of those polled thought BBC TV gave the best coverage of the war, 30 per cent ITV, and only 13 per cent the newspapers.[8] Another poll found that 38 per cent said that the BBC 'stood up best for Britain in reporting the crisis', ITN 26 per cent, the *Sun* 9 per cent and the *Daily Mirror* 5 per cent.[9]

To summarise, the media's image of the war was determined largely by four factors. Journalists' controlled access to the battle zone and to news from the Ministry of Defence and military censorship all limited the flow of information which the public received. In addition, the jingoistic undertone of the coverage of most popular papers further limited the image.

PUBLIC OPINION

Public opinion was an influence on British policy regarding the Falklands before the Argentine invasion, when London and Buenos Aires attempted to resolve their dispute about the sovereignty of the islands by diplomatic means. The underlying assumption of the FCO policy was that Britain's political and economic interests in Latin America outweighed resistance to Argentinian claims to the islands, and that a compromise on the issue of sovereignty should be aimed for. The Falklands population opposed any compromise. In letters to British newspapers they expressed fears of a British sellout to Argentina, and complained that the British government was not consulting them. The FCO made a number of attempts to reach a settlement with the Argentinians behind 'closed doors', but the Falkland Islands Emergency Committee and its supporters succeeded in publicising the secret deals in the press, notably the *Daily Telegraph* and the *Daily Express*, and in Parliament. These papers rose to the defence of the Falklanders at the slightest mention of an Argentinian deal. The FCO saw that it had failed to explain its position to Parliament and the media.

When the Argentinians launched their invasion many newspapers were critical of the FCO's handling of the Falklands issue, and called for the resignation of Lord Carrington, the foreign secretary. Carrington and John Nott, the minister of defence, were, according to the *Daily Express*, 'Thatcher's guilty men'.[10] 'If he has not the grace to resign', the *Daily Mail* wrote of Carrington, 'she should sack him'.[11] Following a historic debate in the House of Commons on Saturday, 3 April, Carrington did offer his resignation but was persuaded by Mrs Thatcher to stay on. But criticism in the press on Sunday and Monday, in particular a *News of the World* article[12] and an editorial in *The Times* arguing that Carrington should 'do his duty',[13] persuaded him to tender his resignation a second time, when it was accepted. 'The newspapers were all screaming for blood', he said later.[14]

The government received broad public and media support when it launched the naval task force. Until the Cabinet Papers on the war are released it will be difficult to estimate the influence of the media on the progress of the war. British media coverage and comment were followed by the politicians and the military. A summary of British media attitudes, prepared by the spokesman of the MOD, was the third item at each day's

meeting of the chiefs of staff. 'The higher you get the more aware you
are of the great importance of public support and the part that the media
play in providing you with public support and parliamentary support',
Sir Terence Lewin, chief of the defence staff, said.[15] But the media did
not alter military strategy in the campaign, he claimed. 'I can see no
time when I was greatly concerned about items that appeared in the
media. We had our problems. We had our differences, but they were
of a relatively minor nature.'[16]

The main reason for the discussion by the chiefs of staff about the
media was to decide about that day's public statement and whether or
not to release a particular piece of information. Although it is true that
up to the third week of May the government was sustained on a tide
of anger and patriotism – strengthened by the absence of television
pictures of British casualties – from the moment that the task force
achieved a bridgehead on East Falkland there was a noticeable public
mood of impatience with the war's progress. Ministers were pressing
the military to move forward, but John Nott told the House of Commons on 23 May that 'there can be no question of pressing the force
commander to move forward prematurely'. No 10 Downing Street,
however, in a series of disclosures, reassured the media that a breakout
from San Carlos was imminent. Pressure further increased after the
Argentinian sinking of HMS *Sheffield* on 4 May. Indeed, throughout
the campaign there were audible voices of scepticism in both the two
main political parties and in the media. There was, in addition, some
discussion as Lewin indicated about the way policy was presented. It
was in reaction to the use by the BBC and ITN of Argentine television
footage, in the absence of picture reports from British reporters, that,
within two days of the cabinet discussing the subject, the MOD, having
prevaricated for two weeks, took steps to quicken and increase the
quantity of TV pictures brought back to London and released. Another
decision was to reintroduce off-the-record briefings for accredited
defence correspondents and for editors in order to stop some ill-informed
discussion of British strategy.

This public mood of impatience shows how the public's chauvinism
for the war was considerably less than that of the popular media. Despite
the fact that newspapers favouring a strong line against Argentina (the
Sun, Star, Express, Mail and *Telegraph*) outnumbered those favouring
a more cautious line (*Daily Mirror, The Guardian, The Times* and the
Financial Times) by sales of 11 million to 4.5 million, opinion polls suggested the British public did not favour the strong line advocated by
the first group of newspapers. An opinion poll at the end of April found
that three in five Britons were not prepared to lose one serviceman's
life to regain the Falklands, and that one in seven would be prepared

to see 100 or more servicemen lose their lives to win back the islands.[17] A poll in the middle of April, during US Secretary of State Alexander Haig's diplomatic shuttle between London and Buenos Aires, found that despite the rejection of the shuttle by most in the first group of papers, 61 per cent said they strongly favoured a diplomatic solution.[18] This illustrates the danger of policymakers equating media opinion with public opinion. It also raises again the question of the nature of the relationship between the media and the formation of public attitudes.

Did the British media influence the British troops in the South Atlantic? During Suez, British soldiers in the Middle East discovered from the BBC World Service the deep divisions which existed in Parliament, the public, and the media about the British operation. In the case of the Falklands, through the BBC World Service and through the newspapers which reached the South Atlantic much later, the troops were aware of the range of opinions expressed in Britain. While there is no evidence that media and other opinion critical of the war unhinged the troops' military resolve, some soldiers were 'extremely anxious' about what was being said at home, according to a navy education officer who accompanied the troops.[19]

An additional question concerns the Argentinians. When, on receiving intelligence reports that Argentinian ships were heading towards the Falklands, the British government ordered ships and submarines to sail to the South Atlantic in the hope of deterring the Argentines from actually invading, it was thought important by some ministers that calm rather than patriotism dominate. Instead, parliamentary fervour and media publicity about British ships being sent to the South Atlantic created a mood in which the Argentinians were being less deterred and more challenged to invade.

INFORMATION

To what extent did the media provide information to British policymakers? During the war their main source of information was from SIGINT or the interception of radio traffic, which is done at the government's Communication Headquarters at Cheltenham. Other sources of information were HUMINT, or human intelligence, and intelligence received from the United States through the 1947 UKUSA agreement by which the two countries exchange intelligence. Also the media of Britain, the United States, Argentina and other Latin American countries provided additional information. A vivid illustration occurred after HMS *Sheffield* had been abandoned after being hit by the Argentinians. Anxious to know about the ship's condition, Rear Admiral Sir John Woodward, the head of the task force, permitted a BBC cameraman to fly over the ship to photograph it, which Woodward said was 'of immense use to me'.[20]

But the most noteworthy cases of the media serving as a source of information occurred in the months and weeks before the invasion. In planning the invasion, the Argentine government, anxious to test the likely reaction from Britain and other countries, encouraged foreign correspondents of the Argentine media based in London and other capitals to report the likely consequences of an invasion. Their reports indicated that Britain would not intervene militarily to counter an Argentine invasion. These reports can also be seen as designed to make London fear that Argentina would use military means if the diplomatic option failed. British diplomats in Buenos Aires misread the significance of the press articles since similar press campaigns had occurred in earlier years. Although the British Embassy and intelligence knew that General Galtieri attached substantial importance to achieving Argentinian sovereignty over the Falklands by January 1983, the 150th anniversary of British occupation, it was thought that any invasion would not take place until diplomatic negotiations had broken down, and that there would be a progression of measures starting with the withdrawal of existing Argentine services to the islands and increased diplomatic pressure. No full-scale invasion was thought likely to take place before the second half of 1982. Although a wrong assessment was made, the case shows that the media was an important source of information.

The British naval attaché in Buenos Aires first heard of the Argentine naval exercises from 23 to 28 March (from which ships changed course and sailed for the Falklands) on March 31 from the Argentine media. He informed London of these reports, but given the ten days' journey time for ships from London to the South Atlantic, little could be done militarily.[21] That the naval attaché was dependent on the media to learn about the exercises was partly the result of cuts in Britain's intelligence efforts in Latin America, where MI6's two regional head-quarters, dealing with Spanish- and Portuguese-speaking countries respectively, had been reduced to one, in Buenos Aires, involving a single MI6 officer with two military attachés.[22] One of the attachés remarked that his 'section of the embassy neither had the remit nor the capacity to obtain detailed information of military movements' – as opposed to simply Argentina's military capabilities – 'given the country's very long coastline and the distance of the southern Argentine ports from Buenos Aires'.[23]

A government inquiry under Lord Franks, established to review British government actions in the period leading up to the invasion, criticised the structure for its assessment of information and intelligence. Its report suggested that the part-time chairmanship by a senior FCO official of the Joint Intelligence Committee, based in the Cabinet Office, should be replaced by a full-time chairman from outside the FCO, such as a Cabinet Office official, thereby providing an alternative assessment to a given situation from that of the FCO. The report also recommended that the assessments staff of the Joint Intelligence Committee should 'take fully into account both relevant diplomatic and political developments and foreign press treatment of sensitive foreign policy issues'.[24] As argued in Chapter 3, although the media cannot substitute for primary intelligence gathering, their value lies in being a secondary, alternative source of information and interpretation.

INFORMATION AS A WEAPON

As a carrier of information the media may be considered as weapons in a number of senses:

1. The British media as a source of information to the enemy.
2. The use of the media by the British government to misinform the enemy.
3. The media as a bureaucratic weapon in Whitehall interdepartmental infighting.

British officials assumed that just as the British monitored the Argentine media the Argentinians similarly monitored the British media, including videotaping television news and current affairs programmes, in order to find clues to future British moves. The small amount of hard information available to British journalists from the MOD encouraged journalists to speculate about British tactics and intentions. Retired military officers were interviewed to give their expert assessments. As a result there was a mass of information in circulation about ships' movements, the composition of the task force, weapons capabilities, and future operations. Sir Henry Leach, the First Sea Lord, argued that 'If you say "Now, they could land to the north, or to the east, or to the south, or to the west", then you have really covered all the options and one of them was almost certain to be the right one'.[25] The counter-argument is that an enormous amount of information about British weapons systems was already available from unclassified sources, such as Janes' military books and the *Military Balance*, published by the International Institute of Strategic Studies, and that the Argentinians who had in the past purchased considerable military hardware from Britain, such as the Harrier jet, acquired at the same time important information. 'Argentine intelligence just isn't that defective', the director-general of the BBC suggested.[25a] Some journalists took special care in preparing their reports. A television defence correspondent, in using a map in his studio commentaries, ensured that when he pointed to particular places and areas he did so in a vague manner so that if the film was videotaped at a regular or slow speed the enemy could not learn about precise geographical locations.

In misinforming the enemy the military had two objectives: to lower the morale of Argentinian troops on the Falklands, and to misinform their commanders about British military plans and military capabilities. In pursuit of the first objective, the MOD set up *'Radio Antalantico del Sur'* to broadcast in Spanish selected items of bad news such as that imports to Argentina from Brazil had almost stopped, and that sea and air supplies to the 'Malvinas' (the Argentinian name for the Falklands) had been suspended by Argentina. A talk on the military situation emphasised how powerful the British commando rifles were, and that the Argentinian force commander was furious at having to send his young pilots on missions without support from other services. An Argentinian prisoner interviewed complained that 'I never thought we would have to fight when we came here. They only gave me a rifle and six bullets. I don't know why they brought me here.'[26] It is difficult to evaluate the effectiveness of these broadcasts given the shortness of the war; some British officials claimed that some Argentinian prisoners interrogated said that they had heard the broadcasts.*[27]

A number of cases of misinforming the Argentinian military command involved the British media. When reports reached London at the end of March indicating that Argentina was planning some type of military action, the British government leaked the news to the press that HMS *Superb* had sailed from Gibraltar. MOD spokesmen refused to clarify whether the submarine was sailing for the South Atlantic. Some weeks later, in fact, it arrived in Scotland. An unsuccessful attempt at misinformation occurred after a lone RAF Vulcan bomber hit the airfield at Port Stanley, the Falklands capital, on 1 May. In its press statement the MOD spoke of 'aircraft', and the BBC TV correspondent with the task force was shown photographs which gave him the clear impression that the airfield had been badly hit and was not usable for landing aircraft. In fact, only one bomb landed on the runway while the remainder landed to its side. If these photographs were designed to misinform the Argentinian military command about the usability of the runway they were unsuccessful, since the Argentinians in Port Stanley were able to inspect it, and did so.

* The media were also used to broadcast to the Falklands population and to British troops in the South Atlantic. The BBC External Services programme 'Calling the Falklanders' was increased from its weekly broadcast to a daily one. In addition to news, the programme included interviews with government ministers and messages from relatives and friends of the 1800 inhabitants. The British Forces Broadcasting Service transmitted a musical request show for the British troops.

A successful attempt at misinformation occurred on the eve of the British landing at San Carlos Bay when, at an off-the-record briefing for defence correspondents, Sir Frank Cooper, the permanent under-secretary of the MOD, said that they should expect various little raids at different places rather than a D-Day style landing. In fact 3000 British troops went ashore in the biggest British amphibious assault since D-Day in the Second World War. Given the ease with which the landing was achieved, the attempt at misinformation was particularly successful. In another case, after the British landing ships, the *Sir Galahad* and the *Sir Tristram*, were attacked by enemy on 8 June at Bluff Cove, to the south of Port Stanley, which cost the lives of 50 men, military experts believed the casualties to be much higher – from 400 to 900 marines killed or wounded – which gave the Argentinian military command cause to believe that a serious delay had occurred in the expected British assault on Port Stanley. Sir Terence Lewin was told by Sir John Fieldhouse, the Navy's commander in chief, that he wanted the casualties talked up as much as possible. It is significant that the next British target, the capture of Mount Longden, was achieved on 13 June with relative ease. The speculation about the casualty figures aroused so much concern inside Britain that already on 10 June political correspondents were being told by No 10 Downing Street that the true figures were about 43 killed and 120 injured.[28]

The use of the media to misinform the enemy aroused considerable controversy among journalists. Journalists with the task force were told by its commander, Sir John Woodward, that he wanted to use all possible means, including the media, to deceive the enemy.[29] Sir Terence Lewin admitted after the war that the media had been used and were 'quite helpful'.[30] The House of Commons Defence Committee, which investigated the handling of information during the Falklands War, justified misinformation if it was calculated to protect operations of a major nature.[31] The MOD has claimed that it did not publish false 'facts'; rather, the whole truth was suppressed and useful rumours which were not true were not denied. Notwithstanding this, in the case of Cooper's statement before the landing at San Carlos Bay, he later justified denying that a D-Day style landing would take place on the ground that 'I did not expect a D-Day type of invasion because the whole aim of the operation was to get the forces ashore on an unopposed landing. A D-Day type invasion in my mind is actually an opposed landing.'[32] The cost for the government of using the media as a means of misinformation was to bring its credibility into question. The defence correspondent of the Press Association argued that

misinformation has short-term benefits operationally, but in the long term it destroys the whole raison d'être of your operation to deal with the press, because your credibility disappears. I still find myself, months after the Falklands, speaking to the Ministry of Defence over quite trivial things and not actually believing what they say, because the seven weeks inside the Ministry of Defence [during the war] taught me not to believe what they say.[33]

As a weapon in the Whitehall infighting, the most noteworthy case involving the media occurred following the establishment of the bridge-head at San Carlos. With politicians pressing the government for a quick advance on Port Stanley, but with the military anxious not to advance prematurely, No 10 began to apply pressure on the MOD by various means including leaks to the media. No 10 told political correspondents that an attack on Port Stanley was expected 'in a matter of days'. On 26 May, following the sinking of HMS *Sheffield*, correspondents were told by No 10 'to expect news shortly of advances by British land forces'. Since there were only two places for the British troops to break out to from San Carlos, of which the most likely was Goose Green, these leaks had serious military implications. Before the attack, by a parachutist regiment, had begun on Goose Green, an MOD official told the BBC radio defence correspondent that the attack was already under way, and Mrs Thatcher announced in the House of Commons that 'British forces have begun to move forward from their San Carlos bridgehead'. The regiment's commanding officer, Lieutenant Colonel Herbert Jones, heard the news on the BBC World Service before the event had actually occurred. An unusually large number of casualties were suffered in the attack, including eighteen killed, among them Jones, because the Argentinians had reinforced their defence around Goose Green. Whether the leaks, the general speculation in the media, or other factors were responsible for the Argentine reinforcement is unclear; an internal MOD inquiry failed to trace any leak within the ministry and blamed the general speculation.[34]

MOULDING OPINION ABROAD

The importance for Britain of gaining the support of foreign public opinion in the Falklands War was in one sense limited. The remoteness of the area meant that the crisis could reach a conclusion without endangering the international system. The war for the 1800 Falklanders on a distant, windswept island was seen in some countries, including the United States, in comic terms. In another sense, however, foreign opinion was important. US public opinion played a role in Britain gaining the support of the US administration when many in Washington were pressing for a more even-handed approach. In Western Europe, EEC support for economic sanctions against Argentinian exports helped to weaken the junta's self-confidence and contributed to discouraging other Latin American countries from giving economic or military support to Buenos Aires.

In the United States the Falklands crisis was front-page news almost every day of the conflict. At the outset, the American press was unreserved in supporting the British action. The *Washington Post*, in an editorial entitled 'Argentina's Aggression', said that Mrs Thatcher spoke the simple truth when she labelled the Argentinian act 'unprovoked aggression'.[35] The *New York Times*, in an editorial entitled 'Brute force in the Falklands', said that America had no choice but to denounce Argentina's aggression.[36] When it became clear that Britain was serious in using military means to restore the island to British rule, fears began to be expressed in the US media that the US might be drawn into another Vietnam. There was also concern that a humiliation of Argentina might harm US interests in the continent. These fears underlay the refusal of the US government to commit itself publicly to the British side at the beginning of the war. Instead it steered a middle path between London and Buenos Aires. The British embassy in Washington carried out an intensive information effort. The embassy communicated directly with some 60 congressmen at different periods of the war. The influence of the Latino lobby on Capitol Hill was slight and most Congressmen supported Britain. The ambassador, Sir Nicholas Henderson, who gave more than 60 interviews and briefings, 30 of which were for US television or radio stations, became something of a media celebrity. The success of Britain's information work may be gauged from a Harris opinion poll on 29 April which showed that 60 per cent of the American people backed Britain against 19 per cent who backed Argentina.[37]

British officials in Latin America had little hope, but they failed to consider the historic disagreements between Argentina and other states in the continent. These were reflected in voting patterns on the war in the Organisation of American States. Officials therefore did succeed in getting a daily radio programme on the war, which was beamed to North American radio stations, accepted by 13 radio stations in Latin America.

In Western Europe, while governmental support for their fellow EEC partner was positive and correct, this was not reflected throughout the media. In West Germany, for example, while *Der Spiegel* put Mrs Thatcher on the front cover clad as a Wagnerian knight with sword aflame, and the left-of-centre *Die Zeit* said that Britain was exercising its right of self-defence against unprovoked aggression, other papers saw Britain as still living in past colonial glories. The theme of Britain as imperialist was taken up in Spain where there was sympathy for kith and kin in Argentina, as well as a wary eye on Gibraltar which Spain sees as its own Malvinas. Scandinavian opinion, which might have applied pacifist principles against Britain, was generally supportive.

Information policy entailed using the existing agencies, notably the COI and the BBC External Services. The FCO's Information Policy Department monitored and responded to Argentine claims. It produced nearly 90 guidance telegrams, advising Britain's missions abroad on the line to take, and twelve background papers on such topics as life on the islands under Argentinian occupation, militarism and repression in Argentina, misinformation by the Argentinian government, and international press comment on the invasion. In addition to a daily news programme, comprising news and ministerial interviews, beamed to North America, two films on life on the islands were produced and distributed to foreign television stations and shown inside British missions to invited audiences. Information work by the local post, such as responding to cases of bias, depended on the post's accessibility to the media. In Spain, for example, no member of the British embassy in Madrid was interviewed on radio or television throughout the war.

The BBC's Spanish-language Latin American Service increased its broadcasts from four to five hours daily. The BBC World Service broadcasts eight hours to Latin America. An indication of the former's perceived success was that for the first time in the 44-year history of BBC Spanish transmissions, broadcasts were jammed by the Argentinians. BBC Spanish-language broadcasts to Spain had been axed in 1981 to save £181,000 per annum. So had the Italian Service, and the Brazilian Service had been reduced. The opposition in those countries to Britain's case strengthens the BBC argument that a language service cannot be started up once a crisis has broken but requires to have built up a following beforehand. A noteworthy feature of external broadcasting in this war was that there was no attempt at governmental interference, as there had been in the case of Suez.[38]

The Falklands War was the first military operation, apart from Northern Ireland, since the 1977 Berrill Report laid bare the fact that much of the country's image is determined less by local information work done by British posts abroad and more by the foreign press corps in London. This, and the corrective action taken by some government departments since, was ignored in the war, and foreign correspondents had to rely on the British media for their information. Foreign reporters were not included among journalists travelling in the task force. An attempt by ABC to charter an oil tanker from Sao Paulo, which would sail for the Falklands so that the war could be covered from helicopters on the ship, failed to materialise after Britain established its total exclusion zone around the islands. In London, with the exception of some briefings at the end of the war for American correspondents, the MOD gave no off-the-record briefings to foreign correspondents.

While regular briefings for the foreign press at the FCO and at No 10 Downing Street provided the diplomatic and political background to the war, correspondents complained that they lacked the military background to events. The Foreign Press Association complained of the 'high-handed or indifferent attitude of MOD press spokesmen', allegedly much more concerned with domestic British opinion, leading to 'Argentinian sources exercising undue influence in the foreign press'.[39]

The presence in London of the correspondents of the Argentinian media offered the British government a unique but unexploited opportunity to reach the Argentinian public. Another lost opportunity was the capital to be gained via the correspondents of British Commonwealth media from Britain coming to the defence of a colony. The House of Commons Defence Committee said:

The British Government appears to have assumed that diplomatic contacts and the BBC Overseas Service were sufficient to convince the world of the clarity of its case. Given the lack of pictures from London and the somewhat cavalier treatment of the foreign press, this was an extremely risky and short-sighted attitude. In future, British governments should not rely on the sense of fairness and objectivity of the world's media but should appreciate the importance of propaganda.[40]

MOULDING OPINION AT HOME

Governmental attempts to mould British opinion began, abortively, during the series of negotiations between Britain and Argentina. Then came the war, and although the FCO had the brief to explain the diplomatic moves the main focus for moulding attitudes moved across Whitehall to the MOD.

The public relations of the MOD differ from those of the FCO in terms of goals, structure, and size. The FCO's News Department, with only twelve officials, has the limited function of briefing journalists. The MOD not only briefs the media, on a smaller scale, but also has information divisions for print and film publicity and for tours to military bases. The Army, Air Force, and Navy each have a public relations section with their own directors working under the civilian head of the MOD's public relations. For reasons of structure and size public relations at the MOD have been bedevilled by a history of internal conflicts, with each service, for example, trying to improve its own image particularly at times of defence expenditure cuts. In personnel terms, while the FCO News Department is staffed by career diplomats, the MOD is, like other government departments, staffed by information officers. On the one hand, the lack of background in defence policy of the career information officer places him on a lower footing vis-à-vis the policy departments than the News Department official; on the other hand, he should be more au fait with the modern technology of the electronic media.

The MOD's chances to gain public support were weakened by its lack of credibility, caused partly by its not restarting off-the-record briefings with accredited defence correspondents. The decision was initiated by Ian McDonald, the acting spokesman, who is an administrative civil servant rather than a career information officer. It meant that to all intents and purposes the MOD was severing its lifeline with the media when it should have been extending it. As a result of a dispute between McDonald and the correspondents in the preceding months, MOD's credibility had worsened. When the invasion occurred all briefings were, therefore, on-the-record which meant that only the blandest of information came out. With little information in London or from the Falklands, journalists turned to United States sources and retired soldiers for information and comment. McDonald's style as a spokesman confused journalists. If he said, 'We have no reports of any major Argentinian warships or auxiliaries having penetrated the Maritime Exclusion Zone', in the absence of background briefings all the journalists could do, according to one of them, was to treat each statement as a theological text. Were 'reports' from embassy sources, or from military intelligence, or what? Why 'major' warships – did that exclude small ones? How small? And did 'penetrated' mean from the mainland to the islands, or from the islands to the mainland as well?[41]

By the middle of April, two weeks after the invasion, the handling of information at the MOD was causing concern in Whitehall, particularly at No 10 Downing Street, and a respected information officer, Neville Taylor, was appointed to the vacant post of MOD spokesman. When he took over responsibility for the Falklands, in the second week in May, the off-the-record briefings were resumed at a rate of two per week. These were taken by Sir Frank Cooper, the permanent under-secretary, himself. There were two types of briefings: for defence correspondents, divided into journalists from the national and the provincial media respectively, and a briefing for editors which was more a means for discussing, and for journalists complaining, about arrangements for handling information.

There was a lack of coordination between the MOD and No 10 Downing Street. Although information strategy should have been agreed at a daily meeting between the No 10 spokesman, the MOD spokesman, the FCO spokesman, and a COI representative, journalists sensed a battle taking place in Whitehall before many announcements were made, and in some cases journalists were confused as to which was the lead department. Whereas the MOD used the media in order to confuse the enemy, No 10 used them in order to sustain public support at home.

Thus the different casualty claims of the MOD and No 10 over the losses on the *Sir Galahad* and the *Sir Tristram* at Bluff Cove. Thus the leaks from No 10 and elsewhere about the imminent attack on Goose Green. The Whitehall battle had already begun before the naval task force set sail with the MOD initially refusing to take any journalists and the No 10 spokesman, Bernard Ingham, under pressure from news organisations, overruling their refusal. It was in order to improve the rapport between the MOD and No 10 that Cecil Parkinson, chancellor of the Duchy of Lancaster, and a member of the war cabinet, was appointed as information coordinator, but in practice this became limited to presenting the government's case on television and in the press. The lack of coordination thus went unresolved.

The moulding of opinion comprised suppressing, or timing the announcement of, negative information rather than a conscious attempt at overt propaganda. Selection of what information to give out, and what not to, encouraged accusations by journalists that censorship was being used not only for security reasons but also to manipulate public attitudes to the war. The fact that the *General Belgrano* had been torpedoed while it was sailing outside the naval exclusion zone, set up by the British, was suppressed by the government. Dramatic pictures of casualties were in some cases released by censorship after some delay and in some cases never reached their news organisations. Pictures of HMS *Antelope* exploding on 24 May were delayed and a picture of its sinking was never released. The world-famous British photographer Don McCullin was repeatedly refused permission to sail to the Falklands. In the case of television pictures, although there were serious technical difficulties in obtaining satellite transmission from the South Atlantic, there was allegedly also a lack of will to overcome these difficulties. 'The criticism we had in not obtaining television transmission is a drop in the ocean compared to the problems we would have had in dealing with television coverage', Cooper said.[42] Television film of injured sailors from the *Sir Galahad*, showing their burnt skin peeling away, was delayed by censorship until after the war. So were voice reports. The report of the attacks on the *Sir Galahad* and *Sir Tristram* by ITN's Michael Nicholson, which was upbeat, speaking of 'a day of extraordinary heroism', was released without delay. But that by the BBC's Brian Hanrahan, which arrived in London simultaneously with Nicholson's but was more sombre, talking of a 'setback for the British', and including the description 'Other survivors came off unhurt but badly shaken after hearing the cries of men trapped below', was temporarily held up. By the time it was released, with this description removed, the news bulletins were over and both BBC and ITN had been forced to use Nicholson's version.

MD-K

The manner in which the MOD announced the sinking of HMS *Sheffield* is another example. The announcement by McDonald of the sinking was filmed, but the announcement of the casualties was not because the discreet black and white of newsprint was considered more dignified than the glare of television. And film of the survivors and an interview with its captain, filmed on 5 May, and a picture of the ship itself, shot on 7 May, were finally shown in London on 26 and 28 May respectively. By then, the British had landed on East Falkland, fighting had been going on for a week, and the war had moved into a different phase.

Reports and pictures presenting the positive side of the war tended to reach news organisations much quicker. The picture of a San Carlos villager offering a Marine a cup of tea achieved instant currency. News of the British bombing of the airfield at Port Stanley was telephoned to news organisations by the MOD. The reports by the *London Standard*'s Max Hastings, which were relatively more positive and patriotic, reached their destination with greater regularity and speed than those of other reporters.[43]

The BBC claimed that the MOD came very close to the management or manipulation of the news. Had the British operation ended in failure, the suppression of news could have had serious consequences for the Thatcher government. In the event, although the MOD suffered some loss of credibility with the media, and although a greater credence than might otherwise have been was accorded to the reports from Buenos Aires, the MOD's manipulation of the media achieved its objective of maintaining broad public support for the war.

THE INFORMATION DEBATE

A debate about informational aspects of the conflict began soon after the invasion and continued for months after the recapture of the islands. The House of Commons Defence Committee examined the handling of press and public information during the conflict, and the MOD sponsored studies on military censorship and on government-media relations in wartime. Academic studies included research on how journalists reported the war, the image conveyed of it, and the use of retired officers as military commentators.[44]

For journalists specific complaints included the inadequate number of places to accompany the task force and the unfairness of the procedure for distributing them; the absence of direct television coverage from the battle zone; inconsistent vetting by military censorship of correspondents' reports; and the lack of background briefings in London during the first half of the war. These complaints reflected the lack of contingency planning by the MOD and the military: answers to such basic questions as how many reporters to take, how to get copy back to London, and censorship had to be improvised over one weekend as the task force was being assembled. Civilian information officers accompanying the reporters were inexperienced, failing to win the respect of either the journalists or officers. Reporters received no training on the voyage to the South Atlantic on what to do once ashore. Nor did they receive suitable kitting for the rough conditions there. And the foreign media were ignored both in being denied places in the task force and in their treatment in London.

The MOD accepted some of these criticisms. It acknowledged that the cancellation of the background briefings for defence correspondents was an error. The director of the Army's public relations was charged in the aftermath of the war to devise procedures for accommodating the media and providing communication requirements in a future war. But given the need to retain flexibility, the extent and composition of the media in any future operation will depend on the location, whether maritime or land based, and on available transport and communications. The MOD asked news organisations to designate certain reporters who would report a future conflict with a view to taking them on military exercises, which were designed to accustom journalists to the conditions of wartime and the military to fighting a war accompanied by the media. The MOD accepted a proposal made by the House of Commons Defence Committee that in a lengthy or large conflict the minister of defence should appoint one of his ministers to take day-to-day responsibility for the handling of information. It rejected, however, the claim that coordination with No 10 had broken down: 'The Secretary of State of a Department is the focal point for the policies of that Department, and directly responsible for them', it said.[45]

The major points of debate concerned censorship and the manipulation of the media. Most journalists accept the need to withhold information for reasons of operational security. It is the interpretation of 'operational security' which sometimes draws accusations from the media that the government is using it as the reason for not releasing inconvenient pieces of information or as a means to misinform the enemy. It is true that journalists are not always able to appreciate the military significance of a piece of information.

Regarding the use of the media for misinformation, the defence correspondent of *The Economist* argued that it can never be right for a democratic government to use the free press for such purposes.[46] He received backing from a study group on military censorship, sponsored by the MOD, which said that other means than the media should be found for deception of the enemy.[47] These include, to name just three, allowing fake messages to 'fall' into the enemy's hands, deceptive communications or other electronic emissions, and faked troop movements. The House of Commons Defence Committee, however, argued that 'in our judgement the public is, in general, quite ready to tolerate being misled to some extent if the enemy is also misled, thereby contributing to the success of the campaign'. Indeed, more and greater acts of disinformation than occurred in the Falklands War are justified, it said.[48]

Even more contentious was the use of the media to sustain public morale at home. 'We did not produce the full truth and the full story. The news is handled by everybody in politics in a way which rebounds to their advantage', Sir Frank Cooper said.[49] In normal circumstances, when a journalist has other sources of information, this may be so, but in war the media are more dependent on the government for access to the battle zone. While it is legitimate for a government to seek public support for its policies, it is not legitimate to do so by manipulating the media, according to the House of Commons Defence Committee and the Study Group on Censorship. Indeed, 'it was easy to underestimate the resilience of the British people to adversity. The reporting of blitz damage did not lower morale in the last war', the Study Group argued.[50] Nor should it be assumed that in another war, say, in Europe, the MOD will be in any position to monopolise the flow of information. Without this monopoly the only alternative available is for the MOD to open its lines of communication with the media, such as by providing background briefings and facilities for reporting from the battle zone.

The questions about giving journalists access to the battle zone and of manipulating the media are not peculiar to Britain or the Falklands War but concern every open society at war. In the United States, for example, a similar debate has taken place in the aftermath of the military operation in Grenada in 1983 when a ban on reporters was introduced for the first two days. Grenada and the Falklands shared the characteristic of being islands to which access for the media could be controlled. They contrasted with some other wars such as Vietnam and the Lebanon War where controlling access was much less of an option for the governments concerned. The US government justified the press ban in Grenada because of the need for surprise. Public opinion polls supported the government. But partly as a result of wide media criticism the secretary of defence, Caspar Weinberger appointed a commission under General Winant Sidle to draft guidelines for media access to future combat situations. Its report, which was accepted by Weinberger, confirmed the right of the media to cover combat 'to the maximum possible consistent with mission security and the safety of US forces'. The new guidelines oblige the armed forces to provide adequate transportation and other assistance to war correspondents, including communication facilities to send their reports home and officers to escort them in the battle zone. They also create a system of 'pool coverage' whenever the number of journalists must be limited. In certain situations journalists could be obliged to keep information secret even from their own superiors until the operation is safely under way. The British have not gone as far as the Americans in confirming the right of the media 'to the maximum possible'. Indeed, experimental guidelines telling journalists what they could and could not report which were used at military exercises in 1983 were criticised by journalists who participated as being so restrictive as to leave them little to report.

The information debate focussed on official handling of information. Other legitimate questions about the military—media relationship — including criticism by some politicians that some journalists 'confused' their roles as patriot and neutral observer — failed to be addressed, to be forgotten until any future military conflict.

CONCLUSION

The Falklands War illustrated several aspects of media diplomacy.

1. The media coverage. While the media showed great interest in the war, journalists' access to the battle zone was limited and controlled by both the British and the Argentinians.
2. The media's influence on British policy. In the course of the war, the media's impact on policy became evident with politicians anxious for a quick victory.
3. The media were used by the military to misinform the enemy.
4. Governmental explanation of policy. The government's performance in moulding public support abroad was divided between its success in the United States and, to a lesser extent, in Western Europe and its failure in Latin America and certain other Third World countries. Gaining public support at home was facilitated by the government controlling the media's access to the South Atlantic.

CHAPTER TWELVE

THE REVOLUTIONS IN DIPLOMACY AND COMMUNICATIONS

'Before the war I had been drilled to an instant evasive reflex if the press ever hove into sight. Only the mighty ever confronted those coffin-like microphones of the early radio; television did not even exist to panic us. A decade later, we were to run with outstretched hand to meet the press. On tour from overseas head-quarters we were not to shrink from the intrusive hand-mike, or to wince at the inevitable question "What does it feel like ...?"'
– Sir Geoffrey Jackson, former British ambassador[1]

We have seen that the media and diplomacy interact in numerous significant ways, which can sometimes affect the foreign policy of the British government at the formulation and the implementation stages.

Both the overseas and British media are perused regularly by members of diplomatic missions abroad as well as officials and ministers in London. The media are also sources of information for groups indirectly involved with foreign policy, such as interest groups and the wider public. By affecting the perceptions of both policymakers and the interest groups and general public to whom they are responsive, the media influence the course of foreign policy itself.

In addition to their role as sources of information, the media serve as channels of communication both internally and bilaterally. Internally, various elements of the British government use the media to disclose information that will advance or hinder proposed policies. The media are also used, in international negotiations, by Britain and other govern-ments to pressure and manoeuvre one another.

Finally, the media are a means to gain the support of both domestic and foreign publics. Abroad, this entails the fostering by diplomatic missions of relations with the local media, including distributing printed and visual material to them. At home, the British media are used by the government to explain policy to the British public and create favourable perceptions.

Although these are the main ones, there are other types of inter-actions between media and diplomacy. These include the influence of the British media on other governments' relations with Britain. British media reports of elation at the assassination of Mrs Indira Gandhi in October 1984 among members of the Sikh community in Britain created a bad atmosphere in relations between Delhi and London. The broad-casting in Britain of the ITV production 'Death of a Princess' in April 1980, dealing with the execution of a Saudi princess for committing adultery, strained relations between Saudi Arabia and Britain for four months. During the Nigerian Civil War, the publication in the *Sunday Telegraph* of a confidential British government report criticising the federal government, which the British were backing, for its manage-ment of the war produced a short-lived cool in relations between the two governments. Another type of interaction between media and diplomacy is the influence of local media on a foreign government's relations with Britain. Press criticism of British policy in Northern Ireland in certain countries, including the United States, has in some cases contributed to the government concerned taking up the Northern Ireland issue with London. Still another type is the influence which British media has on foreign publics and governments. BBC External Service broadcasts have upset governments. Negative news about the British economy conveyed by the British media discourages foreign investment in Britain.

The influence of media on diplomacy, and the interactions between them, are likely to increase in the future. This concluding chapter will consider some of the prospective developments in the field of media diplomacy, including the call for a new world information order and related international issues; the effects of expanding communication technologies; the changing nature of public opinion; and the likely impacts of all these factors on the future course of British diplomacy.

POLITICAL ISSUES

Media diplomacy should not only be seen in terms of the various roles which the media play in the formulation and implementation of foreign policy, but also in terms of the media themselves as an international issue. The best known case of this is the UNESCO movement for a 'new international information order'.[2] In order to rectify the imbalance in the international flow of news – with Western news agencies being accused of creating a negative image of Third World countries – a number of reforms have been recommended ranging from establishing an independent Third World-based news agency, to licensing foreign correspondents, to establishing a system for correcting reports which were subsequently shown to be incorrect. Western governments, led by the United States, have responded by criticising Third World governments for limiting access to foreign correspondents and for the trend towards a state-controlled media. Some western governments, including Britain, have encouraged the training of journalists from the developing world, and some news organisations, including Reuters, have made attempts to provide a more balanced and comprehensive picture of affairs in the developing world.

Another media issue to reach the international agenda has been the flow of information between West and East. The Soviet Union and some East European states have objected to the western media, in particular foreign broadcasts, and have used various means, political and technical (jamming), to stop these. For the East the broadcasts are an interference in their domestic affairs, and pose a threat to the integrity of their national cultures. Under the 1976 Helsinki accords the East agreed to ease the flow of information, but there has been little real improvement. Radio Free Europe, Radio Liberty, and to a lesser extent the BBC External Services have continued to be jammed at periodic intervals. British correspondents in Moscow and Warsaw have in a number of cases had their freedom to report curtailed.

The trend in many countries towards, if anything, greater control of the media has important implications for media diplomacy. In information gathering by diplomats where 75 to 90 per cent of information has come from published sources, any increase in state control of media, including in the 'threat countries' about whom information is required, will be felt, even though state-controlled media perform a separate function of reflecting shifts in the ruling bureaucracy. The use of reconnaissance satellites enables governments to obtain a certain type of information. For the wider public, major news organisations – which already use communication satellites to beam words and images from one place to another – may use commercial satellites for foreign news gathering (these have already been used for US coverage of the space missions) in a similar way to the governmental use of reconnaissance satellites. In overseas information work, greater state control of the media means that foreign embassies have fewer means to project themselves locally.

The extent to which the media are free will also influence a foreign government's ability to manipulate the media during an international negotiation. Nevertheless, summitry and the role played by the media are likely to continue. 'It is the showmanship, being seen on television in your own home country and host's and international TV, which attracts prime ministers and presidents to do what foreign ministers and career diplomats used to do', according to a diplomat.[3] And this despite the practical need for fundamental issues to be systematically analysed by trained negotiators away from the media's limelight. At the policy planning level the bureaucratic use of the media for competitive leaking is likely to increase given the involvement of home departments in foreign policy. Coordination between the FCO and the Ministry of Defence works fairly well, but in EEC matters where many departments are involved this is less true.

MEDIA TECHNOLOGY

Technological innovation in mass communications has added new dimensions to diplomacy, with instantaneous communication of words and images over vast distances. In news reporting, electronic newsgathering equipment (ENG) – comprising a small colour camera, a video recorder, and mobile satellite transmitters – enables news reports to be 'bounced back' to a satellite ground station from where they are beamed to the news organisation. Before ENG was developed in the early 1970s, television reporting was based on film, which is a slow and costly process. While videotape had been used earlier for producing commercials and live coverage of sporting events, the equipment was too cumbersome for news reporting. Now, miniature videotape recorders requiring three-man crews are being replaced by ones needing only one-man crews. Thus television news, once confined to summarising events that took place earlier, now often cuts into programmes with late-breaking stories. In radio reporting, cordless telephones will enable the reporter to send back his despatches from distant places such as a battlefield.

The development of the satellite has had a number of consequences for media diplomacy. In addition to enabling a reporter, print or broadcast, to send back his despatch instantaneously, the quantity and speed have vastly increased. Whereas in 1975 a foreign reporter could send back a maximum of 1,200 words per minute to his news organisation, by the mid-1980s satellite communications enabled at least ten times this amount to be sent.[4] Under the Eurovision News Exchange, begun in 1960, BBC and ITN receive and send television reports from and to broadcasting organisations in Western Europe, North America and the Middle East. In 1984 the Independent Broadcasting Authority experimented with a schedule of programmes to be beamed via satellite in different languages to West European and Middle Eastern countries. However, owing to the cost (£500–£600 million) and to doubts about the potential market, even a combined consortium, comprising BBC, ITV and five non-broadcasting organisations, failed in 1985 to launch Britain's first direct broadcasting by satellite to Western Europe. A British viewer possessing his own satellite dish receiver is able to pick up television programmes from southern Scandinavia, Belgium, the Netherlands, Germany, France, Spain and Portugal. In newspaper production, the satellite enables dummy pages to be transmitted over long distances, within and beyond national boundaries, to be printed in different places. Among the media printed in this way are the *Financial Times*, the *International Herald Tribune*, the *Wall Street Journal*, *Time*, and *Newsweek*.

The increase in the flow of international news resulting from the new technology creates greater public interest, and therefore greater public pressure on policymakers. This was vividly illustrated in the Falklands War when the BBC and ITN, unable to get picture reports from their own reporters and cameramen in the South Atlantic, turned to using Argentinian television footage. The new technology has also again raised the question about the long-term future of the printed media. With instantaneous television reporting, popular newspapers have given up any pretence to cover international news, concentrating on home, investigative features. The serious newspapers, however – *The Times, Financial Times, The Guardian*, and *Daily Telegraph* – have not reduced their foreign coverage, but have expanded their background analysis to developments. While observation satellites and other technological developments contribute to the flow of information reaching British diplomats and intelligence, the limitations of observation satellites – including the ability of satellites to look in detail only at one area at a time, vagaries of weather, and the inability to judge men's intentions and capabilities – mean that the conventional news media remain important sources of information to policymakers.

The potential role of the satellite as a channel for a government to reach foreign audiences has yet to be fully appreciated. Indeed, the use of film and video in British overseas information work has been limited to commercial publicity, with the political side still done by BBC external radio. The BBC are considering a world satellite television service which would initially transmit two hours of programmes, including 20 minutes of news, to foreign television stations for rebroadcasting. Later, the service would be extended worldwide, 24 hours a day, and would also be beamed directly to viewers' homes. The United States is more advanced in applying the satellite to overseas information work. The United States Information Agency, the equivalent of the Central Office of Information, satellites abroad more than 100 programmes a year. The USIA production 'Let Poland be Poland' was estimated to have been watched by 185 million people, and the programme 'Afghanistan Digest' by an estimated 40 million people in 40 countries. The USIA Worldnet television system, begun in 1983, enables foreign journalists in different capitals to interview US officials simultaneously through one-way video and two-way audio satellite hook-up. For example, on 5 April 1984, 12 hours after President Reagan called for a worldwide ban on chemical weapons, Vice President George Bush, hooked up to US embassies in Western Europe, was explaining the plan to foreign journalists. By 1985 40 US embassies were expected to be linked to the system. Although finance and a lower international profile are both factors against the wide use of the satellite in Britain's information work – the USIA budget for satellite broadcasting in 1984 was $27.5 million – there is the possibility of the required technology being shared among EEC countries.

The satellite has also increased the complexity of political issues in international broadcasting. A 1977 agreement among members of the International Telecommunications Union banned direct broadcasting by satellite across national frontiers on a planned basis without the agreement of the states concerned. While there is nothing stopping, say, the Russians from shooting down the satellite responsible, cross-boundary broadcasting appears likely to continue. If the finances can be found, the development of direct broadcasting by satellite (DBS) will make external television a future possibility. The fears of the communist and developing worlds about DBS may be seen in the 1982 UN resolution establishing rather restrictive principles for it. There is also an ITU agreement under which satellite time is divided up for press use. While countries with large land masses – the USA, Australia, India, China, the USSR and Canada – can regulate their own land stations, smaller countries – including Britain, France, Scandinavia, the Benelux countries, Germany, Austria and Switzerland – need to reach multilateral agreements for press usage of satellite channels. Further developments in telecommunications are likely to increase the instances where the media are the subject of international negotiation and agreement.

The capacity of the computer to store and organise information has contributed to various aspects of media diplomacy. Reporters type their despatches on video display terminals (VDT), which store the despatch until the sub-editor is ready for it, after which the VDT sends the story to be typeset or transmitted. Major news organisations have equipped their foreign and domestic bureaux with them. The more advanced remote job entry (RJE) enables an even greater capacity of transmission between two distant points, between and among computers, terminals, and other devices, and greater independence for the bureaux from the main computer situated in the head office of the news organisation. Already the portable VDT and, to a greater extent, the RJE enable the reporter in the field to send his despatch and pictures by any telephone.

In addition, data base systems enable subscribers to call up a particular page of news on a television screen. In the BBC Ceefax system each page contains 120 words with a maximum of 800 pages (although it can be adapted to transmit an unlimited number). By enabling the interested subscriber to call up international news, data base systems compensate for the lack of international news resulting from editors' perceptions of a lack of public interest. Individual news organisations, including the *Financial Times*, Reuters and UPI, have introduced data base systems. Through its ability to store, sort, and retrieve information the data base system offers the diplomat abroad and the FCO in London revolutionary means for information gathering, political reporting, and analysis – providing that security for transmission between the post and London, and in the opposite direction, can be ensured. So will magnetic tape, and magnetic discs which are faster, and video discs which can be read or written not by a magnet but by a laser, which are still faster and have better storage capacity.

Another technological change in information gathering is the use of video recording machinery by many British posts to monitor local television broadcasting. However, given the expense involved and given that print media can be read by a diplomat at a place of his choosing, the local print media are, depending on their quality and the degree of freedom in each case, likely to remain a preferred source of information. At the level of the wider public, the increase in the number of British homes linked to cable television channels offers the potential for specialised programmes covering international news. Ted Turner's US Cable News Network (CNN), which is a 24-hour-a-day station broadcasting news only, was introduced in Western Europe in 1985 on an experimental basis, and Visnews, the international TV news agency, was in 1985 examining the possibility of a pan-European cable news network.

Although these technological advances have revolutionised the transmission and storage of information, the role of newspapers, radio and TV as gatherers of foreign news will ensure that these remain for the foreseeable future major sources of international news for policymakers. In addition, policymakers will continue to require to monitor these media in order to know what the public are seeing and reading. The role of these media as an information source for policymakers is particularly important during a conflict or diplomatic crisis when as much, and as up-to-date, information as possible is at a premium in order that the most appropriate policy decisions may be taken.

PUBLIC OPINION

The fact that the citizen is able to draw his information from many diverse sources, including television, radio, newspapers, computers and books, makes it more difficult for the policymaker to control the flow of information about foreign affairs from the government. In contrast to the pre-television age when newspaper readers could turn their attention away from foreign news, the viewer of television news is forced to accept the information, and form attitudes on international questions. And debate and discussion, as basic ingredients of broadcasting, encourage this trend. The old situation of only a small informed minority being interested in foreign affairs is likely to make way for a wider public interest, and pressure, on foreign policy. But the lack of background of the mass public on international affairs produces uneducated opinions, swinging between the poles of isolationism and interventionism, making it difficult for the policymaker at the planning stage, and when presenting policy, to assess the likely public reaction. While a greater flow of news has led to some fragmentation of national identity in Britain, and produced less bipartisan support for foreign policy, on basic questions regarding defence of the realm national honour runs deep and can be aroused with little difficulty by politicians and opinion-formers. Despite the questions about the economic and diplomatic value to be gained from fighting for the Falkland Islands, the majority of British public opinion supported the British response to the Argentinian action.

There is no reason to believe that greater public interest will be so intense as to alter the substance of foreign policy. The greater interdependency of states, in economic as well as in other terms, means that external pressures, and the 'national interest' as perceived by policymakers, rather than domestic pressures from the media and the public will determine the substance of foreign policy. Despite the establishment of the House of Commons Select Committee on Foreign Affairs, the executive, notably the FCO and Cabinet Office, dominates foreign policymaking. And the ever growing complexity of modern government means that the civil servant remains in an influential position *vis-à-vis* his minister. Still, there remains a need to widen the access of interest groups and the wider public. The few debates in Parliament on foreign policy fail to cover the entire gamut of international questions, with the result that the legislature fails to fulfil its constitutional role of representing public attitudes on international matters. One means used by the US State Department after the Second World War was to create a division of public opinion studies to analyse public attitudes based on available poll data. Its division of public correspondence reads and responds to letters from the public, some of which are reprinted in the State Department's internal newspaper.

Increased public interest will also produce a need for more information and explanation by the FCO of foreign policy decisions. There are some indications that the FCO are already aware of this. Its relations with the media are less tightly controlled than they were. Part of the work of the News Department is to advise the geographical and functional departments when planning policy on likely media and public reactions, and to plan themselves how to react to events. Of course, not all international events are predictable. Although the problem of the FCO's public responsiveness has been, and remains, attitudinal, it is also a legislative one. A reform of the Official Secrets Act is unlikely to affect the flow of information from the government about foreign policy because matters affecting defence and security would probably still be covered by the act. The onus of proof rests with the media. Under a Freedom of Information Act, however, there would be access to a welter of analytical and factual material. Although matters of security would be excluded, the onus of proof would rest with the government. The Labour government's 1978 White Paper, which replied to the Berrill Report on overseas representation, accepted the principle of making foreign policy less secretive:

The Government, in support of their overall objective of providing a more open and accessible administration, are making a special effort to explain publicly the objectives of our foreign policy. This is done in Parliament, through the media and in a multiplicity of international bodies.[5]

While the background papers produced by the FCO, as well as the Select Committee on Foreign Affairs, have resulted in more information there remains a lack of debate about basic policy assumptions, such as the special relationship with the USA or with the Commonwealth. The FCO responds to, rather than initiates, any debate about policy. Officials say this belongs to the ministerial domain, but given the day-to-day duties of the minister in government, Parliament, and his party, this is more theory than practice. Officials claim (correctly) that being less secretive would entail more work in preparing press releases and so on, and thus more staff. They also fear that greater access by the media, and the public, will result in criticism of government policy. Although the relationship between a democratic government and a free media is, by definition, antagonistic, it is incorrect to assume that only criticism of policy would result, rather than understanding or praise as well.

Some of the attitudinal problem would be overcome by certain changes in the administrative structure of the News Department. While there is a 'News' Department to handle inquiries from news organisations, there is no Public Affairs Office to deal with inquiries from the public. The State Department has a number of divisions responsible for public liaison. One prepares printed and film material for distribution to interested groups, educational institutions, and the wider public. Another supplies these with speakers from the department's staff.

The structural changes which would enable the FCO to supply these public services (as well as those for receiving inputs from the public and interest groups, referred to earlier) could be achieved in three ways:

1. The existing News Department could be enlarged to become the Public Affairs and News Media Department, incorporating four units for (a) the analysis of public trends and responding to letters from the public; (b) liaison between the Office and interested groups; (c) preparation and distribution of printed, tape, and film material on foreign policy issues; and (d) the existing News Department function of briefing journalists. Such a department would have a staff of 25 officials, plus support staff, and would include the existing News Department spokesmen (about 12), four or five officials to liaise with interest groups, two or three for preparing public opinion studies, and four or five for the distribution of material and for arranging FCO staff to address interested groups and educational institutions.

2. The News Department would continue to function as at present. Given its function, the unit for liaison with interested groups and the wider public would best be situated in the office of the foreign secretary, as would the unit analysing public opinion trends. Alternatively, these could be part of the permanent under-secretary's department. A unit or department responsible for producing and distributing information materials could be located within the Information Policy Department.

3. Most of the officials in the News Department would be moved to the geographical and functional departments, leaving a small department of three or four officials headed by the spokesman. By having the spokesman who specialises in certain regions situated in the relevant department/s, he or she is better informed about policy and the flow of policy decisions, and better able to provide daily input into the relevant department's discussions. Given the differences in outlook between those in the News Department responsible for explaining foreign policy at home and those in the Information Policy Department responsible for overseas information, he or she will be able to provide a coordinating role. This proposal is based on the State Department's structure. It is true that the present structure of the News Department ensures that inquiries from the media are centralised to one point in the Office and that a single line is given out. However, there is coordination between

the State Department's press office and the public affairs officials in the various bureaux. In addition to its coordinatory function, a News Department reduced in size would be responsible for the Office's statements, for directing inquiries to the relevant officials, and for advising the foreign secretary on media trends.

With the exception of a separate unit producing and distributing information materials, these changes could be achieved without financial outlay.

The level of understanding of international affairs is not only determined by the FCO. The public's image is also determined by the media. If the popular press and some broadcasting fail to give time and space to international news, complaints by the media and others about the lack of access to the FCO lose some of their validity. If editors complain that their hands are tied by a lack of public interest, part of the solution lies in encouraging school education in contemporary international politics. While courses in history, geography and the social sciences include some aspects of international politics, the subject's complexity requires that specific analytical tools and topics, including defence doctrines, alliances, arms control approaches, and the role of international organisations, to name but a few, be understood by the student within the framework of a school course on International Relations.

BRITISH DIPLOMACY

Other developments in media diplomacy will be the results of change in the machinery and profession of diplomacy, in the nature of the international news media, and in the condition of world politics and British foreign policy goals. The reduction in Britain's international position means that there is less need to gather information comprehensively from all parts of the world. Its information requirements include those regarding its bilateral relations, the European Economic Community, and those countries posing a threat to its interests, including the Soviet Union and certain Third World countries.

Britain's information programme abroad is more complex. Cuts in information programmes have been based partly on a perceived lesser need to disseminate information given the reduction in Britain's role. The emphasis on commercial publicity, however, is appropriate not simply because of the importance of export promotion but also because economic power is a primary determinant of a state's international position. The dilemma reflects the wider question about Britain's future overseas representation. Although the diplomatic service accounts for only 0.5 per cent of public expenditure, some, including the Berrill

Report, have argued that Britain's decline abroad would suggest less excellent Excellencies.[6] Yet, there are those who argue that the reduction in Britain's territorial power abroad requires that other forms of influence be discovered to replace it, which would call for increased rather than reduced information work. Furthermore, some generalised image projection, in addition to the commercial publicity, is required because unless there is a high regard for Britain the information machinery will be unable to perform its task effectively when particular policy objectives do arise.

The dilemma about information work also partly reflects doubts about, and difficulties in measuring, its effectiveness. While listener surveys of external broadcasting may measure audiences for these programmes, there is a need to relate listening to its effect on relations with Britain. The number of inquiries or sales of a particular product do indicate the success of a publicity campaign. An accumulation of such studies, whether about products or about political or cultural information work, enable some general inferences about information effectiveness to be drawn. Britain's membership in the EEC has, surprisingly, not produced substantial change in the information programme. Patterns of external broadcasting among member countries have not altered. Plans for a programme on European affairs, to be jointly produced and broadcast in the various countries, failed to materialise. EEC governments jointly produce a 30-minute programme for distribution in the developing world. There is a case for greater coordination in some countries, including many Third World and communist countries, where EEC countries do not need to project a national image but rather a western, or European, image extolling such values as democracy and freedom. EEC countries should concentrate on those countries and regions where they are most credible, e.g. Britain in East Africa and France in West Africa.

What type of training should tomorrow's 'media diplomat' be given? Whereas post-war recruits to Britain's diplomatic service have learnt about public relations mostly on the job, the sophistication of mass communications argues for a specific course of training for all diplomats. It would include simulating interviews and speeches on closed circuit television on an array of topics such as British policy in Northern Ireland, EEC policy, or the virtues of British products. Public relations experts and foreign correspondents should be invited to address the group. Just as it is an error not to train every diplomat, from the ambassador downwards, in media techniques, it is also an error for a diplomat to spend much of his career in different informational functions because of the need to gain the intellectual roughage of thinking about policy — the diplomat's basic job — which can only be done in the geographical or functional departments at home or their equivalent in the embassy abroad.

Among those responsible for information policy there is an appreciation of only some of the strategic dimensions of propaganda. It took until the Berrill Report to bring home the obvious key role which foreign correspondents in London play in moulding Britain's image. Or, while officials recognise that some of Britain's negative image abroad as a place to invest in is caused by the British media seen abroad, few solutions have been found. Even government inquiries on overseas representation and on the information agencies failed to discuss the positive and negative roles played by media exports from Britain. Partly, this is due to a lack of long-term planning and coordination. Overseas information work is planned separately from the daily reactive work of the News Department. And the effects of the media are assessed elsewhere, in the geographical and functional departments. The supervising under-secretary responsible for the information departments at whose level long-term planning should be done has tended to be concerned about matters which could be dealt with at the departmental level, including whether there are adequate facilities for the foreign press corps in London, and responding to complaints by foreign governments over BBC broadcasts.[7] But partly, the absence of planning is to be traced to the notion of minimal interference, or keeping government involvement in the media at home and abroad to a minimum. Indeed, the BBC's success in maintaining a worldwide audience despite Britain's decline abroad is a result of the perception that the government does not control its editorial output. This lesson has not been lost in Washington where some officials advocate a weakening of government control over the information agencies including the Voice of America. And partly the absence of planning is explained by the fact that a government cannot entirely control its image abroad. A former under-secretary for information noted:

From time to time we used to produce papers defining the sort of image it was that we wanted this country to present to the world at large, or some particular part of it. But the pieces from which this image was to be created in day-to-day propaganda could not be produced at will; at best they could only be selected as and when suitable items became available in the news, and there would always be some awkward pieces lying around which just did not fit into the picture we wanted to present.[8]

The relationship between the media and diplomacy is already reaching its optimum. Notwithstanding future technological innovation, the flow of international news has reached a peak with instant live coverage of foreign events, and with specialist media dealing with international affairs. In terms of the image of the world conveyed, more coverage of the Third World as a result of the UNESCO debate and a wider range of themes as a result of rising educational standards may produce a more accurate image, contributing to greater understanding across national boundaries and less chauvinism. But this will be limited by the natural human interest in crisis and war, and by limitations of access imposed by governments on foreign journalists. Whatever the increase in public interest in international affairs, the media's influence on foreign policy will be limited by Britain's growing interdependency with other countries. There will remain a need to explain foreign policy to the public at home, and while the principle of secrecy in diplomacy has been truly breached, a Freedom of Information Act is required to make the principle of open government a meaningful one. Abroad, the idea that every diplomat, not just 'the spokesman', is involved in public relations is accepted. The world of media diplomacy has become a global information village in which the public utterances of a government official are picked up instantly in foreign capitals. The glamour associated with meetings of heads of state will ensure that such meetings have a long life ahead of them. Yet the greater media exposure, and public pressures resulting therefrom, have resulted in a tendency among diplomats who are involved in planning policy and in negotiation towards ultra-secretiveness.

NOTES

CHAPTER ONE – INTRODUCTION

1. Joe Haines, *The Politics of Power*, London, Jonathan Cape 1977, pp. 74–81, 92–3.
2. Terence Prittie, *Through Irish Eyes: a journalist's memoirs*, London, Bachman & Turner 1977, p. 269. The Soames affair is also discussed in Richard Crossman, *The Diaries of a Cabinet Minister*, Vol. 3, London, Hamish Hamilton and Jonathan Cape 1977, pp. 378–9; Uwe Kitzinger, *Diplomacy and Persuasion*, London, Thames & Hudson 1973; Kenneth Lamb, 'Disclosure, Discretion, and Dissemblement; Broadcasting and the National Interest in the Perspective of a Publicly Owned Medium' in Thomas Franck and Edward Weisband, eds., *Secrecy and Foreign Policy*, New York, Oxford 1974, pp. 233–4; and Harold Wilson, *The Labour Government 1964–70: A Personal Record*, London, Weidenfeld & Nicolson and Michael Joseph 1971, p. 618.
3. For example, John C. Farrell and Asa P. Smith, eds., *Images and Reality in World Politics*, New York, Columbia University Press 1967.
4. Jeremy Tunstall, *Journalists at Work*, London, Constable 1971.
5. Leon V. Sigal, *Reporters and Officials*, Lexington, Mass., D.C. Heath 1973.
6. Chris Argyris, *Behind the Front Page*, San Francisco, Jossey Bass 1974.
7. Gabriel Almond, *The American People and Foreign Policy*, New York, Praeger 1960, pp. 137–9.
8. William L. Rivers, Susan Miller and Oscar Gandy, 'Government and the Media', in Steven H. Chaffee, ed., *Political Communication: Issues and Strategies for Research*, California, Sage 1975.
9. Dan Nimmo, *Newsgathering in Washington*, New York, Prentice-Hall 1964.
10. William O. Chittick, *State Department, press and pressure groups*, New York, John Wiley 1970.
11. James Rosenau, *Public Opinion and Foreign Policy*, New York, Random House 1961.
12. Colin Seymour-Ure, *The political impact of mass media*, London, Constable 1974.
13. The main academic studies dealing with foreign policymaking in Britain are James Barber, *Who Makes British Foreign Policy?*, Milton Keynes, The Open University Press 1976; Donald Bishop, *The Administration of British Foreign Relations*, Syracuse, Syracuse University Press 1961; Robert Boardman and A. J. R. Groom, eds., *The Management of Britain's External Relations*, London, Macmillan 1972; David Vital, *The Making of British Foreign Policy*, London, George Allen & Unwin 1968; William Wallace, *The Foreign Policy Process in Britain*, London, George Allen & Unwin 1976. Three government inquiries examined the machinery of Britain's overseas representation: the 1962–3 *Committee on Representational Services Overseas* (the Plowden Report), London, HMSO 1964, the 1968–9 *Review Committee on Overseas Representation* (the Duncan Report), London, HMSO 1969, and the 1976–7 *Review of Overseas Representation* (the Berrill Report), London, HMSO 1977. An early post-war study of the work of the Foreign Office is by Lord Strang, a former permanent under-secretary of the Foreign Office: *The Foreign Office*, London, George Allen & Unwin 1955. A more popular work is Geoffrey Moorhouse's *The Diplomats: The Foreign Office Today*, London, Jonathan Cape 1977. Of all these studies, only Barber, Bishop, and Boardman and Groom have chapters dealing specifically with the media. Barber discusses the image of the world conveyed by the media, and the relationship between the media and public opinion. Bishop, whose book is based on historical sources, considers the influence of public opinion. Elliott and Golding, who contributed the chapter on the media in Boardman and Groom, concentrate on the media's image of the world.

With the exception of Wallace, none of the academic studies examine the use of the media as a source of information in foreign policymaking, because they regard the media as just one of various contributors to the information flow. Nor is it examined in the government inquiries. In addition to Elliott and Golding, and to Barber, Denis Quail has researched the image of foreign affairs of the British national daily press ('Foreign Affairs Content in National Daily and 2 Scottish Newspapers 1975' in *Analysis of Newspaper Content*, the 1977 Royal Commission on the Press, London, HMSO 1977).

The roles of public opinion, interest groups, and Parliament in the formulation of British foreign policy have been dealt with. The relationship of the media to each of these is mostly ignored. Peter G. Richards (*Parliament and Foreign Affairs*, London, George Allen & Unwin 1967) fails to discuss the use of the media by MPs as a source of information or as a channel to the public. Barber, and Wallace, who deal with the role of interest groups, do not discuss their use of the media to gain public support. Barber, Joseph Frankel (*British Foreign Policy 1945–73*, London, Oxford 1975), and Wallace in considering the role of public opinion fail to relate the formulation of public opinion to the media. Christopher Hill ('Public Opinion and British Foreign Policy since 1945: Research in Progress', *Millenium*, Vol. 10, No. 1, 1981) has bemoaned the unrigorous treatment of public opinion in research on British foreign policy.

The use by ministers and officials of disclosures to the media to advance or hinder foreign policy objectives has not been dealt with. The extensive use of disclosures in British domestic politics is discussed by Richard Crossman (*The Diaries of a Cabinet Minister*, Vol. 2 and 3, London, Hamish Hamilton and Jonathan Cape 1976 and 1977), by Colin Seymour-Ure (*The Press, Politics and the Media*, London, Methuen 1968), by Jeremy Tunstall (*The Westminster Lobby Correspondents*, London, Routledge 1970), and Michael Cockerell, Peter Hennessy and David Walker (*Sources Close to the Prime Minister*, London, Macmillan 1984).

Whereas most of the academic studies discuss in depth the formulation of foreign policy, few discuss its implementation. Thus the role of the media in, for example, signalling to other governments or manoeuvring during international negotiation, is not dealt with. The objectives, structure, and costs of the overseas information services are discussed by the Plowden, Duncan, and Berrill reports, and by the 1954 *Summary of the Report of the Independent Committee of Inquiry into the Overseas Information Service* (the Drogheda Report), London, HMSO 1954. Literature dealing with specific branches of the information programme, including the BBC External Services and the Central Office of Information, adds to the picture. Publications on the BBC External Services include Gerald Mansell, *Let the Truth Be Told: 50 Years of BBC External Broadcasting*, London, Weidenfeld & Nicolson 1982; Gerald Mansell, *Broadcasting to the world: forty years of BBC External Services*, London, BBC 1973; Gerald Mansell, *Why External Broadcasting?*, BBC Lunchtime Lecture 11.3.1976; James Monahan, *Broadcasting to Europe*, BBC Lunchtime Lecture 9.10.1963; Robert Gregson, *Broadcasting and the Third World*, BBC Lunchtime Lecture 23.11.1976. Publications dealing with the Central Office of Information include Sir Fife Clark, *The Central Office of Information*, London, George Allen & Unwin 1970; and Marjorie Ogilvy-Webb, *The Government Explains*, London, George Allen & Unwin 1965. Sir Douglas Marett (*Through the Back Door*, Oxford, Pergamon 1968), who spent his working life in information work in the Foreign Office, provides a useful insider's account of information work. The relationship between the FCO News Department and the diplomatic correspondents of the British media is described by Bishop, Seymour-Ure and Cockerell, Hennessy and Walker.

The dearth of literature on media diplomacy in Britain contrasts with the United States where a number of studies dealing specifically with the subject have appeared. Yet gaps remain there as well. As the title suggests, Bernard C. Cohen's *The Press and Foreign Policy*, Princeton, Princeton University Press 1963, concentrates on the press. He does not examine the differences between the effects of the press and those of radio, television, and news agencies; nor do Chittick, op. cit., Sigal, op. cit. Other aspects of media diplomacy not dealt with by these authors include the roles of overseas media as a source of information and in information work. Least covered is the bureaucratic use of the media among competing policymakers. Exceptions include Chittick, op. cit., and Morton Halperin,

Bureaucratic Politics and Foreign Policy, Washington DC, The Brookings Institute 1974. Nor is the usage of the media by governments to signal, and manoeuvre, examined widely. Exceptions include Sigal, op. cit. and W. Phillips Davison, 'News media and international negotiations', *Public Opinion Quarterly*, Summer 1974.

CHAPTER TWO – ORIGINS

1. Quoted in Sir Arthur Willert, 'Publicity and Propaganda in International Affairs', *International Affairs*, Nov.–Dec. 1938, p. 810.
2. Michael Palmer, 'The British press and international news, 1851–99: of agencies and newspapers', in George Boyce, James Curran and Pauline Wingate, eds., *Newspaper history: from the 17th century to the present day*, London, Constable 1978.
3. Phillip Knightley, *The First Casualty. From the Crimea to Vietnam: The War Correspondent as Hero, Propagandist and Mythmaker*, New York, Harcourt Brace and Jovanovitch 1975.
4. Philip Schlesinger, *Putting reality together: BBC news*, London, Constable 1978, Ch. 2.
5. Hans Morgenthau, 'The Permanent Values in the Old Diplomacy', in I. Kersetz and M. A. Fitzsimmons, eds., *Diplomacy in a Changing World*, Indiana, University of Notre Dame Press 1959.
6. R. B. Mowat, *Diplomacy and Peace*, London, Williams & Norgate 1935, Ch. 4.
7. Zarah Steiner, *The Foreign Office and Foreign Policy 1898–1914*, London, Cambridge 1969, pp. 186–8.
8. Sir Robert Marett, *Through the Back Door: An Inside View of Britain's Overseas Information Services*, Oxford, Pergamon 1968, pp. 123–7.
9. Kennedy Jones, *Fleet Street and Downing Street*, London, Hutchinson 1919, pp. 96–7.
10. *Parliamentary Debates*, House of Commons, 11 Nov. 1911, Vol. 32, Column 564.
11. Miss Shaw later married a Captain Lugard who had been a colonial administrator in Aden and India. As Lord Lugard he was appointed governor of British territory in West Africa. The territory had no name and Miss Shaw, now Lady Lugard, gave it the name of 'Nigeria'.
12. Thomas Barman, 'A Diplomatic correspondent's look back', *The Listener* 4.1.1967.
13. Colin Lovelace, 'British press censorship during the First World War' in Boyce, Curran and Wingate, op. cit.
14. Donald McLachlan, *In the Chair: Barrington-Ward of The Times*, London, Weidenfeld & Nicolson 1971, pp. 128–9.
15. John Douglas Pringle, *Have Pen: Will Travel*, London, Chatto & Windus 1973, p. 61.
16. Thomas Barman, *Diplomatic Correspondent*, London, Hamish Hamilton 1968, p. 192.
17. William Clark, 'Cabinet Secrecy, Collective Responsibility and the British Public's Right to Know and Participate in Foreign Policy', in Thomas M. Franck and Edward Weisband, eds., *Secrecy and Foreign Policy*, New York, Oxford 1974, p. 207.

CHAPTER THREE – INFORMATION

1. *The Times*, 16.4.1984.
1a. *The Guardian*, 17.6.1971.
2. William Wallace, *The Foreign Policy Process in Britain*, London, Royal Institute of International Affairs and George Allen & Unwin 1976, p. 63.
2a. Cord Meyer, 'The Collectors', in *Facing Reality: From World Federalism to the CIA*, New York, Harper & Row 1980.
3. Survey by Freedom House, New York, reported *UK Press Gazette*, 8.1.1979.
4. Sir Humphrey Trevelyan, *Diplomatic Channels*, London, Macmillan, 1973.
5. Bernard C. Cohen, *The Press and Foreign Policy*, Princeton, Princeton University Press 1963, p. 141.
6. Nils Orvik et al., *Departmental Decision-making*, Oslo, Universitetsforlaget 1972, Ch. 7.
7. W. E. Skurnick, *The Foreign Policy of Senegal*, Evanston, Northwestern University Press 1972, pp. 73–4.

8. Frederick Forsyth, *The Biafra Story*, London, Penguin, 1969, p. 224.
9. Terence Prittie, *Through Irish Eyes: a journalist's memoirs*, London, Bachman & Turner 1977, p. 267.
10. *Review Committee on Overseas Representation*, London, HMSO 1969, pp. 53–4.
11. Central Policy Review Staff, *Review of Overseas Representation*, London, HMSO 1977, Ch. 15 Para. 19, and Ch. 7 Para. 24a.
12. *Review Committee on Overseas Representation*, op. cit., p. 54.
13. Written evidence to the House of Commons Defence and External Affairs Subcommittee in *Fourth Report from the Expenditure Committee*, Session 1977–8, *The Central Policy Review Staff of Overseas Representation; Volume II: Minutes of Evidence and Appendices*, London, HMSO, 1978, p. 55.
14. Trevelyan, op. cit., p. 85.
15. Based on Denis McQuail's content analysis of foreign news coverage of the British press over a two-week period in 1975 (*Analysis of Newspaper Content*, Research Series 4 of the 1977 Royal Commission on the Press), the usefulness of the media for the various departments of the FCO and for the different types of work was examined.

In terms of the diplomatic reporting of Britain's bilateral and multilateral relations there is no evidence that the media could substitute for it. Of the 2,520 items on foreign affairs which appeared during this two-week period, those concerning British bilateral and multilateral relations were: Britain and the Soviet Union, 35 items; Britain and the EEC, 21; Britain and Africa, 21; Britain and the USA, 14; Britain and France, 13; Britain and Eastern Europe, 11; and Britain and the Middle East, 10. A further 321 items about events occurring abroad involved Britain or British people or interests, and 154 items occurring in Britain had a foreign angle.

As regards supplying background information, 60% of the 2,520 items concerned international, political, economic, or defence subjects; the other 40% concerned entertainment, crime, and legal matters. FCO departments responsible for European and North American affairs are able to rely on the media because 58% of the 1500 items on international political, economic, or defence subjects were located there. However, those departments responsible for Latin American and Australasian affairs are unable to rely on the media. Only 3% of the items were located in Latin America and 3% in Australasia. 12% of the items were located in Africa, 11% in Asia, and 10% in the Middle East.

In the case of the FCO's functional departments, 19% of the 1500 items covered trade, economic, financial, and industrial subjects, 8% military and defence subjects, and 1% aid and development. Those departments concerned with these subjects do not require as many alternative sources of information as other departments including Science and Technology, Marine and Transport, and Western Organisations. All of the functional departments are able to draw on a broad range of more specialised and technical media.

The media have a particular contribution to make during crises. 33% of the 2,520 items in the sample concerned foreign policy: 20% for international, political or diplomatic, 5% for violent or revolutionary conflict, 4% for non-violent, constitutional conflict or crisis, 3% for armed conflict, and 1% for peace moves. With a wider definition of 'foreign policy' as being about a foreign event or action, the number of items in this category was 59% of the total.

The post-war years have seen a large increase in the economic work of overseas representation, which now includes export promotion, capital flows to and from Britain, and representational functions at such international organisations as the EEC, IMF, and UNCTAD. Home government departments and the Bank of England require data about international economics and finance in planning and managing economic, fiscal and industrial policy. Much of the data required are available from the IMF, OECD, IBRD, foreign governments, and central banks but the British national and specialised press are important secondary sources of information. These include the *Financial Times, The Times*, and *The Economist*; 19% of all items concerned economic, trade, financial, and industrial subjects.

In defence work there is a need for information about the armed forces of countries with which there is a possibility of Britain becoming involved militarily, such as East European countries, neighbouring states to Britain's remaining dependent territories, and countries where Britain is involved in peacemaking operations. There is in addition a need for limited background information about the armed forces of other countries. The national media are unable to provide adequate information for any of these; of the items examined only 205 items or 8% concerned defence or military matters. Specialised journals, however, such as *Flight International*, may be useful for some background reporting.

16. Patrick Gordon Walker, 'Secrecy and Openness in Foreign Policy Decisionmaking; a British Cabinet Perspective', in Thomas Franck and Edward Weisband, eds., *Secrecy and Foreign Policy*, New York, Oxford 1974, p. 44.

17. In early 1967 the prime minister, Harold Wilson, and the foreign secretary, George Brown, toured West European capitals to sound out opinion about the possibility and conditions for British entry. At the cabinet meeting following their return Denis Healey and Barbara Castle criticised the Wilson and Brown account of their visit as making too much of their success. Richard Crossman wrote of the cabinet meeting of April 23 that 'I said that one of the things we should certainly want to know more than anything else is the assessment of the situation in Europe made by our Ambassadors in the various capitals. Should we not recall them for a special meeting with the Cabinet? This raised the alarm that I was told that it would alert the general public. I had asked for the (cabinet) meeting because I'd been reading the telegrams from Paris and Bonn very carefully and I've noticed that for weeks there's been nothing in them about either the European reaction to our entry or the Ambassadors' assessments of our chances. I now gather that a special instruction was sent out cutting off the confidential telegrams on this subject for four or five weeks. I have tried to insist that everything relevant should be collected and presented to us before next Saturday's Common Market meeting but I know that it won't be' (Richard Crossman, *The Diaries of a Cabinet Minister*, Vol. 2, London, Hamish Hamilton and Jonathan Cape, 1976).

    Wilson and Brown, writing before the Crossman Diaries were published, denied that information to the cabinet was suppressed. George Brown noted that 'voluminous records of all our talks had to be taken to satisfy suspicious colleagues in the Cabinet' (George Brown, *In My Way*, London, Gollancz, 1971, pp. 21, 219). Harold Wilson wrote that after he returned from Europe 'colleagues had by this time had the opportunity to study every word of the discussions in the six capitals. A further series of authoritative papers, some of them very lengthy and on almost every issue raised, was prepared for circulation'. With one exception 'all the papers were prepared, without ministerial intervention by the special unit I had set up in the Cabinet Office under Mr (later Sir) William Neild with experts drawn from the departments. Individual ministers who wanted to circulate their own papers were not precluded from doing so ... Where any asked for more information, or a further paper – or for a matter to come back to us for reconsideration – this was agreed ... By the last week of April I felt that the Cabinet discussions were reaching the point where my colleagues would soon be ready to take a decision. Even those who pressed for more and more information were silent' (Harold Wilson, *The Labour Government 1964–70: A personal record*, op. cit., pp. 386–8).

18. BBC Audience Research Report: *Studies of the Impact of the Radio and Television Coverage of the EEC Referendum Campaign*, London, BBC, Jan. 1976, pp. 35–6.

19. Social and Community Planning Research, *Attitudes to the Press*, Research Series 3; 1977 Royal Commission on the Press, London, HMSO 1977, p. 31.

20. *European Business Readership Survey 1978*, based on a survey among 1,455 of 43,924 senior British businessmen.

21. Anthony Barker and Michael Rush, *The Member of Parliament and his Information*, London, George Allen and Unwin 1970, pp. 35–6.

22. Bernard C. Cohen, op. cit., p. 216.

23. R. M. Punnett, *Front Bench Opposition*, London, Heinemann 1973, pp. 278–285.

24. Barker and Rush, op. cit., p. 245.

25. Finance can also be a factor in the number of British publications subscribed to. The United Nations Association in 1979 considered cancelling its subscription to *The Economist* in order to subscribe to the *International Herald Tribune*.

CHAPTER FOUR – IMAGE OF THE WORLD

1. A survey of space/time given to foreign affairs during one week in April 1971 found that 37% each of BBC TV's nine o'clock news and ITN's 'News at Ten' was given to foreign affairs, 34% of BBC Radio 4's 'The World Tonight', 22% of quality newspapers, and 10% of popular papers. Philip Elliott and Peter Golding, 'News Media and Foreign Affairs' in Robert Boardman and A. J. R. Groom, eds., *The Management of Britain's External Relations*, London, Macmillan 1973, p. 31.

2. Television was considered the most useful source of foreign affairs information by 58% of people, the national daily morning press by 24%, the national Sunday press by 5%, national radio by 8%, the local evening press by 2%, the local weekly press by less than 1%, and local radio and magazines each by 1%. Social and Community Planning Research, *Attitudes to the Press*, Research Series 3, 1977, 1977 Royal Commission on the Press, London, HMSO 1977, p. 31.

3. A study by the author of BBC World Service news bulletins during the first twenty-four hours of the 1973 Arab-Israeli war found that although the BBC received 34 despatches from its own correspondents in the Middle East and major world capitals (comprising 18 despatches from BBC correspondents in Jerusalem and Beirut, and the remainder from Cairo, Washington, the UN, London, and Paris) the news sources used in preparing news bulletins were chiefly news agencies. Correspondents were used to interpret developments within news bulletins, in 'Radio Newsreel' and other programmes.

4. John Crawley, *The Work of a BBC Foreign Correspondent*, BBC Lunchtime Lecture, 14.10.1974, p. 9.

5. Edwin Samuel, 'The Administration of The Times' in *Public Administration in Israel and Abroad*, Vol. 14, 1973, pp. 224–7.

6. International Press Institute, *IPI Report*, June 1978, p. 16.

7. 'South Africa turns screw on pressmen', *Sunday Times*, 31.10.1976.

8. Desmond Taylor, Editor of BBC News and Current Affairs, addressing the Broadcasting and Press Guild, Daily Telegraph, 15.9.1976.

9. Confidential minutes of meetings of BBC news and current affairs executives, chaired by the BBC Director-General, 18.1.1976, pp. 10–11; and *BBC Handbook 1977*.

10. Ibid., 18.6.1976, pp. 1–2.

11. Denis McQuail, *Analysis of Newspaper Content*, Research Series 4 of the 1977 Royal Commission on the Press, London, HMSO 1977, pp. 251–2.

12. Ibid., p. 262.

13. Ibid., p. 272.

14. Ibid., p. 254.

15. Elliott and Golding, op. cit., p. 318.

16. Chris Mullin, 'The war Smith is winning', *New Statesman*, 19.1.1979.

17. L. N. Gould, *The ENDC and the Press*, Stockholm, Almquist and Wiksell 1969.

18. North America was the second most covered region in Reuters, UPI, and AFP. Western Europe and North America accounted for over half of all despatches on Reuters, AP, and UPI. Reuters and AP gave approximately equal attention to the Middle East and Far East (8–12% of despatches) and UPI gave considerably more attention to the Middle East and Africa than the Far East. AFP gave considerable coverage to the Far East and Africa accounting for about a fifth of total output. Eastern Europe received little attention (4–10% of all despatches) although more than Latin America (2–7%). Australasia and Oceania received 0–1%. Oliver Boyd Barrett, 'The Collection of Foreign News in the British Press', in *Studies on the Press*, 1977 Royal Commission on the Press, London, HMSO, pp. 41–2. Of *The Times'* 15 foreign correspondents in 1984 seven were based in Western Europe and North America. The remainder were in Argentina, India, Israel, Lebanon, Poland, Singapore, South Africa, and the Soviet Union.

19. Boyd Barrett, op. cit.

20. The imbalance in the distribution of staff correspondents was somewhat redressed by the distribution of the part-time stringer correspondents. According to Boyd Barrett's study, carried out in 1976, 28% of the stringers of *The Times*, the *Financial Times*, *The Guardian*, and the *Daily Telegraph* were based in Western Europe, 19% in the Far East, 16% in Africa,

10% in Latin America, 11% in the Middle East, 6% in Australasia/Oceania, 5% in North America and 3% in the Soviet Union and Eastern Europe (Boyd Barrett, op. cit., pp. 21–2). Since, however, much of the copy received and used by the newspapers tends to come from staff correspondents, whose output has to justify the heavy investment made by the news organisation, the imbalance in the image of the world presented to readers remains.

21. Social and Community Planning Research, *Attitudes to the Press*, 1977 Royal Commission on the Press, Research Series 3, London, HMSO 1977, p. 29.
22. Connie M. Kristiansen, Gary Fowlie and Susan J. Spencer, 'Britain's Broadcast Coverage of the Soviet Invasion of Afghanistan', *Journalism Quarterly*, Winter 1982.
23. British Business for World Markets (an anti-EEC interest group), *The Press and the Common Market*, March 1975.
24. BBC Audience Research Report: *Studies of the Impact of the Radio and Television Coverage of the EEC Referendum Campaign*, London, BBC, Jan. 1976.
25. Glasgow University Media Group, *Really Bad News*, London, Writers' and Readers' Publishing Cooperative 1982, pp. 14–15.
26. Articles by John Birt and Peter Jay, *The Times*, 28.2.1975, 30.9.1975, 1.10.1975, 2.9.1976 and 3.9.1976.
27. BBC General Advisory Council, *The task of broadcasting news*, London, BBC, 1976, pp. 15–17.
28. For a discussion of the Birt–Jay thesis see Philip Schlesinger *Putting 'reality' together: BBC News*, London, Constable 1978, Ch. 9.
29. Boyd Barrett, op. cit., p. 16. In 1983 the BBC desired to appoint a staff correspondent in West Africa based in Lagos. But the Nigerian government asked the BBC for an initial deposit of £¼ m comprising five years rent in advance. Unwilling to pay, the BBC based their correspondent instead in Abidjan, the Ivory Coast.
30. Elihu Katz, 'Media Events: The Sense of Occasion', paper presented at the Second World Encounter on Communication, Acapulco, July 1979.
31. Marshall McLuhan, *Understanding Media*, New York, McGraw Hill, 1964.

CHAPTER FIVE – PUBLIC OPINION

1. David Vital, *The Making of British Foreign Policy*, London, George Allen & Unwin 1968, pp. 84–5.
2. Dr Chaim Weizmann, a science lecturer at Manchester University, met C. P. Scott for the first time at a tea party in Manchester in 1914. As a result of this and of subsequent meetings Scott became a keen advocate of the Zionist cause. In December 1914 Scott put Weizmann in touch with Lloyd George. Advising Weizmann how to obtain an appointment with the latter, Scott said 'Lloyd George attends to telegrams, he does not attend to letters'. In January 1916 Scott advised Weizmann, 'Now was the time for pressing the matter when British troops were actually on Palestine soil'. Scott persuaded Weizmann not to leave London for Egypt as he had planned until the British government committed itself to a declaration of policy in favour of Britain keeping Palestine rather than exchanging it with the French for other parts of the Ottoman empire.

As a result of his contacts and sources, Scott informed Weizmann of the planned Sykes–Picot agreement by which Britain and France were planning to divide up Palestine in a way which might be detrimental to Jewish plans for a homeland. Scott subsequently made inquiries to Lord Milner, the colonial secretary, about the proposed agreement. The answer convinced Scott that only a provisional agreement was in the air, which could be set aside.

When Weizmann moved to London to work at the Ministry of Munitions, where he made some important breakthroughs in the use of acetone, Scott and Weizmann still met and corresponded fairly frequently. 'It became a practice with me, whenever I happened to be in London, and Mr Scott came up on the night train, to meet him at Euston Station', Weizmann wrote. From Aug. 1914 to Oct. 1917 (a month before the British government announced the Balfour Declaration granting a homeland to the Jews in Palestine), the two men corresponded 31 times, 11 of them in the 10 months leading up to the Declaration.

Scott met Lloyd George on 43 occasions from Aug. 1914 to Nov. 1917, usually for lunch or breakfast. Lloyd George looked on Scott as an adviser. At most of these meetings the main topic of conversation was the ongoing war. Zionism and Palestine was discussed at five of them but was never the sole topic of conversation between the two men. Sometimes Scott brought a guest to these meetings; he brought Weizmann to six of them, although Zionism only came up at three of them. Weizmann's progress in researching acetone came up at four. The closest Scott appears to have come to influencing the Balfour Declaration was at lunch in Spring 1917 when Scott pressed Lloyd George for a definite statement by the government in favour of Palestine being a home for the Jews. It would be wrong to exaggerate Scott's role in the developments leading to the Balfour Declaration in light of Zionist activity involving other individuals, including another journalist, Herbert Sidebotham of *The Times*. But the case of C. P. Scott offers an insight into the overlap between interest groups, the press, and politicians.

(David Ayerst, *Guardian: Biography of a Newspaper*, London, Collins 1971, pp. 381−6; Meyer W. Weisgal, ed., *The Letters and Papers of Chaim Weizmann, Volume VII, Series A, August 1914 − November 1917*, London, Oxford 1975; Chaim Weizmann, *Trial and Error*, Greenwood, Conn. 1972, p. 150; Trevor Wilson, ed., *The Diaries of C. P. Scott 1911−1928*, London, Collins 1970, p. 258; S. H. Zebel, *Balfour: a political biography*, Cambridge 1973, p. 242).

3. William O. Chittick, *State Department, press and pressure groups*, New York, John Wiley 1970, pp. 222−5 and 262−7.

4. *The Times* dislikes publishing letters on something that an MP could say in the House of Commons, and prefers letters from MPs on something which has appeared in the newspaper. Jeremy Tunstall, 'Letters to the Editor', in *Studies on the Press*, 1977 Royal Commission on the Press, London, HMSO, p. 243.

5. One Conservative MP said: 'If the government were Labour I would write to *The Times*. If the government were Conservative I would write to the *Daily Telegraph*, and write to the minister enclosing a copy of my letter and tell him the response I had to it. The *Daily Telegraph* is read almost exclusively by Tories; a Conservative government has to pay more attention to what its people say. The *Telegraph* is also read by four or five times more people. *Daily Telegraph* readers may not be so academically advanced but *The Times* on balance is really a club writing for each other and one wants to write for a wider circle'.

6. Christopher Mayhew and Michael Adams, *Publish it Not ...*, London, Longman 1975, p. 67.

7. *The Times* 5.2.1976.

8. Kenneth Younger, 'Public Opinion and Foreign Policy', in *British Journal of Sociology*, 1975, pp. 172−3.

9. William Wallace, *Foreign Policy and the Political Process*, London, Macmillan, 1981, p. 50.

10. Younger, op. cit.

11. For discussion of the relationship between mass media and public opinion see, for example, Bernard Berelson, 'Communication and Public Opinion', in Wilbur Schramm, ed., *The Process and Effects of Mass Communication*, University of Illinois Press, 1954; and Robert Carlson, ed., *Communications and Public Opinion*, New York, Praeger 1975.

12. BBC Audience Research Report: *Studies of the Impact of the Radio and Television Coverage of the EEC Referendum Campaign*, London, BBC, January 1976, p. iv.

13. Social and Community Planning Research, *Attitudes to the Press*, Research Series 3, 1977 Royal Commission on the Press, London, HMSO, p. 29.

14. Lord Carrington, 'My job', *The Listener*, 1.4.1982.

15. James Barber, in Ch. 12 of *Who Makes British Foreign Policy?* Milton Keynes, Open University Press 1976, develops this theme.

16. Christopher Hill, 'Public Opinion and British Foreign Policy Since 1945: Research in Progress?' *Millennium*, Vol. 10, No. 1, Spring 1981. The author also argues that the paradox of rare interference of public opinion in British foreign policy and yet policymakers' obsession with it cannot be resolved by focusing on the mechanics of power and influence. Research has rather to focus on the importance of perception because images of public volatility are both influenced by leadership and help to shape its actions.

17. Kenneth N. Waltz, *Foreign Policy and Democratic Politics*, London, Longman 1968, p. 171.

18. Harold Wilson, *The Labour Government 1964–70: A personal record*, London, Weidenfeld & Nicolson and Michael Joseph 1971, pp. 557–9.
19. Werner Levi, 'The Relative Irrelevance of Moral Norms in International Politics', *Social Forces*, Vol. XLIV (1968).

CHAPTER SIX – INTERNATIONAL NEGOTIATION

1. Sir Humphrey Trevelyan, *Diplomatic Channels*, London, Macmillan, 1973, p. 60.
2. Colin Seymour-Ure, '*The Times* and the appeasement of Hitler', in *The political impact of mass media*, London, Constable 1974, p. 77.
3. *The Foreign Relations of the United States 1944, Volume V, Near East and South Asia*, pp. 239–40.
4. Ibid.
5. In the case of the leak to *The Guardian* in October 1983, by Sarah Tisdall, a Foreign Office clerical officer, of a confidential document by Michael Heseltine, Minister of Defence, on publicity and the arrival of cruise missiles in Britain, *The Economist* (31.3.1984) calculated that the number of ministers and officials, apart from clerical officers, who had access to the document was at least 55.
6. David Vital, *The Making of British Foreign Policy*, London, George Allen & Unwin 1968, p. 46.
7. Lawrence W. Martin, 'The Market for Strategic Ideas in Britain: the Sandys Era' in Richard Rose, ed., *Policymaking in Britain*, London, Macmillan 1969, pp. 261–2.
8. Harold Wilson, *The Labour Government 1964–70: A personal record*, London, Weidenfeld & Nicolson and Michael Joseph 1971, p. 473.
9. The 44 volumes of *The Foreign Relations of the United States* which were examined were: *FRUS 1943 Volumes I–IV; The Conferences at Washington and Quebec 1943; The Conference at Cairo and Tehran 1943; FRUS 1944 Volumes I–VII; The Conference at Quebec 1944; FRUS 1945 Volumes I–IX; The Conferences at Malta and Yalta 1945; The Conference of Berlin (Potsdam) 1945 Volumes I–II; FRUS 1946 Volumes I–IX; FRUS 1947 Volumes I–IX.*
10. Leonard Miall, 'How the Marshall Plan Started', in *The Listener* 4.5.1961.
11. Rene MacColl, *Deadline and Dateline*, London, Oldbourne Press 1956, p. 174.
12. Ibid., p. 175.
13. Memorandum by C. P. Kindleberger in *The Foreign Relations of the United States 1947, Volume III British Commonwealth and Europe*, Washington 1965, pp. 244–7.
14. Andrew Boyle, *The Climate of Treason*, London, Hutchinson 1979, p. 282.
15. Miall, op. cit.
16. MacColl, op. cit.
17. *FRUS 1945 Volume VIII, Near East and Africa*, p. 1266.
18. David Martin and Laurence Marks, 'Man who saved Rhodesia deal', *The Observer*, 9.12.1979.
19. *The Guardian*, 24.–26.1.1978.
20. Fred Charles Ikle, 'Bargaining and Communication' in Ithiel de Sola Pool and Wilbur Schramm, eds., *Handbook of Communication*, pp. 837–8.
21. *The Economist*, 15.5.1982.
22. Kindleberger, op. cit.

CHAPTER SEVEN – MOULDING OPINION ABROAD

1. *Middle East Decisionmakers Survey 1978*, prepared by McCann Erickson for the *Financial Times* and others.
2. *Report of the Committee on Representational Services Overseas*, London, HMSO 1964, Para. 264.
3. *Review Committee on Overseas Representation*, London, HMSO 1969, Ch. 8 Para. 8.
4. Ibid., Ch. 8 Para. 9.

5 Central Policy Review Staff, *Review of Overseas Representation*, London, HMSO 1977, Ch. 14 Para. 12.

6. In a BBC memorandum submitted to the House of Commons Defence and External Affairs Subcommittee, in *Fourth Report from the Expenditure Committee*, Session 1977–8, *The Central Policy Review Staff Committee of Overseas Representation, Volume II: Minutes of Evidence and Appendices*, London, HMSO, p. 105.

7. Survey by Radio Free Europe based on Polish visitors to the West, taken prior to martial law in December 1981. International Press Institute *IPI Report*, Aug. 1982.

8. Gerard Mansell, *Let the Truth Be Told: 50 years of BBC External Broadcasting*, London, Weidenfeld & Nicolson 1982, pp. 250–1.

9. *Summary of the Report of the Independent Committee of Inquiry into the Overseas Information Service*, London, HMSO 1954, p. 13.

10. Sir Douglas Marett, *Through the Back Door*, Oxford, Pergamon 1968, p. 198.

11. *Report of the Committee on Representational Services Overseas*, op. cit., Paras. 266–7.

12. Marett, op. cit., p. 175.

13. *BBC Handbook*, London, BBC 1980, p. 178.

14. John B. Black, *Organising the Propaganda Instrument: the British Experience*, The Hague, Martinus Nijhoff 1975, p. 64.

15. Kenneth Lamb, 'Disclosure, Discretion and Dissemblement: Broadcasting and the National Interest in the Perspective of a Publicly Owned Medium', in Thomas M. Franck and Edward Weisband, eds., *Secrecy and Foreign Policy*, New York, Oxford 1974.

16. Harman Grisewood, *One thing at a time* (Mr Grisewood was Chief Assistant to the BBC Director-General during the Suez Crisis).

17. F. R. Mackenzie, 'Eden, Suez and the BBC – A Reassessment', *The Listener* 18.12.1969. Other material on the BBC and Suez includes Barbara Castle, 'The Fiasco of Shaq-al-Adna', *New Statesman* 29.12.1956; and Gordon Walterfield, 'Suez and the role of broadcasting', *The Listener* 29.12.1966.

18. In evidence to the House of Commons Defence and External Affairs Subcommittee, in *Fourth Report from the Expenditure Committee, The Central Policy Review Staff Review of Overseas Representation*, Vol. II, op. cit., p. 114.

19. Ibid.

CHAPTER EIGHT – MOULDING OPINION AT HOME

1. Terence Prittie, *Through Irish Eyes: a journalist's memoirs*, London, Bachman & Turner 1977, pp. 265–6.

2. Home Office, *Departmental Committee on Section 2 of the Official Secrets Act 1911*, London, HMSO 1972, Vol. 1, p. 49 (The Franks Report).

3. W. E. H. Whyte, 'The FCO and the media', in Annabelle May and Kathryn Rowan, eds., *Inside Government: British government and the media*, London, Constable 1982, p. 195.

4. Prittie, op. cit.

5. Whyte, op. cit.

6. Alastair Hetherington, *Guardian Years*, London, Chatto & Windus 1981, p. 48.

7. The formation of the groups is partly determined by the degree of confidentiality with which the FCO is prepared to brief particular journalists and news organisations. A good example occurred at a foreign ministers' meeting in Geneva in May 1959 when the *Daily Worker*'s diplomatic correspondent, Sam Russell, was excluded from the briefing given by the Foreign Office's spokesman, Peter Hope. Hope said that in view of the presence of people who were not normally present at such briefings in London he could not speak confidentially. All eyes turned on the *Daily Worker* correspondent. The following morning Russell was told by the *Daily Herald*'s correspondent, who was recognised as the head of the group of diplomatic correspondents, that it would be better if he did not attend the briefings; the decision had been taken by Hope, the *Herald* man claimed. Hope, however, told Russell later that he was entirely in the hands of the correspondents and that it was up to them to decide who was to be admitted to the 'magic circle'. 'I informed them that the *Daily Worker* refused to accept this blatant discrimination and rejects the

"offer" of a deal under which the *Daily Worker* will be given what can only be an emasculated and carefully doctored version of what other British correspondents are told', Russell wrote in his paper (*Daily Worker* 13 and 14.5.1959).

8. David Gow, 'The EEC and the management of the news' in *Media, Culture & Society*, Vol. 1 No. 1, Jan. 1979.
9. Anthony Sampson, 'Secrecy, News Management, and the British Press', in Thomas M. Franck and Edward Weisband, eds., *Secrecy and Foreign Policy*, New York, Oxford 1974, p. 221.

CHAPTER NINE – REPORTING A HIJACKING

1. *The Guardian*, 22.6.1985.
2. *The Listener*, 31.1.1985. According to John Simpson, BBC TV Diplomatic Correspondent, reporting from Beirut, 'there were rules about walking down the street: take at least one person, preferably two, with you, locals rather than Westerners, since, though they might not prevent your being kidnapped, they would at least have an idea which one of dozens of organisations had done it. When driving, take two cars, so that the rear one could block any attempt to head you off the road.' Ibid., 25.5.1985.
3. Interviewed on '24 Hours', BBC World Service, 29.5.1985.
4. *The Times*, 21.6.1985.
5. Michael J. Kelley and Thomas H. Mitchell, 'Transnational Terrorism and the Western Elite Press', *Political Communication and Persuasion*, Vol. 1, No. 3, 1981.
6. J. Bowyer Bell, 'Terrorist scripts and live action spectaculars', *Columbia Journalism Review*, May/June 1978.
7. Kelly and Mitchell, op. cit.
8. *UK Press Gazette*, 22.7.1985.
9. An ITN cameraman managed to smuggle a minicam camera to the back of the embassy building without the knowledge of the police, sending live pictures back to ITN. The pictures of the rescue were held back and broadcast in a commercial break some four minutes later. Clutterbuck argues that hostages' lives would have been risked had the pictures been broadcast live. Richard Clutterbuck, *The Media and Political Violence*, London, Macmillan, 1981, pp. 138–40.
10. Philip Schlesinger, Graham Murdock and Philip Elliott, *'Televising Terrorism': political violence in popular culture*, London, Comedia 1983, p. 118.
11. Clutterbuck, op. cit., p. 135.
12. For example Grant Wardlaw, *Political Terrorism: Theory, tactics, and counter-measures*, Cambridge, C.U.P., 1982, Chapter 9.
13. Alex P. Schmid and Janny de Graaf, *Violence as Communication: Insurgent Terrorism and the Western News Media*, London and Beverly Hills, Sage 1982, p. 162.
14. *Television Today*, 15.8.1985.
15. Quoted in Schlesinger, Murdock and Elliott, op. cit., p. 131.
16. *Sunday Times*, 11.8.1985.
17. Michael Sommer, 'Nation's police chiefs, media differ on television coverage, year-long study shows', news release, California State University, 1978; quoted in Schmid and de Graaf, op. cit., p. 170.
18. David L. Paletz, John Z. Ayanian and Peter A. Fozzard, 'Terrorism on TV News: The IRA, the FALN, and the Red Brigade' in William C. Adams (ed.), *Television Coverage of International Affairs*, New Jersey, Ablex, 1982, p. 152.
19. Schlesinger, Murdock and Elliott, ibid.

CHAPTER TEN – LEBANON: IMAGES AND INTEREST GROUPS

1. Vincent Hanna in *The Journalist*, Sept. 1982.
2. *Daily Express* 10.6.1982.
3. *The Guardian* 22.6.1982.
4. *Yorkshire Post* 30.7.1982.

5. *Daily Mirror* 3.8.1982.
6. *Daily Mail* 20.9.1982.
7. *The Guardian* 21.9.1982.
8. *Jerusalem Post Magazine* 14.1.1983.
9. Hanna, op. cit.
10. *Daily Mirror*, 9.8.1982.
11. For a general survey of the Lebanon War and mass media see Yoel Cohen and Jacob Reuveny, *The Lebanon War and Western News Media*, Research Report Nos 6 and 7, Institute of Jewish Affairs, London, July 1984.
12. Poll by Market and Opinion Research International (MORI) *Jerusalem Post*, 29.8.1984.
13. For a discussion of the influence of media on British policy on the Arab–Israeli conflict, as well as other aspects of media diplomacy in British–Israeli relations, see Yoel Cohen, 'Media Diplomacy: A Case Study of Anglo-Israel Relations', in *Crossroads* (Israel Research Institute of Contemporary Society, Jerusalem), 1984.
14. Survey obtained from the Board of Deputies of British Jews. Based on calculating the number of letters appearing in the British press from June until the middle of October 1982, the survey was broken down to national daily and Sunday newspapers with 147 against Israel and 103 for; provincial morning newspapers with 46 against Israel and 26 for; provincial evening newspapers, 59 against and 18 for Israel; and weekly local newspapers, 47 against and 23 for Israel.
15. Council for the Advancement of Arab–British Understanding, *CAABU's Tenth Anniversary*, London 1977, p. 7.
16. *Jewish Chronicle* 2.7.1982.
17. At a symposium on the media's coverage of the war held by the Institute of Jewish Affairs, London. *Jewish Chronicle* 13.5.1983.
18. *The Times* 16.5.1982.
19. *The Guardian* 8.7.1982.
20. *The Times* 18.6.1982.
21. Simon Freeman, 'British Jews fear backlash after Beirut', *Sunday Times* 15.8.1982.
22. *Jewish Chronicle* 16.7.1982.
23. *Jewish Chronicle* 24.9.1982.

CHAPTER ELEVEN – THE FALKLANDS WAR

1. Memorandum by the Press Association to the House of Commons Defence Committee, *The Handling of Press and Public Information during the Falklands Conflict*, Vol. II, Minutes of Evidence, London, HMSO 1982, p. 308.
2. Ibid., p. 63.
3. For a discussion of military and media attitudes about each other see Chapters 12 and 13 of Alan Hooper, *The Military and the Media*, Aldershot, Gower 1982.
4. *The Sun* 4.5.1982.
5. *The Sun* 20.5.1982.
6. *The Sun* 7.5.1982.
7. *Daily Mirror* 8.5.1982.
8. BBC audience selection poll, *The Guardian* 20.5.1982.
9. Unpublished poll carried out by *The Sun. The Guardian* ibid.
10. *Daily Express* 5.4.1982.
11. *Daily Mail* 5.4.1982.
12. *News of the World* 4.4.1982.
13. *The Times* 5.4.1982.
14. Interview with Lord Carrington, *The Times* 19.1.1983.
15. *The Handling of Press and Public Information during the Falklands Conflict*, Vol. II, op. cit., Question 1385.
16. Ibid., Question 1364.
17. *Sunday Times* 2.5.1982.
18. *The Times*, 16.4.1982.

19. Commander Nicholl, an education officer, in conversation with Peter Preston, editor of *The Guardian,* in *The Handling of Press and Public Information during the Falklands Conflict*, Vol. II, op. cit., Question 1385.
20. Ibid., Question 1199.
21. *The Franks Report*, London, HMSO 1983, Cmnd 8787, Paras. 263, 313.
22. *The Times* 1.7.1982; Jonathan Bloch and Patrick Fitzgerald, *British Intelligence and Covert Action*, London, Junction Books 1983, p. 15.
23. *The Franks Report*, op. cit., Para. 312.
24. Ibid., Para. 317.
25. *The Handling of Press and Public Information during the Falklands Conflict*, Vol. II, op. cit., Question 1425.
25a. Robert Harris, *Gotcha! The Media, The Government and the Falklands Crisis*, London, Faber and Faber, 1983, p. 80.
26. *The Observer* 30.5.1982.
27. *The Handling of Press and Public Information during the Falklands Conflict*, Vol. II, op. cit., Question 1892.
28. Ibid., p. 418.
29. Ibid., according to Brian Hanrahan of the BBC, Question 334.
30. Robert Harris, *Gotcha! The Media, The Government and the Falklands Crisis*, op. cit., p. 93.
31. The House of Commons, Defence Committee, *The Handling of Press and Public Information during the Falklands Conflict*, Vol. I, Report and Minutes of Proceedings, London, HMSO 1982, Para. 27.
32. *The Handling of Press and Public Information during the Falklands Conflict*, Vol. II, op. cit., Question 40.
33. Ibid., Question 1254.
34. Interdepartmental infighting also occurred in American policymaking on the crisis. Alexander Haig, the US secretary of state, complained that inaccurate leaks from the White House threatened to upset the diplomatic negotiations he was conducting between London and Buenos Aires. A report on ABC's 'Nightline' programme that the US was offering extraordinary intelligence to the British 'very nearly wrecked the talks', he wrote. Alexander Haig, *CAVEAT: Realism, Reagan and Foreign Policy*, London, Weidenfeld and Nicolson 1984, p. 285.
35. *The Washington Post* 4.4.1982.
36. *The New York Times* 4.4.1982.
37. Max Hastings and Simon Jenkins, *The Battle for the Falklands*, London, Michael Joseph 1983, p. 113.
38. Douglas Muggeridge (Managing Director, BBC External Services) 'BBC External Broadcasting: An Organisation which tells the truth and is believed', *The Listener* 2.9.1982.
39. Memorandum of the Foreign Press Association to the House of Commons Defence Committee, *The Handling of Press and Public Information during the Falklands Conflict*, Vol. II, op. cit., p. 127.
40. *The Handling of Press and Public Information during the Falklands Conflict*, Vol. I, op. cit., Para. 8.
41. Christopher Wain (BBC TV Defence Correspondent), in *The Listener*, 6.5.1982.
42. *The Handling of Press and Public Information during the Falklands Conflict*, Vol. II, op. cit., Question 76.
43. Harris, op. cit., pp. 135–8.
44. A journalistic account of the debate is Robert Harris, *Gotcha! The Media, The Government and the Falklands Crisis*, op. cit.
45. Ministry of Defence, *The Handling of Press and Public Information during the Falklands Conflict: Observations presented by the Secretary of State for Defence on the First Report from the Defence Committee*, House of Commons papers 17-I-II 1982–83, London, HMSO 1983.
46. *The Handling of Press and Public Information during the Falklands Conflict*, Vol. II, op. cit., Questions 735–6.

47. Ministry of Defence, *The Protection of Military Information: Report of the Study Group on Censorship*, London, HMSO 1983, Para. 155.
48. *The Handling of Press and Public Information during the Falklands Conflict*, Vol. I, op. cit., Paras. 26–7.
49. *The Handling of Press and Public Information during the Falklands Conflict*, Vol. II, op. cit., Question 104.
50. *The Protection of Military Information: Report of the Study Group on Censorship*, op. cit., Para. 143.

CHAPTER TWELVE – THE REVOLUTIONS IN DIPLOMACY AND COMMUNICATIONS

1. Sir Geoffrey Jackson, *Concorde Diplomacy*, London, Hamish Hamilton 1981, pp. 191–2.
2. For an account of the UNESCO debate, and of the international politics of telecommunications, see Anthony Smith, *The Geopolitics of Information*, New York, Oxford 1980.
3. Jackson, op. cit., p. 21.
4. For an assessment of technological developments in news gathering during wartime see Ministry of Defence, *The Protection of Military Information: Report of the Study Group on Censorship*, London, HMSO 1983, Paras. 111–26.
5. *The United Kingdom's Overseas Representation*, London, HMSO 1978, pp. 8–9.
6. For a discussion about the diplomatic machinery of the future, see Zarah Steiner, 'Foreign ministries old and new', *International Journal*, Vol. 37, No. 3, 1982.
7. The Plowden Report criticised the extent to which under-secretaries in the FCO were taken up with day-to-day matters. Their function, it argued, is responsibility for the higher management of policy with 'time to think about profitable policy trends in their areas, to maintain touch with outside bodies such as the universities and learned associations and generally to act in a supervisory role – to guide, to stimulate and to restrain'. *Review of the Committee on Representational Services Overseas*, London, HMSO 1964, Para. 201.
8. Sir Douglas Marett, *Through the Back Door*, Oxford, Pergamon 1968, p. 175.

BIBLIOGRAPHY

A. *Selected list of persons interviewed*

The positions given for the interviewees on this list were the ones regarding which they were interviewed

Adams, Cecil	FCO
Aitken, Jonathan	MP
Alan, James	Head, Overseas Information Department, FCO
Amar, Benny	Journalist, BBC External Services
Avis, Peter	Diplomatic correspondent, *Morning Star*
Bannerman, Patrick	Deputy head, Research Department, FCO
Barnes, Sir John	Ambassador
Bell, Martin	United States correspondent, BBC TV
Bennett, Sir Frederic	MP
Bottomley, Arthur	Minister for Overseas Development
Boyce, Graham	FCO
Brandon, Henry	Washington correspondent, *Sunday Times*
Brazier, Kenneth	Editor, BBC External Services News
Brazier, Peter	Deputy press secretary, 10 Downing Street
Briley, Harold	Political correspondent, BBC External Services
Brunson, Michael	Journalist, Independent Television News
Bulloch, John	Diplomatic staff, *Daily Telegraph*
Carroll, Nicholas	Diplomatic correspondent, *Sunday Times*
Cooper, Jack	Central Office of Information
Critchley, Julian	MP
Davidson, Jonathan	FCO
Dickie, John	Diplomatic correspondent, *Daily Mail*
Doigt, David	Clerk, Defence and External Affairs Subcommittee, House of Commons
Ellison, John	Foreign editor and diplomatic correspondent, *Daily Express*
Everett, Brian	Deputy head, Information Policy Department, FCO
Faulkner, Alex	Chief United States correspondent, *Daily Telegraph*
Finsberg, Geoffrey	MP
Foster, Monica	Central Office of Information
Gilmour, Sir Ian	Deputy foreign secretary
Greenhill, Lord	Permanent Under-Secretary, FCO
Hadow, Sir Michael	Head of News Department, FCO
Hodgson, Larry	Editor, BBC Radio News
Home, Lord	Prime Minister and Foreign Secretary
Hooley, Frank	MP
Hurd, Douglas	Minister of State, FCO
Jackson, Sir Geoffrey	Ambassador
James, Michael	Deputy head, Information Policy Department, FCO
Jenkins, Simon	Political editor, *The Economist*
Joynes, C. A.	Research Department, Conservative Party
Keatley, Patrick	Diplomatic correspondent, *The Guardian*
Kelley, E. R.	Overseas controller, Central Office of Information
Leahy, Sir John	Under-secretary for Information, FCO

Ledwidge, Sir Bernard   Ambassador
Little, Jenny   International Department, Labour Party
Luard, Evan   Parliamentary Under-Secretary, FCO
Mackenzie, Angus   FCO
MacLeod, Alexander   Diplomatic correspondent, *The Scotsman*
Mason, Sir John   Ambassador
McAffrey, Sir Tom   Press secretary, 10 Downing Street
Meacham, Jim   Defence correspondent, *The Economist*
Milner, Donald   Diplomatic correspondent, BBC Radio
Mortimer, Edward   Journalist, FCO
Palliser, Sir Michael   Permanent Under-Secretary, FCO
Paynting, W. A.   Diplomatic correspondent, BBC External Services
Rhodes James, Robert   MP
Richard, Ivor   Ambassador
Roberts, Ivor   Deputy head of News Department, FCO
Roper, John   MP
Rutherford, Malcolm   Journalist, *Financial Times*
Sandelson, Neville   MP
Scicluna, Martin   Chief of Public Relations, Ministry of Defence
Sells, David   Journalist, BBC TV
Simpson-Orlebar, M.K.   FCO
Snow, Peter   Journalist, BBC TV
Spanier, David   Diplomatic correspondent, Independent Radio News
Stark, Michael   FCO
Steele, Jonathan   Journalist, *The Guardian*
Stewart, Michael   Foreign Secretary
Stewart, Morley   Ministry of Defence
Thomas, Anthony   Journalist, *The Economist*
Wain, Christopher   Defence correspondent, BBC TV
Walker, David   FCO
Walker, Andrew   Commonwealth correspondent, BBC External Services
Wall, Patrick   MP
Whitney, Ray   MP
Whyte, Hamilton   Head of News Department, FCO
Wood, Richard   Minister for Overseas Development
Wright, Steven   FCO
Younger, George   Minister of State, Ministry of Defence

B. *Official reports and other published sources*

Philip Abrams, 'Social Structure, Social Change, and British Foreign Policy' in Kaiser and Morgan (eds.) *Britain and West Germany changing societies and the future of foreign policy*, London, Oxford 1971.

Acorn Study Group, *The United Nations and the Press*, London, The United Nations Association 1967.

Jonathan Aitken, *Officially Secret*, London, Weidenfeld & Nicolson 1971.

Gabriel Almond, *The American People and Foreign Policy*, New York, Praeger 1960.

Chris Argyris, *Behind the Front Page*, San Francisco, Jossey-Bass 1974.

David Ayerst, *Guardian: Biography of a Newspaper*, London, Collins 1971.

BBC Audience Research Report, *Studies of the Impact of the Radio and Television Coverage of the EEC Referendum Campaign*, BBC, January 1976.

BBC Audience Research Report, *News Broadcasting and the Public*, London, BBC 1970.

Michael Balfour, *Propaganda in War 1939–45: Organisations, Policies and Publics in Britain and Germany*, London, Routledge 1971.

James Barber, *Who Makes British Foreign Policy?* Milton Keynes, Open University Press 1976.

Anthony Barker and Michael Rush, *The Member of Parliament and his Information*, London, George Allen & Unwin, 1970.

Thomas Barman, 'A Diplomatic Correspondent's look back', *The Listener*, 5.1.1967.

Thomas Barman, *Diplomatic Correspondent*, London, Hamish Hamilton 1968.

Lee Becker, 'Foreign Policy and Press Performance' in *Journalism Quarterly*, Vol. 54, Summer 1967.

Bernard Berelson, 'Communication and Public Opinion', in Wilbur Schramm (ed.), *The Process and Effects of Mass Communication*, University of Illinois Press 1954.

(The Berrill Report), Central Policy Review Staff, *Review of Overseas Representation*, London, HMSO 1977.

Roger Berthoud, 'Making Whitehall a happier hunting ground for foreign correspondents', *The Times* 12.2.1977.

Donald Bishop, *The Administration of British Foreign Relations*, Syracuse, Syracuse University Press 1961.

John B. Black, *Organising the Propaganda Instrument: The British Experience*, The Hague, Martinus Nijhoff 1975.

Jay Blumler and Elihu Katz (eds.) *The Uses of Mass Communications*, Beverly Hills and London, Sage 1975.

Robert Boardman and A. J. R. Groom (eds.), *The Management of Britain's External Relations*, London, Macmillan, 1972.

Lee Bogart, 'The overseas newsman: a 1967 profile study', *Journalism Quarterly*, Vol. 45, pp. 293–306.

Oliver Boyd Barrett, Colin Seymour-Ure, and Jeremy Tunstall, *Studies on the Press*, Working Paper 3 of the 1977 Royal Commission on the Press, London, HMSO 1977.

Oliver Boyd Barrett, *The international news agencies*, London, Constable 1980.

Robert Carlson (ed.) *Communications and Public Opinion*, New York, Praeger 1975.

Barbara Castle, 'The Fiasco of Shaq-al-Adna', *New Statesman* 29.12.1956.

William O. Chittick, *State Department, press and pressure groups: a role analysis*, New York, John Wiley-InterScience 1970.

Sir Fife Clark, *The Central Office of Information*, London, George Allen & Unwin 1970.

Richard Clutterbuck, *The Media and Political Violence*, London, Macmillan, 1981.

Michael Cockerell, Peter Hennessy and David Walker, *Sources close to the Prime Minister*, London, Macmillan, 1984.

Bernard C. Cohen, *The Press and Foreign Policy*, Princeton, Princeton University Press 1963.

Bernard C. Cohen, *The Public's Impact on Foreign Policy*, Boston, Little Brown 1973.

Yoel Cohen, 'Media Diplomacy: A Case Study of Anglo-Israeli Relations' *Crossroads* (Israel Research Institute of Contemporary Society, Jerusalem), 1984, No. 11.

Yoel Cohen and Jacob Reuveny, 'The Lebanon War and Western News Media' Research Report Nos 6 and 7, London, Institute of Jewish Affairs 1984.

John Crawley, *The Work of a BBC Foreign Correspondent*, BBC Lunchtime Lecture 14.10.1974.

Charles Cruickshank, *The Fourth Arm: Psychological Warfare 1938–45*, London, Oxford 1981.

E. Davis, *Government and the Press in Britain since the Second World War*, Cornell University PhD thesis, 1950.

W. Phillips Davison, *International Political Communication*, New York, Praeger 1965.

W. Phillips Davison, 'News media and international negotiation', *Public Opinion Quarterly*, Summer 1974.

W. Phillips Davison, 'Mass Communication and Diplomacy', in James Rosenau, Kenneth Thompson and Gavin Boyd (eds.), *World Politics*, New York, Free Press 1976.

(The Drogheda Report), *Summary of the Report of the Inquiry into the Overseas Information Service*, London, HMSO 1954, Cmnd 9138.

(The Duncan Report), *Review Committee on Overseas Representation*, London, HMSO 1969, Cmnd 4107.

Leon D. Epstein, *British Politics in the Suez Crisis*, 1964.

Fourth Report from the Expenditure Committee, Session 1977–8, The Central Policy Review Staff Review of Overseas Representation, Vols. I and II, London, HMSO 1978, pp. 286-I and 286-II.

Thomas Franck and Edward Weisband (eds.) *Secrecy and Foreign Policy*, New York, Oxford University Press 1974.

Joseph Frankel, *The Making of Foreign Policy*, London, Oxford University Press 1971.

Joseph Frankel, *British Foreign Policy 1945–73*, London, Oxford University Press 1973.

Frederick Forsyth, *The Biafra Story*, London, Penguin 1969.

John Galtung and Mari Holmboe Ruge, 'The Structure of Foreign News: The Presentation of the Congo, Cuba and Cyprus Crises in Four Foreign Newspapers', *Journal of International Peace Research* Vol. 1 1965.

Loyal N. Gould, *The ENDC and The Press*, Almquist and Wiksell, Stockholm Institute for Peace Research (SIPRI) 1969.

David Gow, 'The EEC and the management of news', *Media, Culture and Society*, Vol. I, No. 1, 1979.

Robert Gregson, *Broadcasting and the Third World*, BBC Lunchtime Lecture, 23.11. 1976.

Bill Grundy, 'Who sprang the leak?' *The Spectator* 10.5.1975.

Joe Haines, *The politics of power*, London, Jonathan Cape 1977.

Julian Hale, *Radio Power*, London, Paul Elek 1975.

Morton Halperin, *Bureaucratic Politics and Foreign Policy*, Washington, The Brookings Institute 1974.

Robert Harris, *Gotcha! The Media, The Government and the Falklands Crisis*, London, Faber and Faber 1983.

Jim A. Hart, 'Foreign News in US and English Daily Newspapers: A Comparison', *Journalism Quarterly*, Vol. 43, No. 3.

Alastair Hetherington, *Guardian Years*, London, Chatto & Windus 1981.

Christopher Hill, 'Public Opinion and British Foreign Policy since 1945: Research in Progress', *Millennium* Vol. 10, No. 1, 1981.

Frederick B. Hill, 'Media Diplomacy: Crisis Management with an eye on the TV screen,' *Washington Journalism Review* May 1981.

Lord Hill of Luton, *Both Sides of the Hill*, London, Heinemann 1971.

Christopher Hitchens, 'How they tried to bend the BBC', *New Statesman* 2.3.1979.

Alan Hooper, *The Military and the Media*, Aldershot, Gower 1982.

House of Commons Defence Committee, *The Handling of Press and Public Information during the Falklands Conflict*, Vols I and II, London, HMSO 1982.

Fred Charles Ikle, 'Bargaining and Communication' in Ithiel de Sola Pool and Wilbur Schramm (eds.) *Handbook of Communication*.

Robert Jervis, *The Logic of Images in International Relations*, Princeton, Princeton University Press 1970.

Kennedy Jones, *Fleet Street and Downing Street*, London, Hutchinson 1919.

Sir Geoffrey Jackson, *Concorde Diplomacy*, London, Hamish Hamilton 1981.

Patricia A. Karl, 'Media Diplomacy', in Gerald Benjamin (ed.) *The Communications Revolution in Politics*, Proceedings of the Academy of Political Science, Vol. 34 No. 4, New York 1981–2.

Elihu Katz and Paul Lazarsfeld, *Personal Influence*, Glencoe, Free Press, 1955.

Michael J. Kelley and Thomas H. Mitchell, 'Transnational and the Western Elite Press', *Political Communication and Persuasion*, Vol. 1, No. 3, 1981.

I. Kertesz and M. A. Fitzsimmons (eds.) *Diplomacy in a Changing World*, Indiana, University of Notre Dame Press 1959.

Uwe Kitzinger, *Diplomacy and Persuasion*, London, Thames & Hudson 1973.

Phillip Knightley, *The First Casualty. From the Crimea to Vietnam: The War Correspondent as Hero, Propagandist, and Myth Maker*, New York and London, Harcourt Brace Jovanovitch, 1975.

Connie M. Kristiansen, Gary Fowlie and Susan J. Spencer, 'Britain's Broadcast Coverage of the Soviet Invasion of Afghanistan' *Journalism Quarterly*, Winter 1982.

Theodore E. Kruglak, *The Foreign Correspondents*, Geneva, Libraire E. Droz 1955.

Maurice Latey, *Broadcasting to the USSR and Eastern Europe*, BBC Lunchtime Lecture 11.11.1964.

David Leigh, 'Death of the department that never was', *The Guardian* 27.1.1978.

Walter Lippmann, *Public Opinion*, New York, Harcourt Brace 1922.
Colin Lovelace, 'British press censorship during the First World War' in George Boyce, James Curran and Pauline Wingate (eds.) *Newspaper history: from the 17th century to the present day*, London, Constable 1978.
F. R. Mackenzie, 'Eden, Suez and the BBC – A Reassessment', *The Listener*, 18.12.1969.
Gerard Mansell, *Broadcasting to the World: forty years of BBC External Services*, London, BBC 1973.
Gerard Mansell, *Why External Broadcasting?* BBC Lunchtime Lecture 11.3.1976.
Gerard Mansell, *Let the Truth Be Told: 50 Years of External Broadcasting*, London, Weidenfeld & Nicolson 1982.
Sir Douglas Marett, *Through the Back Door: An Inside View of Britain's Overseas Information Services*, Oxford, Pergamon 1968.
David Martin and Laurence Marks, 'Man who saved Rhodesia deal', *The Observer* 9.12.1979.
Laurence W. Martin, 'The Market for Strategic Ideas in Britain: The Sandys Era', in Richard Rose (ed.) *Policymaking in Britain*, London, Macmillan 1969.
Annabelle May and Kathryn Rowan (eds.), *Inside information: British government and the media*, London, Constable 1982.
Iverach McDonald, *A Man of The Times*, London, Hamish Hamilton 1976.
Donald McLachlan, *In the Chair: Barrington-Ward of The Times*, London, Weidenfeld & Nicolson 1971.
Denis McQuail, 'Foreign Affairs Content in National Daily and 2 Scottish Newspapers 1975' in *Analysis of Newspaper Content*, Research Series 4 of the 1977 Royal Commission on the Press, London HMSO.
Ian McLaine, *Ministry of Morale*, London, George Allen & Unwin 1979.
Richard L. Merritt (ed.) *Communication in International Politics*, Urbana, Chicago, University of Illinois Press 1972.
Leonard Miall, 'How the Marshall Plan Started', *The Listener* 4.5.1961.
Ministry of Defence, *The Protection of Military Information: Report of the Study Group on Censorship*, London, HMSO, Cmnd 9112, 1983.
Ministry of Defence, *The Handling of Press and Public Information during the Falklands Conflict: Observations presented by the Secretary of State for Defence in the First Report from the Defence Committee*, House of Commons paper 17-I-II 1982–3, London, HMSO 1983, Cmnd 8820.
James Monahan, *Broadcasting to Europe*, BBC Lunchtime Lecture 9.10.1963.
Geoffrey Moorhouse, *The Diplomats: The Foreign Office Today*, London, Jonathan Cape 1977.
Michael D. Mossettig, 'The Revolution in Communications and Diplomacy', in *Proceedings of the Academy of Political Science*, Vol. 34, No. 2, New York 1981–2.
R. B. Mowat, *Diplomacy and Peace*, London, Williams and Norgate 1935.
Chris Mullin, 'The war Smith is winning', *New Statesman*, 19.1.1979.
Harold Nicolson, *Diplomacy*, London, Oxford 1967.
Dan Nimmo, *Newsgathering in Washington*, New York, Atherton Press 1964.
Marjorie Ogilvy-Webb, *The Government Explains*, London, George Allen & Unwin 1961.
E. Ostgaard, 'Factors influencing the flow of news', *Journal of International Peace Research*, Vol. 1 1965.
Michael Palmer, 'The British press and international news, 1851–99: of agencies and newspapers' in George Boyce, James Curran and Pauline Wingate (eds.) *Newspaper history: from the 17th century to the present day*, London, Constable 1978.
(The Plowden Report) *Report of the Committee on Representational Services Overseas*, London, HMSO 1964, Cmnd 2276.
The Political Quarterly, Vol. 54, No. 2, 1983, special issue on the information age.
Nicholas Pronay and D. W. Spring (eds.) *Propaganda, Politics & Film 1918–1945*, London, Macmillan 1982.
A. M. Rendel, 'Policymakers and Opinion', *International Journal*, Vol. 30, No. 1, Winter 1974–5.
Review of the BBC External Services, Report by the Review Team to the Board of Governors of the BBC and the Secretary of State for Foreign and Commonwealth Affairs, London, BBC 1984.

Peter G. Richards, *Parliament and Foreign Affairs*, London, George Allen & Unwin 1967.
William L. Rivers, Susan Miller and Oscar Gandy, 'Government and the Media' in Steven H. Chafee (ed.) *Political Communication: Issues and Strategies for Research*, Beverly Hills and London, Sage 1975.
James Rosenau, *Public Opinion and Foreign Policy*, New York, Random House 1961.
Edwin Samuel, 'The Administration of The Times', *Public Administration in Israel and Abroad*, Vol. 14, 1973.
Paddy Scannell, 'The BBC and foreign affairs: 1935–1939', *Media, Culture and Society*, Vol. 6, 1984.
Philip Schlesinger, *Putting reality together: BBC news*, London, Constable 1978.
Philip Schlesinger, Graham Murdock and Philip Elliott, *Televising 'Terrorism': political violence and popular culture*, London, Comedia 1983.
Alex P. Schmid and Janny de Graaf, *Violence as Communication: Insurgent Terrorism and the Western News Media*, London and Beverly Hills, Sage 1982.
Selected Public Expenditure Programmes: Central Office of Information Home Publicity, London, HMSO 282-i-iv (Session 1977–8).
Colin Seymour-Ure, *The political impact of mass media*, London, Constable 1974.
Colin Seymour-Ure, *The Press, Politics, and the Public*, London, Methuen 1968.
Geoffrey Sheridan, ' "A sense of betrayal" as BBC comes under fire for broadcasts to Portugal', *The Times* 30.12.1975.
Charles E. Sherman and John Ruby, 'The Eurovision News Exchange', *Journalism Quarterly*, Summer 1974.
Leon V. Sigal, *Reporters and Officials*, Lexington, D.C. Heath 1973.
Anthony Smith, *The Politics of Information: Problems of Policy in Modern Media*, London, Macmillan 1978.
Anthony Smith, *The Geopolitics of Information: How Western Culture Dominates the World*, New York, Oxford 1980.
William P. Snyder, *The Politics of British Defence Policy 1945–1962*, Ohio, Ohio State University Press, 1964.
Social and Community Planning Research, *Attitudes to the Press*, Research Series 3, 1977 Royal Commission on the Press, London, HMSO Cmnd 6810–3, 1977.
Zarah Steiner, *The Foreign Office and Foreign Policy 1898–1914*, London, Cambridge 1969.
J. D. Stewart, *British Pressure Groups and the House of Commons*, London, Oxford, 1958.
Lord Strang, *The Foreign Office*, London, George Allen & Unwin 1955.
Philip M. Taylor, *The Projection of Britain*, London, Cambridge 1981.
Sir John Tilley and Stephen Gaselee, *The Foreign Office*, London, Putnam 1933.
Jeremy Tunstall, *The Westminster Lobby Correspondents*, London, Routledge 1970.
Jeremy Tunstall, *Journalists at Work*, London, Constable 1971.
Jeremy Tunstall, *The media in Britain*, London, Constable 1983.
David Vital, *The Making of British Foreign Policy*, London, George Allen & Unwin 1968.
William Wallace, *The Foreign Policy Process in Britain*, London, George Allen & Unwin 1976.
Gordon Walterfield, 'Suez and the role of broadcasting', *The Listener* 29.12.1966.
Kenneth N. Waltz, *Foreign Policy and Democratic Politics: The American and British Experience*, Boston, Little Brown 1967.
C. H. Weiss, 'What America's leaders read', *Public Opinion Quarterly*, Vol. 38.
Sir Arthur Willert, 'Publicity and Propaganda in International Affairs', *International Affairs*, November–December 1938.
Lord Francis Williams, 'The Government Information Services', *Public Administration*, Vol. 43, Autumn 1965.
Kenneth Younger, 'Public Opinion and Foreign Policy', *British Journal of Sociology*, Vol. 6, 1955.
Kenneth Younger, 'Public Opinion and British Foreign Policy', *International Affairs*, Vol. 40, No. 1, 1964.

INDEX